ELEMENTARY BATTLE OF THE BOOKS

Sybilla Cook, Frances Corcoran, Beverley Fonnesbeck, Roz Goodman
with the Alaska Association of School Librarians

Fort Atkinson, Wisconsin

Dedications

*To all passionate readers—past, present and future—including
Tom, Ana, Alyssa, Matt and Avery.*
—S. C.

*To all the school and public librarians and teachers
from Chicago to Hawaii who shared their enthusiasm for
literature and encouraged me to carry that banner. Mahalo nui loa.*
—F. C.

*To my grandson John and his fellow five-year-olds.
May their tribe increase, and may their adventures with books abound.*
—B. F.

*To the members of the Alaska Association of School Librarians
who, over the past twenty years, have collaborated with students,
teachers, administrators, parents, public librarians and numerous
other literacy advocates to continually refine and improve
Alaska's original 1984 statewide Battle of the Books program.*
—R. G.

Published by **UpstartBooks**
W5527 Highway 106
P.O. Box 800
Fort Atkinson, Wisconsin 53538-0800
1-800-558-2110

© Sybilla Cook, Frances Corcoran, Beverley Fonnesbeck and Roz Goodman, 2005

Cover design: Debra Neu

The paper used in this publication meets the minimum requirements of American National Standard for Information Science — Permanence of Paper for Printed Library Material. ANSI/NISO Z39.48-1992.

All rights reserved. Printed in the United States of America.
The purchase of this book entitles the individual librarian or teacher to reproduce copies for use in the library or classroom. The reproduction of any part for an entire school system or for commercial use is strictly prohibited. No form of this work may be reproduced or transmitted or recorded without written permission from the publisher.

Contents

Foreword	5
Acknowledgments	6
Introduction	7

1. Battle of the Books: A Success Story — 9
Seventy Years of Success — 9
Elementary Battles as a Reading Incentive Program — 10
Competition or Cooperation? — 11
Variations on the Program — 11

2. Literacy and Learning Connections — 13
Literacy — 13
National Programs: Reading Excellence Act, No Child Left Behind — 14
Information Power — 14
Standards and Benchmarks — 15
Reading Assessment in the Library — 15

3. Contests: Begin with the Basics — 17
Goals — 17
Format — 18
Organizing and Planning — 20
Choosing Participants and Teams — 20
Introducing the Contest — 21
Team Selection — 21
Guidelines, Rules and Scores — 22
Incentives and Rewards — 25
Arranging the Setting — 26

4. The Books and the Questions — 28
Choosing the Books — 28
Writing the Questions — 30

5. All About Books: Reading Activities   33

Activities Supporting the Curriculum and
Performance Standards   34

"Reading" the Books   34

Reading Enhancements   35

Language Activities   37

Visual Literacy   38

Story Elements   40

6. All About Books: Writing and Research Activities   42

Story Elements   42

Writing About Books   44

Research Enhancements   46

7. Activities for Fun and Learning   49

Library Media Center and Classroom Activities   49

Parent Involvement and Take-Home Activities   51

Book Report Variations   52

Games, Puzzles and Other Amusements   52

All-School Activities   54

8. Public Relations   57

Teachers   57

Administrators   58

Parents   58

Community   59

District Publicity and Web Pages   60

Media   60

9. Battle Books and Questions   61

Appendix 1: Bibliography   163

Appendix 2: Webliography   165

Appendix 3: Other Resources   167

Author, Subject and Award Index   169

Foreword

A top goal of every school is to have students learn to read and enjoy doing so. As a requested follow-up to their middle school book, these four authors have brought you some wonderful new ways to get younger students interested and excited about books and reading. They have excellent credentials as writers and librarians, having worked in school districts in Alaska, California, Illinois, Hawaii and Oregon. They have used and refined numerous ideas, putting together a grab bag to encourage and extend the pleasures of reading for kindergartners through fifth graders.

I was introduced to the book's central idea, Battle of the Books, in 1985, when Roz Goodman from Alaska sent a description of it to *The School Librarian's Workshop*. Intrigued by her article, I began doing Battle of the Books at Southern Boulevard School in Chatham, New Jersey, receiving a delighted response from students and their parents, all of whom loved the program. I met Roz in person when she talked about this activity at our state EMAnj library conference that same year, after which it became popular in many New Jersey schools.

As the program spread to various states, it has proven that all students, not just the top ones, can succeed. As long as they read the books (or have parents help them at home), they can share a common experience, work cooperatively as a team to find the answers and even make up questions to which other groups will respond. As the authors point out in Chapter 2, "any … activity that encourages students to read, comprehend, analyze, synthesize and communicate information found in quality children's literature is definitely worth a try."

Also featured are a potpourri of other reading activities, all of which promote information literacy skills so important to learning, including "accessing, utilizing and evaluating fiction and nonfiction resources." This book gives you the option of choosing and adapting ideas that will work best with your students.

Chapter 9 offers two lists of possible Battle of the Books selections by title—one with 178 books for grades K–3 and a second of 129 titles for grades 4–5. Both include bibliographic information, URLs, subjects, awards won and five battle questions for each book. Here you receive a veritable treasure trove of information, continued in the Appendix sections which record bibliographies and Webliographies (book selection, author and illustrator information, literature guides, lessons and activities). These provide excellent references to round out your program.

As you refer to this book over and over again, rest assured that when you try some of its multiple selections you will succeed and your students will learn to love reading more than ever!

Ruth Toor
School Library Consultant
Editor, *The School Librarian's Workshop*
Former President of the American Association of School Librarians

Acknowledgements

This particular book could not have been written without the members of the Alaska Association of School Librarians. Over the past 20 years they have collaborated with students, teachers, administrators, parents, public librarians and numerous other literacy advocates to continually refine and improve Alaska's statewide Battle of the Books program.

All of us wish to thank those who have shared their ideas and expertise with us. They come from many backgrounds, libraries and places, and each has contributed to the programs and this book. We're sure we have left many people out, but do want to credit the following school librarians, public librarians and teachers whose ideas are found on the pages of this book.

Mahalo nui loa, thanks so very much.

Alaska

Michelle Andrews, Chevak School Library, Chevak; Barbara Bryson, Hermon Hutchens Elementary School, Valdez; Mollie Bynum, Retired School Librarian, Anchorage; Dianne Crandall, Mountain Village School, Mountain Village; Audrey Drew, Bayshore Elementary, Anchorage; Michael Dickens, Skagway City Schools, Skagway; Funa Hornberger, Newhalen School Library, Newhalen; Susan Koike, Chugiak Elementary, Chugiak; Tiki Levinson, Delta Junction School Library, Delta Junction; Shelly Logsdon, Wasilla High School Library, Wasilla; Florence Manier, Thorne Bay School Library, Thorne Bay; Donna Morrow, Arctic Light School, Ft. Wainwright, Fairbanks; Marty Osredker, Retired School Librarian, Anchorage; Lois Petersen, Media Specialist, Bering Strait School District, Unalakleet; Judy Redmond, Russian Jack Elementary School, Anchorage; Sue Sherif, School Library and Youth Services Coordinator, Alaska State Library, Anchorage; Tracy Swaim, Computer Resource Librarian, Alaska State Library, Anchorage; Nancy Vait, Homer Middle School, Homer.

California

Jamie Boston, Birch Lane Elementary, Davis.

Canada

Randi Hermans, East Chilliwack Elementary, Chilliwack, BC; Jane Salmon, Barrie Public Library, Barrie, ON.

Hawaii

Dayna Hironaka, Kahaluu Elementary School; Dr. Kathleen Carstensen, Sharon Cole, Betty Ito, Caroline Oda and Cheri Woods, all of St. Andrew's Priory School; St. Andrew's parents Mrs. Nakamura, Mrs. Leong, Mrs. Tsutsui, Mrs. Shishido and Mrs. Fujimoto, who developed a reading club for their daughters and share in their girls' interests in reading, thinking and discussing ideas.

Illinois

Dianne Lockridge, Kildeer Countryside School, Long Grove; Linda Lucke, District 7, Butterfield School, Libertyville; Anne Shimojima, Braeside School, Highland Park.

Maine

Nancy Tanner, South Hiram Elementary School, South Hiram.

New Jersey

Ruth Toor, Library Learning Resources, Inc., Berkeley Heights; Hilda K. Weisburg, Library Learning Resources, Inc., Berkeley Heights.

North Carolina

Linda Hurley, Knightdale Elementary School, Raleigh.

Oregon

Libby Hamler Dupras and De Ann Orand, Meyer School, Salem; Marilyn Coxon and Dan White, Douglas County Library; Cheri Page, Mary McClintock and others in the Roseburg school district; Penny Clark and all those who took the Battle of the Books program to heart.

Rhode Island

Wheeler School, Providence.

Introduction

"Battle of the Books is one of the best things that ever happened to our school. My kids really became readers."
Bonnie Leon, parent, Glide Elementary School, Glide, Oregon

Why this book?

Because reading should be fun! With many classrooms being transformed into centers of "teach, drill and test," the library may be one of the few places in the school where a child can read just for sheer pleasure.

Public and school librarians[1] are required to have advanced study in traditional and modern children's literature, as well as in a variety of reading curricula and activities. The concepts and activities in this book have been created and shared by librarians across the country. Many can be used in individual classrooms or at home. These ideas will make books and reading attractive to children so they will become lifelong learners. Chapter 2 describes how these ideas and activities—including contests—connect to specific professional, district, state and national reading and literacy goals.

Through reading, children become familiar with a great many words and their meanings. Listening, visual, comprehension and fluency skills are the core of elementary reading programs. The 1998 Reading Excellence Act[2] defines reading as "the ability to read fluently" and "the development and maintenance of a motivation to read." Library activities are generally planned to develop and encourage fluency and comprehension through oral and silent reading. Yet, like any skill, reading requires practice to perfect. The desire to practice reading is related to ones' motivation to read. The plethora of ideas and activities in this book are designed to motivate young readers.

The more interesting an activity is, the more it's likely to be practiced. As students gain skills and confidence, they are motivated to master more sophisticated literacy skills and become successful independent learners. Competitive activities, such as contests, also add a social element to reading. Cooperation, collaboration and teamwork are encouraged, giving the non-athletic child the same values encouraged in sports programs. A well-designed and well-run reading contest promotes confidence and pride when students are recognized and rewarded for their reading efforts.

Since contests are enjoyable, they often attract students who are not habitual readers. The emphasis should be on cooperation, fun and increasing reading proficiency. All participants learn to work with others who have different interests and ability levels. It is important to remember the goal of a reading contest should always be reading for enjoyment, rather than victory over another child.

Is it worth spending time on contests like Battle of the Books?

Yes, it is! Book contests:

- make reading a social activity as well as a private one

- motivate both readers and nonreaders to discuss books with their peers

- encourage students and teachers to expand their knowledge of new titles, authors, illustrators and a variety of literary genres

- involve parents and other community members in school and public library programs

As its title suggests, our first book, *Battle of the Books and More: Reading Activities for Middle School Students*, was intended for grades 6–8. Many librarians said they would like a similar book on this subject for the lower grades. This book is for teachers and librarians who work with K–5 students. Some details—but not all—from the previous book are repeated here because they are pertinent to all levels. The titles and questions, however, are completely different.

Several chapters have been added with specific ideas for reading, writing and research enhancements. Many of these activities come out of our collective personal experiences in a variety of private and public schools located in rural, suburban and urban areas. Through the years we've also collected numerous ideas from others, adapting them to our own libraries.

This book emphasizes the Battle of the Books Program. Perhaps the most ambitious and structured battle program is the one developed during the last 20 years by the Alaska Association of School Librarians. At their annual library conferences, school and public librarians choose titles, share ideas and structure the program to meet the needs of all schools in their geographically large state. Many of the activities in this book come from this group of dedicated professionals. We are fortunate to be able to include their collective experience.

As in the previous book, we've included five sample questions for more than 300 books likely to be found in any standard library collection—178 books meet the interests and reading levels of children in grades K–3 and 129 titles are for children in grades 4–5. These selections should not be viewed as the perfect collection of books to use "as is." Great new books are constantly being published, while others go out of print all too soon.

Your choice of reading contests and books should be based on your students, your needs and your own collections. Our suggestions are meant to get you up and running with a minimum amount of time. We hope that the ideas here, along with the extensive list of resources, reading lists and questions to use, will help you successfully implement a reading contest in your own school or public library.

Endnotes

1. The term "librarian" refers to both professional librarians and information specialists in the public library and library media specialists in the schools. The term "library" refers to public and school libraries, whether called Instructional Materials Center, Media Center, etc.
2. U.S. House. Title VIII, Reading Excellence Act, Part C, Section 2252. 105th Congress, 2nd sess., HR 2614. Congressional Record (October 8, 1997) H10386-10392.

Battle of the Books: A Success Story

"…the Battle of the Books has made my three boys into constant readers. They were very athletic and competitive, and rarely read on their own, although they would listen for hours, literally, while we read to them…

The quality of books chosen has been high, so they became used to reading well-written stories, which is a plus. Now all three boys spend hours reading, usually at night in bed, and that was not happening before the Battles got them hooked. I'm a true believer. It is one of the reasons I cannot pull my kids out of public school, even though almost all our friends' children are in private schools. It's an idea that needs to spread!"

Dr. Ann Mozell[1]

Seventy Years of Success

The Battle of the Books began in the early 1930s as a radio program sponsored by the Chicago public schools and the Carson Pirie Scott department store. In the 1970s Joanne Kelly, a former participant, became a school librarian in Urbana, Illinois. She reconstructed the program as a reading incentive activity for her library program, and reports of this successful activity spread to other schools in Illinois.

In 1981 she presented the idea at the American Association of School Librarians Conference. This inspired school librarians in other states to develop similar plans as a means of building enthusiasm for recreational reading among their students.

Why has the program survived for 70 years without publisher advertising, sales reps or government interest? Because it's fun for students. It's exciting to watch. It's flexible—it's done differently from school to school, district to district, state to state. And … because it works!

The program:

- highlights and rewards reading as a valuable and important student activity
- makes reading fun, challenging and engaging
- involves students from a variety of academic levels—not just the super readers
- encourages nonreaders to read and enjoy reading
- encourages teachers and students to read more books and explore different genres

- gets parents and families involved in the reading and learning process and introduces them to quality literature, authors and illustrators
- encourages students, teachers and parents to talk about books
- adds worthwhile, noteworthy children's books to classroom and library collections
- is a springboard for many reading, writing and research activities
- directly supports district, state and national reading, language arts and library literacy standards

Elementary Battles as a Reading Incentive Program

Some children become avid readers at an early age, needing little or no motivation beyond the satisfaction the printed page provides. These readers immerse themselves in books, developing decoding and interpretive skills on their own. Competence comes through their reading practice as they devour literature of their own choosing.

Children who find books unappealing become absorbed in other activities—sports, television, video games, etc. They need exposure to and participation in reading programs that highlight reading as an enjoyable and worthwhile activity. This should happen in the early elementary grades. It becomes increasingly difficult to inculcate the habit of reading for pleasure as students move into the middle grades.

Long ago, May Hill Arbuthnot, a pioneer in the field of children's literature, noted children enjoy having fun but also want to feel competent. Sports, games and hobbies may answer these needs, but reading can be equally fulfilling. Reading teaches them to use their imaginations and to empathize with others who may live very different lives. In books, minds and horizons are expanded, roles are tested, values weighed. Beauty and truth are explored, barriers destroyed, imagination set free. Nothing can touch the importance of books and reading in children's lives.

The best learning often happens when children are actively involved in sharing ideas with each other. A book contest is "action learning"—a winning strategy to entice reluctant readers. It's an enjoyable activity for those already immersed in reading. Interaction with peers and the satisfaction of contributing to a team effort provide the same excitement offered by sports and other competitive academic activities.

Children who are not early readers often avoid books because of limitations in their decoding, fluency, vocabulary and/or comprehension abilities. Discussions among team members and opportunities to re-read material several times for legitimate purposes provide strong reinforcement for reading skills. Working with others provides fun and teaches collaboration.

The intensive reading of age-appropriate literature almost always brings pleasure that reluctant or nonreaders have not known before. It creates a desire to keep reading. Children can read difficult materials if they are motivated, and if the books are exciting. Just look at Harry Potter! The books became popular before the media created the hype, but after the big publishing blitz, almost every child felt it necessary to have a copy. They took great pride in being able to read such a long and difficult book.

Competition or Cooperation?

One Battle of the Books critic accused the program of preparing children for war. This is an extreme example of many critics of competitive activities. They feel these activities emphasize winning at all costs.[2]

Unguided competition can be detrimental, especially with young children. However, when the emphasis is placed on the joy of mastering literacy skills in cooperation with others, children learn to respect their own accomplishments as well as the abilities of their classmates. The emphasis needs to be on intrinsic rewards, not the prizes that come from outside.

Children on teams learn to cooperate with each other in order to achieve mutual goals. They contribute their own skills and abilities as part of a joint effort with others, and find they can do more together than by themselves. "This is the best school day of my life!" said the spokesperson of a winning fifth/sixth-grade team in Teller, Alaska. "We've all been reading these books and we're really working together as a team!" added another.

Variations on the Program

Chapter 3 describes how to conduct a full-blown Battle of the Books program. However, there are numerous other less-structured methods of engaging children in a book contest. Classroom book contests can involve all the children. One called Book Charades is fun and creative, since children must figure out how to use mime actions to describe a book title, character or setting. While one team of students uses motions to act out their clue, members of the other team try to guess the answer.

Book Quizzes provide an opportunity for students who do not choose to be on a battle team to participate in a "paper" battle and be rewarded for their efforts. The number of questions depends on the number of books on the booklist and the grade level of the child.

Questions can be read aloud by a reading buddy in grades K–2. The response sheet should include a line after each question to record a key word from the title and the author's last name. To encourage more students to participate, particularly those who shy away from reading activities, offer students the option of consulting the booklist to determine the correct title and author.

Points are earned for correct answers and determine what kind of participation certificate the student receives, such as a basic certificate for participation with different colored stickers for the number of points earned. Parent volunteers can score the quizzes. Although this may seem time consuming, the payoff is getting more students excited about reading books on a list.

There are multiple ways to schedule a Battle of the Books program. The school day at Judson Middle School in Salem, Oregon, has no breaks when teams from all classes can get together. Consequently, their librarian does a version of Battle of the Books in the library at noon for teams of students sharing a common lunch hour. The librarian reads the questions aloud. Each team sits together at a table, and chooses one person to record the answers. These are scored later by the librarian.

A school librarian in Dallas, Oregon, heard about Battle of the Books in a phone conversation with her sister in California. From this conversation, she developed her own program that has been copied by librarians in several nearby districts. The title and author of the assigned book are given before the questioner asks a question on the book. (For example: In the book *Anansi and the Moss Covered Rock* by Eric A. Kimmel, what animal tricks Anansi? Answer: Little Bush Deer.) Points are given for the correct answer. As questions are prepared, the page where the answer can be found is listed with every question, in case there are challenges while the game is going on.

A school in Libertyville, Illinois, uses Battle of the Books as an integral component of their overall reading incentive program. Students earn individual points for reading books on the state Rebecca Caudill Young Readers Book Award list. Twenty of these books are chosen for the school's Battle of the Books booklist, and children also gain points on the quizzes in the Scholastic Reading Counts[3] program.

There are statewide Battle of the Books programs in Alaska, California, New Mexico, North Carolina and Wisconsin. Some programs have spun off from the original idea. America's Battle of the Books,[4] a national nonprofit program, was originally developed in 1986 by Emma Wentland, a librarian in New Mexico. When she moved to California she began the California Battle of the Books program, and later adapted her program into a national one. It is now directed by her son and any school can register.

Computerized programs such as Accelerated Reader[5] and Reading Counts also support these programs. Both offer quizzes on quality children's books. Children read for points and take the quizzes on the computer. Both programs offer customized disks with quizzes for titles of your choice, assuming the titles are in their databases.

Use this book as a guide to get started, but don't feel it is the be-all and end-all of possibilities. Talk it over with your own staff and see if this is a program for you. Adapt it to your own needs. No matter how you adapt a Battle of the Books program to your school or district, "There's no sweeter music than the compliments you hear at the end of a successful Battle of the Books program."[6]

Endnotes
1. Mozell, Ann, e-mail message to Sybilla A. Cook. Sunday, March 7, 2004.
2. Sather, Jeanne. "Compete or Cooperate: Who Wins?" MSN Encarta Web site. Accessed March 11, 2002.
3. Reading Counts, Scholastic, src.scholastic.com/ecatalog/readingcounts.
4. Battleofthebooks.org.
5. Accelerated Reader Software. Renaissance Learning, www.renlearn.com/ar.
6. Aikin, Louisa. "A Bigger Battle." *School Library Journal*, September 2001: 43.

Literacy and Learning Connections

2

"The more children read, the better they get.
Reading exposes children to rich language.
Reading makes all of us smarter."
E. Cunningham and K. E. Stanovich[1]

Unfortunately—or fortunately—the twenty-first century will require everyone to be able to read fluently and be proficient in comprehension. Until now, those who were illiterate could still manage by using their native intelligence and other skills. This is no longer true in our information-based society. The ability to read is a necessity. Our goal in this book is to highlight programs and activities which build a positive attitude toward the communication and use of information and ideas for personal interest and instructional tasks.

The mission statement relating to information literacy and the school library as stated in the IFLA United Nations Educational, Scientific and Cultural Organization (UNESCO) states: "It has been demonstrated that, when librarians and teachers work together, students achieve higher levels of literacy, reading, learning, problem-solving and information and communication technology skills."[2]

Literacy

The report of the National Reading Panel states that "Fluent readers are able to read orally with speed, accuracy and proper expression."[3] Literacy has grown from the definition of the ability to read and write to the broader idea of understanding and dealing with the world of media and information. Today the term literacy is dependent upon the background of the listener for definition. A few examples are computer literacy, functional literacy and information literacy. Skills required for information literacy include how to access, evaluate, communicate and produce information.

Reading enriches children's understanding of the world, beyond what is in their immediate environment. Students need a large vocabulary as well. In her book *Teacher,* Sylvia Ashton-Warner notes children easily learn words that are personally important to them.[4] According to Elfrieda Hiebert, one reason for moving children beyond the basic readers is to provide them with "high-content" words—interesting words with rich meanings.[5]

Competition is an incentive for some children. Others enjoy exploring new ideas, or may become interested in a book because of the questions related to it. Books give a reader vicarious experiences in life situations and unfamiliar settings. They supply possible actions to challenging predicaments while the reader is safe and comfortable in a familiar place. These situations and settings in books stimulate the imagination and encourage the child—whether a competitive participant or an interested observer—to learn more about the world. One of the outcomes of a Battle of the Books program is to build a positive attitude toward the use and communication of information and ideas for personal interest and instructional tasks.

National Programs: Reading Excellence Act, No Child Left Behind

President Bush signed the No Child Left Behind Act (NCLB), a reauthorized version of the Elementary and Secondary Education Act (ESEA), which focuses on the importance of reading skills developed from kindergarten to third grade.[6] Reading First is the challenge since test scores indicate 40 percent of the fourth graders in impoverished areas cannot read at their grade level.

The Reading Excellence Act (REA)[7] awarded more than $327 million to help improve the reading skills of students in kindergarten through third grade. The focus is on tutoring and family literacy as well as professional development and transition programs for kindergarten students.

The original ESEA TITLE II program funded elementary school libraries as a support to the classroom curriculum. With this government encouragement, school districts across the country established libraries staffed with professional school librarians. Because these school library media specialists understood the school curriculum, and the reading and interest levels of their materials, they could easily collaborate with classroom teachers to answer the curricular and literacy needs of different children.

Information Power

Connecting the strands of learning so a student can file each new idea in a connected way with what he or she already knows is part of the collaborative planning between teacher and librarian. Reading, which includes decoding, fluency, comprehension and vocabulary building, is the basis for independent learning. *Information Power: Building Partnerships for Learning*,[8] the handbook developed by the Association of School Librarians and the Association for Educational Communications and Technology, has guidelines for nine information literacy standards for student learning. It emphasizes the awareness that information and ideas are communicated in many different ways: visually, aurally and through a variety of media.

Standard 4 states "the student who is an independent learner is information literate and pursues information related to personal interests." Standard 5 states "an independent learner is information literate and appreciates literature and other creative expressions of literature."

Standards and Benchmarks

"A Developmental Path To Reading," the Summer 2000 issue of the *ERIC Review*,[9] contains several very readable articles about reading benchmarks, from infancy to third grade. This is an issue that parents and teachers may find very useful. The National Reading Panel[10] is another useful source for articles on the development of these benchmarks.

Benchmarks that also apply to the library program are competence in skills and strategies of the reading process in a variety of literature such as:

- reads aloud familiar stories, poems and passages with attention to rhythm, flow and meter
- applies reading skills and strategies—identifies setting, main characters, main events and problems in stories and solution
- applies skills in reading different genres
- identifies favorite books
- identifies story elements
- demonstrates understanding of sequence of events
- uses a picture dictionary to determine word meanings
- identifies the main ideas or theme of the story
- relates story to personal experiences
- makes simple inferences regarding possible outcomes of a story

Reading Assessment in the Library

The reading assessments may come informally by asking the student to:

- retell a story
- summarize a story
- sequence events in a story
- relate a story to a personal experience
- discuss a story with others
- give an opinion of a story
- extend reading through related projects by creating dioramas, puppet plays, posters to advertise a book, etc.

Many states have a favorite book contest each year where students read from a selected list and vote on their favorite title. A list of awards for children's and YA books by state can be located at www.carr.org/read/stateAwardbks.htm. Booktalking and discussion of the titles lead to the question: What kind of books do I like and why?

A social studies standard of the understanding and knowledge of how to analyze chronological relationships and patterns can be the basis for many library activities. The 1942 Newbery Honor Book, *George Washington's World* by Genevieve Foster, is an excellent example of the connectedness between music, art, science and social studies. The American Girl series has a historic addendum at the end of each book that relates to the world outside the book. *Cobblestone* magazine emphasizes relationships among different viewpoints of the same events.

The Six Trait Writing Assessments (or other writing processes) can be discussed and applied to books. Voice, Ideas and Content, Sentence Fluency, Word Choice, Organization and Convention rubrics can be located on the Web at *Six Traits Writing Assessment*.[11] Students can use the writing rubrics to analyze the works of well-known authors.

So what does all this have to do with a Battle of the Books program? Emphasis is being placed on the value and importance of reading today. Many students are struggling to acquire and demonstrate their knowledge of reading skills at an appropriate level. Any reading activity that encourages students to read, comprehend, analyze, synthesize and communicate information found in quality children's literature is definitely worth a try. The Battle of the Books program offers both challenge and opportunity.

In addition, a book contest or a Battle of the Books program provides a golden opportunity for the school librarian to impact student learning in a fun and creative way. It's a chance to collaborate with teachers and parents as they help students acquire and practice reading and other literacy skills. In the process of organizing and implementing a Battle program, a school librarian can put into practice the three basic ideas—collaboration, leadership and technology—which underline the vision of library media programs presented in *Information Power: Building Partnerships for Learning*.[12]

Endnotes
1. Gambrell, Linda. "Motivating Kids to Read." *The Art of Teaching*, a supplement to *Instructor*, 2003.
2. IFLS/UNESCO School Library Manifestion: Section of School at www.ifla.org/VII/s11/pubs/manifest.htm.
3. Report of the National Reading Panel: Teaching Children to Read. Publication Number EX 0115P. National Institute for Literacy, EdPubs, P.O. Box 1398, Jessup, MD 20794-1398.
4. Ashton-Warner, Sylvia. *Teacher*. Simon & Schuster, 2001.
5. Hiebert, Elfrieda. Text Matters in Learning to Read. CIERA Report#1-001. Center for the Improvement of Early Reading Achievement, University of Michigan (1998).
6. Information on NCLB can be found at www.ed.gov/nclb/landing.jthml.
7. www.ed.gov/offices/OESE/REA/index.html.
8. American Library Association, 1998.
9. Published by the Educational Resources Information Center, National Library of Education, Office of Educational Research and Improvement, U.S. Department of Education.
10. nationalreadingpanel.org.
11. www.cyberspaces.net/6traits/. Other sites, including NWREL (the developer of the Six Traits Writing Assessment), are linked from this page. Many of the books listed under the Books to Help Teach the Traits section would make excellent battle books. Students can use the writing rubrics to analyze the works of well-known authors.
12. American Library Association, 1998.

Contests: Begin with the Basics   3

"When I look back over the 20 years I've been associated with the program, I look at the children who read one or more of the list titles, the parents who spend time with their children reading the books and the teachers who use the books as readalouds in their classes. I look at the infusion of carefully selected titles added to library collections and the composure and cooperation of the students as they participate in a battle. Is the program worthwhile? A resounding **yes***. I cannot think of any other reading incentive program that has impacted so many children in Alaska."*
Sue Sherif, School Library/Youth Services Coordinator, Alaska State Library

Once you decide to add a book contest to your program, it's time to make some decisions. Colleagues and supporters must be enlisted so you can collaborate on how you are going to conduct the contest. This will include selecting participants, choosing books, developing questions and establishing procedures and rules. Once these are in place, you can work on inspiring enthusiasm and commitment in your students.

Goals

Reading contests serve many purposes. They supply an incentive for students to read, bring undiscovered titles to their attention, promote books as a topic of conversation and inspire interaction among participants. Contests teach problem-solving skills and help members engage in cooperative learning. They create community interest and support for reading and library programs. Implementing a book contest can strengthen connections among teachers and librarians as well as between schools and public libraries.

Most important of all, book contests kindle a flame of enthusiasm for reading that will continue to burn long after the contest is over. One librarian described a neat thing she noticed when acting as bus monitor was hearing students talk about the books to each other as they waited to board the bus. They often had excited discussions about the characters, plots, settings or solutions to problems. Reading the same books also creates a bond between students, even when they are in different grades or reading at different levels.

Another benefit comes when students move from one school to another or to another school district. They immediately have something in common with classmates in their new school. And when friends who attend different schools are reading books from a similar booklist, their common literary connection may lead to an in-depth discussion of books beyond the school setting.

Which of these goals do you pursue by adding a book contest to your school or library reading program? Are you a classroom teacher who wants children to know that reading is fun, a librarian with great books that need to circulate or a principal or parent association president promoting community involvement and interaction? Book contests range in structure from simple one-time bees in single classrooms to statewide contests involving entire school districts. The format you choose will be determined by which goals you want to achieve.

Format

The first step in creating a book contest is choosing a format. Remember the old KISS formula—keep it as simple as possible in the beginning. If you confine your first reading contest to one classroom, only you and the teacher are involved in the planning. You might decide to start small with the circle format that gives every child a chance to respond to questions, or some simple library book game such as the "Jeopardy" adaptation developed by Rosemary Trotier.[1] As other teachers get interested you can all share ideas and then collaborate to plan a more elaborate program.

Teachers often use baseball, basketball, football or other team sports as models for motivational games that can be played by two teams of students. Arrange three bases plus home plate around the room (if the library is big enough) or on a transparency to project in front of the class. Use baseball rules to determine "runs" and "outs." The leader or "pitcher" reads a question about a book that can be answered with the title and author. If the correct title is given the player advances one base. If the correct author is given the player advances two bases. If incorrect answers are given, the student is "out" and the next "batter" answers a question. After three outs the other team comes up to bat. Students who answer questions correctly may advance paper footballs on a chalkboard field, shoot sponge basketballs into a net or move around the room from chairs representing bases.

Book bees or book circles are other useful formats. The book bee is arranged like a standard spelling bee with children divided into two teams that stand on opposite sides of a room. Questions are asked of one child. If the question is answered correctly, the next question goes to another member of the same team. If the question is missed, the child who misses it sits down, and the next one is asked of the other team. (Some schools give each student a chance to answer two questions before they have to sit down.) The questions continue until only one child remains standing.

Joanne Kelly creates teams within a classroom situation by drawing an imaginary line across the room. Children sitting on one side of the line are on one team.[2] The circle format has all participants sitting in a circle around the classroom. The teacher gives the question to the first student. If that child cannot answer, the next child has a chance to try, and so on around the circle until the question is answered. A new question is then asked of another student. This is a bit less threatening than the bee, because everyone remains in the circle, no matter how many questions are missed.

One advantage of the bee and circle formats is that everyone in a class is involved, rather than a chosen few. A disadvantage is that students know when they will be expected to answer, and may not pay attention until near their turn. Amber, a student who participated in a circle format pointed out another disadvantage. She was always seated on the right of Kayla, a top reader. As the questions went around the circle, Kayla was usually able to answer. Therefore, Amber almost always received a brand new question with little time to think about it.

One way of solving these problems is to have the student who answers the question choose a student to begin the next round of questioning. If the questions usually travel in a clockwise direction, they can be switched to travel counterclockwise occasionally. In a school in Mesa, Arizona, children draw lots for their seating positions.[3] You can also shuffle children at a given signal, or have children change seats every so often.

The bowl and battle format requires teams. Primary teachers usually make team assignments, because they know each child's reading ability and which children work well together. Children at the intermediate level or above usually choose their own teammates. They may be from the same classroom or grade, but this is not necessary. The varied educational experiences of multigrade and other heterogeneous teams can give teams a real advantage. To accommodate children reading well above or below their actual grade level, they can be given the option to read books on a list more appropriate to their actual reading levels.

If you decide to begin with a formal battle structure involving several classes, you will need to consult at the earliest possible time with other teachers and the school principal. While competition is important and fun for students in the intermediate grades, it still needs to be kept fairly low-key so as to prevent a high anxiety level. Encourage children to do their personal best and contribute to the team performance, rather than concentrating solely on total scores. Remind children they are all winners just by reading so many good books.

Practice battles provide **all** students an opportunity to participate in the program. Questions can be read aloud to large or small groups of students. Older students can conduct battles for younger students. Practice battles can be limited to only certain titles, rather than the entire list and can take place before, during or after the instructional school day. They can be held in local public libraries or other community buildings during evening hours, holidays or weekend days. By inviting parents and other community members to attend these practices, they can see firsthand what the program is all about and how they can encourage their own children to read books on the list.

If other schools are involved, and especially if the contest will be conducted district-wide, you need to consult with administrators and any other personnel that may be called upon to assist. The more advanced planning, the fewer glitches and unpleasant surprises. The more people involved the better. Running a battle program is a time consuming job. It's important to delegate responsibilities to others.

The more complex your program, the more help you'll need. The more people participating, the wider the circle of school supporters in the community. Potential helpers may be individual parents, the parent association, senior volunteers, the public library, the local media and independent bookstores or merchants willing to provide incentives for reading.

Alaska, with its schools hundreds of miles apart, has pioneered the use of audio conferencing equipment for their state battles. An in-state telecommunicator company supports the program by offering special rates for the statewide battles. Some districts are also using video conferencing technology to conduct district battles. This adds another whole dimension, since teams can actually "see" the teams they are battling. This can be both good and bad. It adds pressure because of the wider audience—everyone can see what's going on at the various sites—but it also gives the contest excitement and appeals to school spirit in the same way that athletic contests do.

Organizing and Planning

Organization is the basis for successful planning. A simple filing system, either paper or computer, with folders for each aspect of the program, is an easy way to keep track of the many ideas you will collect and use. Suggested titles include Goals and Outcomes, Contests and Programs, Book Selection, Questions, Arrangements, People, Publicity & Public Relations, Forms and Time Lines and Book Activities. These files will grow as your program progresses and should be updated from year to year.

As you present your book contest proposal to your administrator and others whom you hope to interest, support your plan with information from your files. Describe your goals, explain how the program works and how you will evaluate it. Be ready to give examples of successful programs in other districts as well as praises for the program. A list of states and districts currently implementing a Battle of the Books program can be found in the appendix.

Pep assemblies for Battle of the Books teams can be held just before a battle tournament begins. Each school team participates in a mock battle featuring questions from all of the various booklists. Any team can answer a question. The teams are under no pressure and the audience gets to see how battles are conducted and cheer for each team as they would for a sports team. Children who prefer academic rather than athletic team events have a chance to shine and be recognized.

Choosing Participants and Teams

The goals of your program will, of course, determine how participants are chosen. Frequently extra activities in a school are thought to be exclusively for high achievers who require enrichment. Our experience and research[4] indicate that all children gain from reading incentive programs that encourage children to engage in independent reading. Less proficient readers get excited to be teamed up with classmates who are more proficient in reading and will make heroic efforts to read books and answer questions for the sake of the team. What a wonderful opportunity to encourage cooperative learning and team spirit!

For younger children, still essentially "me-centered" a book contest may be their first introduction to the skills of team participation and cooperative learning. Often primary grade teachers or librarians hold contests in which everyone must take part. The most successful programs in the intermediate grades are generally those that introduce the concept to all of the children and encourage those who have a genuine interest to take part.

If the goal of your program is to make every child an avid reader, then all children should be encouraged to be on a team or at least read books on the list in case they decide to be on a team at a later time.

Introducing the Contest

A good introduction is essential to success. To make sure your contest fulfills its goals, it is important that participants see its potential for learning as well as for fun. Children are quick to jump on whatever bandwagon is passing by. All children should be encouraged to participate in some way.

Booktalking the selected titles for all the students in each level is a good way to begin because it engages not only potential participants but other readers as well. Have copies of each book available for children to check out. Involve the entire district in booktalks. In Thorne Bay, Alaska, the librarian asks each teacher to select one of the books on the list and read it over the summer. Then, at the fall staff development program, she sets up a video camera as each person—one by one—gives a five-minute booktalk.

Each booktalk is unique. One teacher dressed up as a character and gave a summary of the story without telling the ending. Another gave some historical background to the story and after the summary explained why the book was so meaningful to her. Once the video is edited it can be circulated to classroom and schools throughout a district. This is a great way to get staff involved in the program and becomes a great motivational tool for students.

One of the best ways to "show" children what a battle book is like is to show a videotape of a battle in action. You could also present a "mock" battle where teachers or older children are recruited to be on teams.

Team Selection

In lower elementary grades, teachers often read the battle books aloud in the classroom so all children including nonreaders, emergent readers and readers are exposed to the stories and can participate in the battles. Most K–3 battles will take place in a single classroom, or involve one or two other rooms. Teachers often select the children for each of the teams. Besides balancing reading proficiencies, teachers use the opportunities to enhance social skills as children interact with each other and the books they choose to read. Some cultures discourage competition. One librarian brings them in by telling them that "You don't know if you'll like it until you try it."

Not all children are required to read every book on a list, but the entire team must know them well enough so someone on the team can answer a given question. This is one way in which less proficient readers can work with more proficient readers. Since the majority of the K–3 books are heavily illustrated, children with keen visual skills have a chance to shine and contribute answers.

Another approach for K–3 contests is to have an entire class be a team. All students participate in determining the answer to each question and a spokesperson states the group answer. Any team with the correct answer earns points, so all teams are winners.

In some schools, teachers choose different teams for each battle, often by counting out, drawing straws or another random method. In other schools, children select their own team members. The teacher or librarian may intercede if a child has moved away, causing a team to be short a member. In that case the teacher or librarian may suggest that another child joins the team. Sometimes it works well to merge two smaller teams.

Team selection in the intermediate grades also involves careful consideration. Teams here usually range from two to five members (with one or two alternates who can fill in if a regular team member is absent on the Battle day). Before any teams are selected, it is important to meet with all of the students who are interested in participating in the contest. It helps to collaborate with teachers of these students so they can participate in the selection process. Next schedule an introductory meeting with students. It is a good idea to send information home to parents asking them to sign a permission slip before their child can take part.

In some schools, interested students put their names in a box. The teacher or librarian determines the teams from these submitted names. In other schools, children choose their own teams. They may choose from within their classroom, within their grade level or from all the participating grades. Meyer Elementary in Salem, Oregon, lets children pick their own teams and their team captain. Once a team is chosen, the members stay together on the team throughout the school year.

Another useful method for team selection, if children are well acquainted, is for the teacher or librarian—or the group, by vote—to select the required number of team leaders. These chosen leaders then create teams from the pool of interested students. When the lists are completed, leaders draw for the team members they will captain. This helps eliminate favoritism.

Before team choices are made, discuss the reasons for having the contest, the importance of giving everyone a chance and what is fair for all. Fourth and fifth graders like to choose their own partners, and this option works well as long as teachers and librarians are aware of potential problems and give some guidance in the process.

Some judicious counseling may also be needed once teams are formed in order to create more balance, include more players and ward off potential problems. In some schools, teacher approval of team rosters has worked successfully in establishing teams that can work well together.

After the teams are chosen, you need to meet with all teams to be sure the responsibilities and expectations for all participants are well understood. For example, team captains are responsible to make sure the members of their teams keep reading and that they arrive on time when battles are scheduled. Team members are responsible for reading assigned titles and learning the official title and author names.

Literary jewelry is one way to identify different teams and build team spirit. Necklaces, bracelets or key rings can be made from shrinky dinks.[5] The team name and a literary representation from one or more of the books is drawn on the special shrinky dink paper. A hole is punched in the top to hang from a chain or to be linked to other parts of a necklace or bracelet, and then shrunk in the oven. Larger images can be used as a window hanging or mobile to identify teams during a battle.

Guidelines, Rules and Scores

You will have to determine a time when the battles can take place within the school schedule. Some schools conduct battles after regular school hours. Some work them in during the lunch hour, which may influence which grades can battle at a particular time. Some schools schedule a particular time for all reading classes, so children can read with others at the same level. Battles fit nicely into this hour. Sometimes battles take place between two or more classrooms at a mutually agreed upon time by the teachers involved. Inter-school or inter-district battles require more collaboration and planning so the needs and interests of all participants are considered and accommodated. If the public library staff will be involved in the program they should also be involved in the initial planning meetings. In Alaska, the dates for the state battles are determined in March for the following school year so districts can determine dates for district battles giving district champs at least a week to prepare for the state battles. Schools within the district determine their own schedules that identify winning teams at least a week before the district battles.

It is a good idea to have all school, district and state battle dates set as early in the school year as possible. This allows dates to be posted on school, district or public library calendars and gives all participants ample time to prepare. Glitches, such as conflicting dates with other school or public library programs or the scheduling of rooms or audiovisual equipment, can be ironed out as quickly as possible.

Elementary children are overwhelmingly concerned with what is fair. A well-conducted contest can be an important means of developing this concept, especially for younger children, whose perceptions tend to be somewhat self-serving. Rules should be established and carefully followed in even the simplest class contest.

You also need to decide how much time you will give students to respond. Usually 30 seconds is enough time for students to come up with their answer. If a team misses the question, the question goes to the other team. They have only five seconds to come up with the answer since they have already heard this question. Some schools give three points for a partially complete answer, and only two points to the other team if they are the ones to answer correctly. Some deduct points for wrong answers.

For the sake of fairness, the Alaska Association of School Librarians no longer gives different questions to different teams in a round. Instead, all teams in a battle receive the same question at the same time for each round. After the teams discuss their answer, the recorder writes down a key word from the title and the author's last name. When the 30-second time limit is up, the spokesperson from each team states the complete title and author. The team's coach or proctor checks the answer sheet to confirm that the stated title and author are the same as those recorded on the answer sheet. This eliminates teams from complaining "the other team got all the easy questions, and our team got all the hard ones." With this variation fewer questions are needed so more quality rather than nitpicky questions are asked.

Many schools are enthusiastic about using buzzer systems to acknowledge team responses. With these, students press the buzzer as soon as they have the correct answer. A beeper sounds and/or a light indicates when the buzzer is pressed, thus ensuring there is no question about who pressed the button first. Using these systems adds even more excitement to a battle, as well as ensuring accuracy. Battles can be done without such equipment, but the lights and sounds certainly add interest to the contests. A list of academic competition systems is included in the appendix.

Contests in the lower elementary grades should promote enjoyable interactions among children and books. Important skills are developed—listening to the question, recalling information and determining which facts are relevant. The focus should be on the learning experience rather than points or scores. When a question is answered, the questioner may then ask the entire group if they agree, keeping all the children engaged. When a child or team does not answer correctly, the general request will avoid placing an individual in the wrong. Most contests in the lower elementary grades permit children who answer incorrectly to remain in the game; they are seldom asked to sit down as in a spelling bee.

In the lower elementary grades, teachers make charts listing the agreed-upon rules. These are discussed before the contest. When a contest is over, children may be asked to decide if they have been successful in following all the rules. It is helpful to conduct numerous practice battles before the real battles begin. Not only does this familiarize team members with the procedures and rules but practice battles can also inspire non-participants to become interested and involved in the game. Easy to answer questions should be used for the battles so students feel successful.

For intermediate grades, and particularly in inter-grade or inter-school contests, you will need to establish more complex rules and be certain that students, teachers and parents understand them. Each contestant should receive a copy and they should be posted in classrooms and the library. If the school or district has a Web site, teachers and parents will appreciate finding them there as well. If a public library is sponsoring a contest, it is sometimes required that children attend a meeting accompanied by a parent so that all questions about the process are fully answered before the competition begins. Rules should be read aloud and explained to younger children.

Here are some rules that have worked well in different schools; you can adapt them to your own situation. You might also want to consult some or all of the Web sites in the appendix which include procedures and rules set by schools and districts from different states.

1. There are 16 or 20 questions to a game.

2. Each team has 30 seconds to come up with the correct answer. They may confer with each other if they wish. The captain gives the answer for the team.

3. Points may be deducted if students are interrupting others.

4. Only questions about the books on a given list may be asked.

5. A team receives five points for each correct answer or title, and three points for the correct name of the author, for a possible total of eight points per question.

6. If, at the end of 30 seconds, the team is unable to answer the question, the opposing team has five seconds in which to give the correct answer. They have only one chance. If they miss, the question goes to the audience. If a buzzer system is used, the team who buzzes first gives the answer. Once it goes off the reader stops reading the question and the team must answer with the incomplete information. If the buzzer is rung early, there will be a five point deduction for an incorrect answer.

7. If the first team is able to give the title of the book (and scores five points) but cannot name the author, the opposing team does not have a chance to answer the question for the additional three points.

8. The audience may not coach members of the team, or talk while the battle is going on. When a question is missed by both teams, the audience may answer any part of the question, either author or title, that has not been answered by either team.

9. All students must remain in their seats at all times.

Questioners need to be fully familiar with the questions and have them arranged to maintain variety and balance. Each team should receive some easier questions and some harder ones. If you give both teams the same questions, easier ones should be used first, then more difficult ones for later rounds. The first set of questions could be easier, to give students confidence. Or have a preliminary rehearsal round using questions already familiar from practice battles.

The final tournament is the culmination of weeks and often months of effort by everyone involved. Plan it as a major celebration. Present certificates or awards to players. Invite the school board, the superintendent and the media. Take pictures or videotape the event. One good shot would be of team leaders shaking hands. Conclude with cheers for all participants, their coaches, sponsors and anyone else worthy of recognition for their support and involvement in the program. Even the book characters and their authors and illustrators can be honored.

Incentives and Rewards

Children need few external rewards for participating in book contests; they are rewarded by its very nature. However, students do value recognition for their effort, such as names on the bulletin board, introductions at an assembly or a listing in a local newspaper or school newsletter or Web site. Team members can give short comments about the contest over the intercom, school radio or TV show.

Although the real reward for reading, understanding and remembering books should be personal satisfaction, many schools offer small prizes to the contestants. Others use more elaborate schemes for motivation and rewards. Recognizing readers both during and at the conclusion of a book contest stimulates interest in the program and honors the reading efforts of all students who participate. Individual, team, classroom or school-wide awards for reading a certain number of books or pages might include the principal or librarian doing something offbeat, free tickets to a school or community event, food coupons, a party, ribbons or certificates.

Everybody enjoys recognition from others when they do a good job. You know your students, your parents and your teachers. Try giving out special passes to the computer lab, gym or "brown bag lunch" passes to the library to practice battle questions. Distribute an invitation to a Battle Book Camp reading marathon in the gym or to a pizza party at the local teen center.

Sleepover Read-a-thons offer students the opportunity to spend a night in the library or other area of the school to enjoy a variety of book-related activities and refreshments. A Battle of the Books Extravaganza sleepover might include practice battles, Thunder Rounds to see how many questions can be answered in 10 minutes, Book Charades, a visit by a local storyteller or battle book games. Individual or groups of students could present book commercials, puppet shows, reader's theater or plays based on battle books. A surprise appearance by a knight in a suit of armor could be a big hit.

Reading Marathons combine the reading talents of students, school staff and parents who form a group to read a particular book. Participants take turns reading aloud for five minutes before passing the book on to another member of the team. The marathon can last for a given amount of time or continue until an entire book is read. Round Robin reading is a similar technique that works well with picture books. A student reads one page before passing the book on to the next reader.

Special Battle of the Books certificates can be awarded to outstanding battlers, perfect-score teams, students who read every book on their grade level list and teams displaying outstanding sportsmanship or team cooperation. Students are nominated for awards by the librarian, teachers and team coaches. Other ideas from different school districts include:

- **Trophies:** For winning teams to be displayed in the library, the front hall of the school or the district office.

- **Permanent badges:** To wear at the battles, and then take home as keepsakes, such as athletic-type letters to wear on a jacket, or small cloisonné buttons that can be worn on a shirt.

- **T-shirt transfers:** Some schools offer T-shirts or pins to identify team members. Some have school trophies inscribed with the names of the members of the winning team. (I was told by the librarian in one school that graduates come back to see if the trophy with their names is still there.) If book battles are established in a district or area, there is often a perpetual trophy with team members' names inscribed. Ice cream or pizza parties or other treats may be provided by local vendors. Independent bookstores might give gift certificates to school, district or state winners.

- **Prizes from sponsors:** Local businesses or sponsors can be asked to donate free passes to a movie, free books or discounts on book purchases. Coupons for free ice cream cones, pizza slices, free admission to skating rinks, bowling alleys or local sporting events. The possibilities are endless.

Arranging the Setting

With the advice of teachers and principals, set the time and place for your final competition at the outset of your planning. Practice sessions and first-round sessions may be called for as the contest proceeds. Discuss with teachers the best ways to provide preparation time, and plan for sharing copies of the books.

Planning the room arrangement is highly important to ensuring a successful battle. Be sure teams are well separated so they can confer without being overhead. Make sure each team can be seen by the audience. Teams can be grouped together around tables with the audience facing the teams in a comfortable setting. Make sure a clock is visible for all to see. Make sure copies of each book are available as a reference for judges or team challenges. Provide a podium and microphone for the questioner and seating for the scorekeeper and judge. If teams are required to record their answers, be sure paper, pencils or writing boards, markers and erasers are available.

Several people are needed to conduct each battle. While they may be recruited from the audience, many librarians have found that peace of mind comes from selecting these assistants ahead of time. A timer is needed to watch the clock and signal when a team's time is up, and a second person is required to keep the score. Someone must be the questioner, and at least one judge is needed to rule on challenges. In some places, students in the audience are invited to volunteer as assistants to the adult facilitators on the day of the battle. It is essential that judges and questioners be thoroughly familiar with the books to be used.

Endnotes
1. Trotier, Rosemary. "Follow this Game Plan." *School Library Journal*, February 1989: 34.
2. Kelly, Joanne. "The Battle of the Books—The Urbana Way." *School Librarian's Workshop*, April 1986: 3.
3. "The Battles Continue." *The School Librarian's Workshop*, November 1986: 8.
4. Krashen, Stephen D. *The Power of Reading, Second Edition: Insights from the Research*. Libraries Unlimited, 2004.
5. www.shrinkydinks.com.

The Books and the Questions

"Four months, five battles, ninety-six questions and six tie-breakers later our team won the district title."

Homer News (Alaska), February 19, 2004

Choosing the Books

With apologies to Margaret Wise Brown,[1] the important thing about a reading contest is that it is about reading. Contests engage children, they contribute to important academic and social skills and they are fun, but the important thing is that they are about reading. A strong book list is your first guarantee of success in raising readers.

A book list must be broad, with appeal for readers who are drawn to different topics and genres and have varied tastes and abilities. It should include books that will bear up under many readings because they have appealing characters, strong plots, positive values and excellent writing. You're more likely to be overwhelmed by the large number of titles to choose from than disappointed by finding too few.

Teachers usually have their own list of favorites for simple book contests. Teachers' manuals will offer many other suggestions. Though these lists become outdated quickly, Web sites abound with up-to-date lists of outstanding books.

You need to be aware of the reading interests and abilities of your teams. Try to include a wide range of genres, types and readability levels. Lists should include books with appeal for girls and boys, and include titles they might not find on their own. Most lists include a classic or two. State regional award lists usually contain books chosen by children from a list of librarian-approved titles. Make sure you include some of the national award winners—not only the Newbery and Caldecotts but also lesser known ones like the Coretta Scott King and John Steptoe awards.[2]

Books on a list can include library titles that correlate to school standards and benchmarks. Such a list will be appreciated by busy teachers and administrators and can also identify you as someone who knows what is going on in the "real world" outside the school library.

Make sure the list contains some books published in the last few years. This helps teachers become aware of current children's literature and adds balance to a list of classics. Include several genres and nonfiction books as well. This gives you, as librarian, a chance to explain the word "genre" to children. Although a challenge for question writing, single poems such as "Casey at the Bat" make good additions to a list.

Including the first title in series books can inspire children to read other titles in the series. Familiar with the main characters, children are then free to concentrate on differences in plots. Mary Pope Osborne's Magic Tree House books, for example, use the same basic plot line in many very different historical settings and events. It can be tricky to write questions for series books because many questions can apply to more than one of these books. You must be doubly careful to make sure they apply only to the particular book chosen.

A booklist can include titles relating to a thematic unit or titles recommended for additional reading in science or social studies units. Biographies, historical fiction or science fiction titles work well for this. Another possibility is to choose books that teachers in your school believe are titles all students should know or read. Books can be selected to expose readers to a variety of well-known and well-loved authors or characters. Literacy skills can be reinforced by including alphabet books, counting books or stories that rhyme.

In creating lists for contests involving several classrooms, schools or districts, it is generally the librarian who takes the lead in gathering suggestions. They do so by consulting professional sources, and compiling a list to meet the needs of participating teachers and their students. Teachers, librarians and parents help select the books for Alaska's statewide book lists. In January, a message board with options for suggesting titles for various levels is set up and posted on the Alaska Association of School Librarian's Battle of the Books Web site. The recommendations are then reviewed by each grade level chairperson who creates a list of possible titles. During a special Battle of the Books meeting scheduled as part of the association's spring conference, participants look over copies of all the books and make their final selection.

The primary list includes picture books where the illustrations carry much of the story, easy readers and chapter books. The books on the intermediate list are for independent readers. These books have a more complicated story structure, which requires more advanced reading skills and enough knowledge and experience to understand the content. Some of these are also suitable for middle schools, while others—the Jean Fritz books for example—are sometimes found on curricular reading lists for younger students.

Some books defy categories, such Debra Fraser's *Miss Alaineus*. While it is designed like a picture book, the topic is vocabulary study in a fifth grade class and 10-year-olds appreciate the story far more than kindergarten children. Other books, like *My Side of the Mountain*, are often read and discussed in a primary classroom and thus become understandable by younger children.

Not all books are right for all children. Books have often been rated on reading levels such as Dolch, Fry and Flesch. Many now also have Lexile scores. More information about these scores can be found at www.lexiles.com. Like the others, these are also based on words and sentence structure, and need to be used with care. One site notes that the Lexile levels for both *Charlotte's Web* and John Grisham's *The Firm* both have Lexile scores of 680—suitable for a proficient reader in fourth grade! Obviously there are other factors to consider.

You know your students best and can factor in such things as age, grade, maturity, background and life experiences. Mix and match from either list, depending on your students' capabilities. But do read the books before recommending them for a battle. Once they are on that list, they become "required reading" and must be suitable for all children taking part in the program.

There are many tools to use in book selection. Resources include professional journals, publications by American Library Association affiliates and lists published by state or regional library and reading associations. Children's literature departments at several universities maintain Web sites devoted to book lists and commentary, as do the majority of children's publishers. Before a book is included, it should be read and reviewed by at least two librarians, teachers or parents.

The number of titles chosen depends upon the complexity of your contest and the number of participants. Most libraries purchase several copies of a title, so the availability of paperback copies may be a criterion for selection. You may also want to survey your school or district for classroom sets of multiple titles. Schools often partner to share sets of books, trading off at intervals until all titles are read.

You need fewer books for simple in-classroom contests. More titles and more copies are needed for school or district tournaments. Alaska, for example, selects an official list of 15 books each for grades K–2, 3–4 and 5–6. All titles must be available in a paperback edition, and at least 25 percent of the titles on the list must be ones used in previous years.

In some bilingual schools, copies may be provided in each language. Frequently, where school book fairs are provided by local vendors, contest books are requested by the librarian or parent association sponsors. Battle books can also be displayed in public libraries and local bookstores.

Writing the Questions

The number of questions you'll need depends upon the length of your book list and the number of players involved. If your list is long, four or five questions for each book may be sufficient; a shorter list requires more questions for each title. You may also want to prepare questions for practice battles, especially in the lower grades where the activity may be totally unfamiliar. Practice battles can be scheduled anytime during the battle program. These informal battles provide students with an opportunity to test their knowledge of books they have already read and whet the appetites of students to keep reading books on the list.

Questions may be used more than once, but students will remember them if they become too familiar, so it is best to have more than you need. A set of new questions should always be provided for the final tournament. In districts where the librarians get together to write questions, they prepare several questions on each book. Some of these are selected for the schools to use, and some are set aside for district or state battles.

The question writing process should be taken seriously to assure fairness during the battles. It is helpful to create a guide for question writing to be used by all writers. (Alaska has a good model for this.) This approach helps identify the most important concepts in a book, and improves the quality and variety of the questions. Take care in your selection of titles to avoid books with similar themes. Sometimes the books chosen are similar in theme or sub-themes, e.g., death of a grandparent, dog as the main character or survival. This can provide difficulty in creating questions pertaining to one of the books because the themes are similar.

Look out for illustrations that depict similar happenings. For example, many picture books show a character reading. Be specific enough to find the answer in only one title. When writing the question, add the number of the page on which the answer can be found. Be open enough to allow for the similar title to be considered correct if you are caught with a non-specific question. Add sticky notes with page numbers to unpaged picture books—it will help the judges check the answer.

Some schools allow teams to challenge questions if they believe another title also answers the question. This makes it important for judges to be thoroughly familiar with all of the books on the list. Book challenges by teams often demonstrate higher level thinking skills and provide students an opportunity to defend their choices. It's also a good idea to review the challenge rule and remind them about good sportsmanship.

The most common questions are knowledge and comprehension questions beginning with "In which book…" that are answered by naming the appropriate book title and author. These questions should be relatively short, using vocabulary understandable to the students or specific idioms used by the author. It is important they fit only one title on the list, but they should be stated in as general terms as possible in reference to places or persons. Use "a character," for example, instead of "a girl"; or "forgot the homework" rather than "forgot his homework." Questions should always be based on the book rather than a film, video or DVD version.

Some schools use a different format for questions. The questioner gives the title and author of the book before the question. For example, the questioner states that the title is *Ramona the Pest* by Beverly Cleary. The question asks "Who gets to be the wake-up fairy?" The expected answer, on page 35 of the book, is "the person who rests most quietly." A similar variation of a question could be "In the book *The Incredible Journey* by Sheila Burnford what are the names of the pets who make the long journey home?" Or "In the book *Curious George* by H. A. Rey what kind of animal is George?"

It's important that questions not descend to trivia. They should relate to the characters, plot, setting or theme. Including unusual and memorable details from the story maintains students' interest and helps them look more closely at the author's style. Questions that emphasize exciting incidents in the plot, without giving away the ending, encourage students in the audience to read the books.

You can ask a question using a quote from the book, but the quote should be one that is used more than one time in the story. For example "In which book does a character say, "I can run away from you, I can! I can!"? (*The Gingerbread Boy* by Paul Galdone.) Or, "In which book does the author address the reader as 'O best beloved'"? (*Just So Stories* by Rudyard Kipling.)

Questions for K–3 books can be asked about pictures in the story, but it is advisable to begin these questions with "In which book do you see a picture of a … ?" Again, questions about pictures should be about pictorial details that are repeated throughout the story. For example, "In which book do you see a picture of alligators wearing black top hats?" (*Mamma Don't Allow* by Thacher Hurd). You may need to identify specific illustrators when you have folktales in several versions.

Students can be involved in writing questions. This practice encourages a deeper look into the structure of a story, and provides practice for writing and thinking skills. When students are taught good question-writing skills, they are often able to write very good questions. If you use this process, provide a form for submitting questions, with a space for recording the question, title, author and page number on which the answer is found. Also include a space for the question writer's name so they can be given credit for their submissions during the battle, if they are used. All questions written by children should be reviewed before use in a battle.

Questions for reading contests can also address one or more of the higher level thinking skills discussed in Bloom's Taxonomy.[3] Ask about comparisons between characters, settings or outcomes for more than one book on the reading list. For example, "In which books do the main characters get married at the end of the story?" (*Mufaro's Beautiful Daughters* by John Steptoe and *Princess Furball* by Charlotte Huck.) These types of questions can be used for fun during practice battles or for tie-breaker rounds during official battles.

It's not surprising that most tournaments, for the sake of simplicity, use factual questions involving memory and comprehension. Some schools use factual questions for the first few rounds of the contest, then use more complex questions for the final rounds. Higher level thinking skills are developed through reading enhancement activities in classrooms or the library. Children spend much time with the contest books, and should profit from all they have to offer.

Endnotes
1. Brown, Margaret Wise. *The Important Book*. HarperCollins, 1951.
2. www.ala.org.
3. Bloom's six cognitive levels of Knowledge, Comprehension, Application, Synthesis, Analysis and Evaluation.

All About Books: Reading Activities 5

"Books are the key to the world of thought;
if you can't do anything else, read all that you can."

Jane Hamilton

In its simplest form, a book contest provides a list of books to read, an incentive for reading the books and time to read the books either as part of or beyond the school day. Activities provide the icing on the cake, the cherry on top of a sundae and the part of the program that makes it come alive. The activities become an important and integral part of the journey—the process by which students really delve into the literature and build their knowledge base of characters, plots, settings and literary themes and conventions as well as develop an appreciation of authors, illustrators and the stories they tell in words and pictures. They ignite a fire under students to read, comprehend and enjoy quality literature.

The possibilities are endless for implementing activities to introduce, promote, extend and enrich the reading of children's literature during any reading contest.

The type of activities you choose depends on:

- the goals of your book contest program
- the number and type of books you select for the program
- the objectives of the program as they relate to the level of involvement and learning outcomes for children
- the amount of time, energy and creativity the school library media specialist, teachers, other instructional staff and parents choose to put into the program

The activities included in chapters 5, 6 and 7 support, enrich and enhance the school curriculum. Some relate to student performance outcomes in literacy and other content areas. Others are more recreational in nature. Of course, an ideal activity is one that combines both fun and learning. Sometimes a simple game using the titles and authors of books or putting together a puzzle to make a picture representing a scene from a book is just plain fun to do. Other activities, such as creating a biography book bag for a favorite character, require much more planning and thinking time to complete and will enrich a student's understanding and appreciation of a piece of literature.

The following activities, which focus on basic literacy skills as well as fluency and vocabulary skills, can be adapted to meet the needs of students at all grade levels. Some work best with individuals or small groups of students, while others are for larger groups or entire classrooms. Some lend themselves to independent student involvement. Others require supervision by the school librarian, classroom teacher, reading teacher or other specialist or parent. Some require little time and effort to initiate and complete, and can be implemented and completed during after-school programs or with the parents at home. Other projects require more direction, more in-depth student involvement and take place during longer periods of time.

Thanks to the Internet, a wealth of literacy activities for most books on a book contest list can be easily accessed. (Check the appendix for the list of resources.) There are also many fine activity books based on children's literature that are easy to incorporate into other projects. Good places to look for these titles are the professional collections in the school or district libraries and in the collections held by reading and writing teachers and specialists. Once you have selected books for your program, it is helpful to set up and maintain a paper and/or electronic folder for each title to store and save the activities you find.

Activities Supporting the Curriculum and Performance Standards

Encouraging students to spend quality time engaged in the reading process for the enjoyment and appreciation of children's literature is the primary focus of any reading incentive program. In addition, the books selected for these programs can also be used as springboards for teaching, supplementing and enhancing the teaching of reading, writing, research and other information literacy skills. By weaving literacy skills instruction into the enjoyment of reading quality children's literature, students are given an opportunity to develop a repertoire of literacy skills in new and different ways. Current trends in education and instructional programs emphasize the importance of improving student performance in these areas, particularly for students in grades K–3. It is also important for students to demonstrate information literacy skills such as accessing, utilizing and evaluating fiction and nonfiction resources to satisfy personal reading interests or solve informational problems. When school librarians and teachers collaborate to provide students with a variety of activities that enable them to practice and improve their reading, writing and research skills in a fun, challenging and engaging way, the potential for creating a "Nation of Readers" increases substantially.

"Reading" the Books

For some students reading titles on a book contest list independently will be a piece of cake. For others, the process is quite challenging for a variety of reasons such as the reading level of the book being too difficult or a lack of interest in a particular type of literature. To help children "read" as many books as possible, consider reading books aloud in the classroom, encouraging parents to read books to or with their children at home and provide access to books on tape (preferably unabridged versions). Groups of students can also benefit from books on tape. For example, one librarian invites small groups of students to select a book they would like to read but find challenging. Each student receives a copy of the book (purchased at a used bookstore) to use during the listening sessions. When students finish listening to the entire story, they are given the book to keep and reread on their own.

Students who qualify for the National Library Service for Blind and Physically Handicapped program[1] are eligible to receive special tape players and copies of books recorded on 4-track audiotapes. In Alaska, the state Battle of the Books lists are given to the librarian in charge of this program and copies of these books—on tape—are sent to qualifying students.

One creative librarian makes her own interactive books on tape. In addition to reading the stories with much expression and voice changes, she includes cues and questions for the listener. For example, after reading, "In the fall we buy some bulbs and plant them in the ground" from *Planting A Rainbow* by Lois Ehlert, she may ask, "Can you count the bulbs that are planted in the ground?" She might also define unusual words in a story or ask the listener to repeat an important phrase or point to something special in an illustration. These homemade tapes can be duplicated and used by students in school, the public library or at home.

Organizing a Book Buddies program provides students who are having trouble reading a particular book the opportunity to spend time with a reading peer who can help the challenged reader get through the book. Book Buddies may also pair older students with younger ones. School staff, parents and other community members can also be recruited to be a Book Buddy.

Reading Enhancements

- **Predictions** are a great way to help readers focus on character development and events in a story. In lower elementary grades, ask students to predict what the book is about by checking for visual clues or words on the cover or title page. Before turning to the next page in the story, ask students "What will happen next?" Older students can make predictions about what individual characters will do in subsequent chapters or what twists and turns the action will take as the story progresses.

- **Book Discussions** introduce readers to a wide variety of books and require students to demonstrate their understanding of what they have read. Discussions can be as simple as unstructured random conversations or more formal and in-depth where students respond to specific questions. They can focus on a single piece of literature or on a variety of books by a single author or a common theme. For more formal discussions it is helpful to brainstorm important questions with students and create a list that will be addressed. By doing this, students can focus their reading on the key questions and take notes to help them during the discussion. For example, if students will be discussing a variety of mystery stories, some key questions for them to consider as they are reading include: What special qualities or skills does the detective in the story have? What are the motives for the villain in the story? What errors did the villain make that caused him or her to be found out? How does the author create suspense? What clues are left out to make it harder for you to solve the mystery? What extra clues are added to confuse you? Is the mystery one that solves a crime, finds something that is missing or has you figure out why the crime has been committed?

  These discussions can also encourage students to think about books in new ways and share their feelings. Some questions to ask students include: Are you glad you read the book? Did you like the way the author told the story? What makes you think the book is so good? How did you feel when the book was over? What was your favorite part of the story? What made the book interesting? What would have made the story more exciting? Did the story seem real?[2]

- **Booktalks** for each of the books on a book contest list are usually developed and presented by the school librarian. One way to involve school staff, students and parents in the book contest is to invite them to create a booktalk for one of the books on the list. Titles can be selected before summer vacation to allow time for reading and preparing a talk. At the start of the new school year, readers are invited into the library to have their booktalk videotaped. Depending on the type of equipment available in your school, the talks can be edited and duplicated in standard video format or DVD. Copies can be distributed to students, teachers and parents so they all become familiar with books on the list. The neat thing about this approach is that each talk is a bit different in format depending on the focus and creativity of the presenter.

    Booktalks can also be aired during local school television or radio programs. When giving booktalks on a theme or genre, book titles can be noted during the talk. "Working Booktalks and Bookchats: Tidbits that Tantalize" by Terrence E. Young Jr. is an excellent article including a definition of a booktalk and a variety of print and online resources on the topic.[3]

- **Compare-and-Contrast Databases or Tables** can be created to help students identify similarities and differences in book characters, settings (time and location), events, themes, genres, awards, etc. Brainstorm with students the fields or headings to include in the database or table. These can encompass all parts of the book or just one area. For example: headings or fields for a database or table on settings might include Title, Location, General Area, Time (month, year, or season) or Important or Not Important to the Story. Headings for a character database or table might include Male or Female, Human or Animal, Child or Adult, Real or Imaginary, Major or Minor to the Story. Headings for a plot database might include Cumulative, Chain or Circular Events, Chronological or Flash Backs, Single or Parallel, Surprise or Expected Ending, Clear-cut/or "I was left hanging" Ending. Other headings might be Point of View (first person or third person), Mood (humorous or dramatic) or Type of Conflict (man against self, nature or society). By using the sort-and-list features, students can find common characteristics in books.

- **Graphing** data found in books is another way students can make connections between books on a list. Students can refer to the list when answering questions such as "How many characters are female?" "How many are male?" "How many are adults?" "How many are animals?" Graphing can also be used to find out how many books represent various genres or subjects or how many books take place in a school, during the winter season or show characters in a tree house. Response to literature surveys can be recorded in a spreadsheet or graphing program and printed out in various visual formats. These include questions such as: Which character is your favorite? Which book did you like the best? Which book made you laugh the most? Which book would you recommend to your best friend?

- **Reader's Theater** provides students an opportunity to select a favorite part of a story and practice reading it with fluency and expression. Individual students can use various voices for different characters or small groups of students can read various character parts. Students need to practice the telling before their final performance. Hand-made puppets or masks can enhance a reader's theater or acting performance and provide shy students an opportunity to perform from behind the stage or incognito. A more complex way to share a story would be for students to act out a favorite scene from a book. Students in grades K–3 can act out entire stories. Rather than announce the name of the book before the performance, let the audience try to guess the book afterwards.[4]

- **A Chain of Events** can be created for each book on a book list. As a student reads a book, each key event is written on a wide strip of paper. Writing should be large and legible. The strips are linked together in sequential order using glue to connect the paper links to form a chain. The first link in the chain should include the title and author of the book. Chains can be displayed in the library, hallways or any other place where students can read the chains.

- **A Poem in a Pocket** allows staff and students to choose short poems that appeal to them. They copy a poem, add names and room numbers and put it in their pocket. During the day, anyone can ask anyone else to trade their poem. Each person reads it to the other, then puts the traded poem in his or her pocket to exchange with someone else. At the end of the day, the classroom teacher lets students read the most recent poem they got in trade and they can see how many different classrooms were involved.

Language Activities

- **Developing Language Concepts** such as recognizing and identifying parts of speech can be reinforced using books on a contest list. As books are read aloud or during guided reading sessions students can be asked to pick out any action words they hear or see. These can be recorded on paper as the student reads or is being read to. Likewise, students can record nouns they identify on a piece of paper divided into three sections—one for nouns that are persons, one for nouns that are places and one for nouns that are things. Emergent readers can listen or look for words that begin with certain consonants (at both the beginning and end of words), phonemes or rhyming words. More advanced readers can look for metaphors, similes or puns.

- **Vocabulary Questions** can be developed to help students focus on unusual, unfamiliar or challenging words. While reading a book, children record any words they don't know on vocabulary posters or in a class notebook (one sheet of paper for each book). They also record the sentence from the book that includes that word and a definition of the word. Students have an opportunity to answer questions that reference these words during practice battles. For example: "In which book does the author use the word 'phosphorescent' to describe the ocean?" (*Amos and Boris* by William Steig).

Visual Literacy

- **Capture a Character on Paper** combines critical reading and character analysis with artistic creativity. Students use paper and other materials to create their favorite book character. After an outline of the character is drawn, a variety of craft materials are used for eyes, hair and clothing to complete the character's appearance as described in the book. Lines are drawn from the character's head, eyes, mouth, hands, heart and feet leading to words describing something the character thought, saw, talked about, did or felt. A backdrop showing a place the character spent time can also be included. The character's name and book title should appear on the top of the paper or on the back if you want others to guess which character is being represented.

- **Character Bags** include items relating to one of the characters in a book. The outside of the bag can be decorated to further identify the character. For example, a character bag for Officer Buckle might include a list of safety tips, a police badge, a dog-training manual, thank-you letters from students and a thumbtack. A card with the character's name and title of the book should be clipped to the bag. Bags can be displayed with or without the identifying card. Students can pull out items from their bag and see who can guess the character, or bags can be passed around and individual students or teams of students can record their guess on paper. These bags can be placed in the library and used as a guessing game for other students. It's a great introduction to biographies.

- **Can You Find?** gives students a chance to locate illustrations or passages and answer a question about a story. This is a great activity to enhance visual literacy. Questions can be asked about one book or several titles on a list. For example, the question "In which book does a tiny mouse peek out at you in every picture?" can be answered with Tomie de Paola's *Charlie Makes a Cloak*. The question "Can you find a part in a story where a character cooks something for someone else?" could be answered by showing a picture of the wolf making pancakes for the chicken and her family in *The Wolf's Chicken Stew* by Keiko Kasza or by reading a segment of the first chapter of *The Stories Julian Tells* by Ann Cameron where the father is making lemon pudding. This activity is a good way for students to get proficient at challenging questions during a battle.

- **Mind Pictures** that visually describe the characters and action for each chapter of a book can be designed by students for all or some of the books they read. A standard 8 ½" x 11" piece of paper can be divided into eight squares. The first square should include the book's title and author. After a student reads or listens to a chapter, time is taken to get a mental image of the characters, setting and action. Once the image is clear in the student's mind, he or she draws that image in the next square. The process continues until there is an image for each chapter of the story. Students keep their mind pictures to jog their memories of the stories they have read. Students in grades K–3 can draw an image for every two to three pages of the story.

- **Be a Picture Detective** encourages readers to look for details in illustrations and make connections between the pictures in a book and the text, both good skills for making predictions and looking for context clues. After reading a page of text found in a picture book, ask students to describe what parts of the picture "show" what the text is saying. For example, after reading "Mr. and Mrs. Mallard were looking for a place to live. But every time Mr. Mallard saw what looked like a nice place, Mrs. Mallard said it was no good. There were sure to be foxes in the woods or turtles in the water,"[5] a student might respond by saying, "In the picture you can see two ducks flying over the land." You can also ask students to suggest any additions to the illustration that would help the reader grasp the meaning of the words. For example, Robert McCloskey could have added a fox running in the woods or a turtle in the water.

- **Rebuses** encourage readers to make mental images of what they are reading. *The Bag I'm Taking to Grandma's* and other books by Shirley Neitzel and illustrated by Nancy Winslow Parker use the rebus concept to help tell the story. Younger students can rewrite a short story and replace visual words with pictures. *The Rebus Treasury* by J. Marzolla can be used to introduce rebuses. A program such as Kidpix lets students mix text and visuals they create. Older students can practice word processing skills or desktop publishing skills by combining text with imported original or clip art images. Pictures can be clipped from old magazines and newspapers and pasted into handwritten stories. Examples of rebus clips from Barrie Public Library Battle of the Books program can be viewed on their library Web site: www.library.barrie.on.ca/kids/Bob/bobclues.htm. Examples of Rebus Rhymes can be found at www.enchantedlearning.com/Rhymes.html.

- **Rebus Stories** based on books can be rewritten on large chart paper leaving blank spots where a picture could go. A Velcro dot is placed in the blank spot. Pictures from magazines are laminated and the other half of the Velcro is affixed to the back of each picture. Each child receives a picture. As the story is read, with pauses at the blank parts, students have to figure out which picture goes in the blank. The person with that picture sticks it to the appropriate spot on the chart.[6] In a story like "Goldilocks and the Three Bears," where there are different size bowls, chairs and beds, students have to analyze their choices and make some informed decisions.

- **Story Quilts** provide an opportunity for students to create images representing the key events in a book that best convey the storyline. The number of squares for the completed quilt will depend on the reading level, the students and the complexity of the story. Squares can be designed using a variety of art techniques. *The Josefina Story Quilt* by Eleanor Coerr can be used to introduce this project. Prior to creating squares, students can also be introduced to a variety of art techniques used by illustrators. A variation of the story quilt is a book quilt including squares with images of the key idea, title and author for each book on a reading list. This quilt can be displayed as a way to help students learn titles and author names for reading contest books. For more quilt activities, see the Jan/Feb 2004 issue of *Instructor*. This includes a pull-out poster of Faith Ringgold's *Tar Beach*.

Story Elements

- **Story Cubes** illustrated with events from a story can be used as prompts for students discussing the story plot. One side of the cube includes the title and author of the story. Other sides include the characters, the setting, the main problem, how the problem is solved and the lesson learned. A story cube can also focus on one character in the story by showing six different stages in the character's life throughout the story. A cube pattern can be found at www.learner.org/catalog/resources/activities/middle/blockpattern.html.

- **Comparisons** of characters within one story or from two or more stories or comparing different books on a similar topic provide students with an opportunity to focus on similarities and differences. The results can be recorded on a chart or using Venn diagrams. Another interesting type of comparison is to note similarities and differences between fictional characters and real ones. For example, referring to *Amos and Boris* by William Steig, ask: "In what way is Amos the mouse like and different from a real mouse?"

- **I Wonder Why?** questions can be developed by students at the end of each chapter. For example, after reading Chapter 1 in Ruth Gannett's *My Father's Dragon*, students might ask: "I wonder why the mother hates cats?" or "I wonder why the cat wanted to weep?" All questions should be recorded (using chart paper works well) so they can be answered as subsequent chapters are read. Some questions will be answered quickly, while others may not be answered until much later in the story. Some questions may never be answered at all.

- **Personality Trait Charts** can be created for any book character. The character's name appears at the top of the page as well as the title of the book. The page is divided into two halves (or sides). Label the top half "Stated," label the other "Implied." As students read a book they add personality traits for a character to the list. If the trait is stated it goes on the the left side or top of the page. If the trait is implied, it goes on the right side or bottom. Some traits might be both stated and implied. The page number(s) where the trait is stated or implied is written next to the trait. A similar activity can be used for the main idea of the book. Readers chart if the theme is stated or implied and where either the statement(s) or the implication(s) are found in the book.

- **Problems, Problems, Problems** charts can be created to track the problems faced by characters in a story. On a paper divided into four sections, students answer these questions: What is the problem? Who is involved in the problem? How is the problem resolved? Why is the solution a good one, or, if it's not, what is the new problem that is created? On the back of the paper or on another page, the readers explain how they would solve the problem. The title and author of the book should appear at the top of the paper.

- **Role Playing** helps students remember the stories and get a better feel for what the characters are thinking, feeling, saying and doing. Parts are assigned to students. If there are more students than characters, more than one student can be assigned to the same character. The librarian or teacher narrates the story. At a part like "'Ah. That feels much better!' said the Well," the student who is the well repeats the phrase while using corresponding actions and expressions to make the story come alive.

- **Photographing the Plot** focuses on identifying and organizing the events in a story. After reading or listening to a story, students talk about the plot and identify each of the key events. Students act out each event and a digital photo is taken to capture each scene. After all of the photos are taken and printed out, individual or small groups of students are given a set of pictures to arrange in sequential order. They then write the text to describe each event.

- **Sequence Pictures** of key events in the story can be drawn by students after a story has been read aloud. Each student draws four to six memorable events from the story on a note card or paper. For older students, a sentence describing the action should be included. All of the cards are collected, then picked out of the pile one at a time and rearranged in the correct order. The set of pictures can be saved and stored in an envelope or Ziplock bag to be rearranged over and over again by other children.

- **Storywebs** or other graphic organizers using words or pictures to identify characters, events in the story, the setting and other important details are good tools to help students focus on key elements of a story. Storywebs—put on display in the library, classroom or hallway—serve as a reminder of the key elements in books on a reading contest list. Webbing can also be used to help students work up in-depth character studies. These include an image of the character and words or pictures describing the physical appearance, thoughts and actions of a character or connections to other characters or events in the story. Software programs such as Kidspiration, Inspiration and PowerPoint work well for this activity. Other graphic organizers can be located at www.graphic.org.

You certainly won't want to try all of these ideas at any one time or for every book on a book contest list! Keep the ideas in mind for those times when you or a teacher need a new or different method of motivating students, beyond the constant pressure to teach, drill and test.

Endnotes
1. www.loc.gov/nls.
2. Shannon, George. Handout, Village Library Workshop, Bethel, Alaska. November 1993.
3. "Nancy Keane's Book Tales Plain and Simple," *Knowledge Quest 32,* no. 1. September/October 2003: 62–63. nancykeane.com/booktalks/default.htm. Includes 1,400 ready-to-use booktalks for children in grades K–12 and tips for preparing and giving booktalks.
4. *Instructor,* January/February 2003: 22–26, 84–85.
5. McCloskey, Robert. *Make Way for Ducklings.* Viking, 1976.
6. Hurley, Linda. Media Coordinator in Knightdale Elementary School, Raleigh, North Carolina.

All About Books: Writing and Research Activities

6

"The student who is information literate accesses information efficiently and effectively, evaluates information critically and competently, and uses information accurately and creatively."

Information Power, page 8, Information Literacy Standards 1, 2, 3

Quality children's books are excellent models to inspire quality student writing. They demonstrate all the elements—characters, setting, dialogue and plot—that a story needs to have. Quality children's books also inspire and challenge students to ask questions and seek additional information about the authors and illustrators who bring them to life. Try these ideas to provide opportunities to practice and improve writing and research skills.

Story Elements

- **What If ... Scenarios** inspire creative and often humorous writing opportunities. Just thinking about possible crossovers from characters or events in books can provide lots of critical thinking and fun. Students respond in writing to questions such as: "What if Hank the cowdog met Kavik the wolf dog?" "What if Big Anthony visited the land of Chewandswallow?" "What if Ramona spent a day in your classroom?" or "What if the BFG became a teacher at Hogwarts School of Witchcraft and Wizardry?"

- **Character Diaries** challenge readers to "become the character." Students design a diary or journal for a particular character. The bookmaking process can be explained at this point. Every time a student stops reading a part of a book, time is taken to write in the character's diary. Entries might include what the character did, thought, felt, said, how the character acted or reacted to a problem or situation and what others in the story have to say about the character.

- **Character Interviews** require readers to brainstorm good interview questions, and then write each question followed by a response from the character. Once written, interviews can be acted out with one student as the reporter and the other as the character. Possible questions might be: How did your thoughts, feelings or attitudes change during the story? If you could change the ending to the story, what would it be? If you could do something different at a critical point in the story, what would that be? What was the most important thing you learned during the story? If the story would continue, what would you do next or what would happen to you?

- **Character Pen Pals** develop critical thinking skills, character analysis and writing skills. Students work with a partner for this activity. Each student chooses a character to represent in a letter writing exchange that is based on the point of view of the character they each represent. The characters can be from the same book or different books. Reader A's character initiates the pen pal letter exchange by writing a letter to reader B's character. The letter writing goes back and forth for any number of exchanges. Students can begin writing while they are reading the book in which their character "lives" or after the book is read. Letters must reflect what the character thinks, says, feels and acts as revealed in the story.

- **Character or Story Poetry** using various poetic formats can be written to capture the essence of a character or book. Forms of Poetry for Children at falcon.jmu.edu/~ramseyil/poeform.htm provides examples from children's literature for limericks, free verse, haiku, cinquian, concrete, ballads, couplets and diamante. After hearing a model in a particular poetic form, students can write their own poems about stories or characters in the books they have read.

- **Character Pyramids** help readers focus on a favorite character, what the character is, the setting in which the character exists and details about the character's appearance, thoughts, feelings and actions. Beginning with the name of the character, the number of words in each successive line increases by one. For example:

Gloria
police dog
visits Napville School
with Safety Officer Buckle
sits at attention upon command
does amazing tricks behind Buckle's back
makes the audience roar and cheer loudly
gives his buddy a kiss on the nose.

From *Officer Buckle and Gloria* by Peggy Rathmann.

- **Matching Text to Pictures** combines prediction skills and writing. Separate the pages of a well-worn or used copy of a picture book. Cover the text with a large note card or lined paper. Assign one page to individual pairs or teams. Have students write a narration for their page of the story. Ask questions like: "What might the characters be saying to each other?" "What is the character thinking about?" or "What is happening in the story on this page?" Encourage students to use dialogue and describe emotions. Students read their text out loud and get feedback before writing their final copy. When each page is complete with narration, the pictures are put in order and the entire story is read aloud. Compare the student-created story with the real story. Pages of the completed book can be laminated and displayed as a "wall book" for all to read.[1]

- **Point of View Stories** encourage readers to think and write about a story from a different perspective. If one person is telling the story, a student can rewrite the story from another character's point of view. For example, in *My Father's Dragon* by Ruth Stiles Gannet, Elmer tells the story. "How would the story be written if Elmer's father, mother, cat or dragon told the story?" "What if the story was written by each of the animals Father encounters along the way?" For longer stories a single scene rather than the entire book can be rewritten from a different perspective. *Fish is Fish* by Leo Lionni and *The True Story of the Three Little Pigs* by Jon Scieszka are good introductions to literary point of view.

- **Readings and Endings** require readers to write an ending to a story after hearing only the first chapter of the book. A new ending can be written after hearing the next chapter of the book. This can continue after each chapter is read. When the entire book has been read aloud, students can share and vote for their favorite ending.

Writing About Books

- **Writing Book Questions** provides students with an opportunity to practice the skill of formulating and writing good questions. A discussion about what makes a good question and the examination of previously used questions should precede the actual writing process. Students can test their questions by asking them of others. All student-written questions should be carefully read by the librarian or a classroom teacher before being used in an actual battle. "Writing Battle Questions" found on page 27 in *Raising Readers: Appealing Approaches & Successful Strategies* by Ruth Toor and Hilda Weisburg describes a question writing assignment requiring critical thinking skills and analysis.

    Another technique to encourage student-written questions is to read a few pages of a story, then stop and ask students to write a question for just that part. Continue reading and have students write more questions. When the book reading is complete, collect the questions, type them up and use them for practice battles. For the lower elementary grades, after reading a page to students, ask them to state a battle question about the words or the pictures in the story. Write down the question to be typed up and used for practice battles.

- **Question Webs** are another way to involve students in the question writing process. Using a graphic organizer program or hand-drawn webs, the title and author of a book are written in the middle with lines webbing out to questions. Question webs can be created for each chapter of a story and posted in the library or hallway. Free graphic organizers including a storyweb are available from Free-ology at www.freeology.com/graphicorgs/.

- **Book Reviews** provide an opportunity for students to practice descriptive or persuasive writing skills. Simple reviews can be a summary of the book's characters, setting, plot, theme and style along with a personal comment about the story. A detailed review may include a more in-depth opinion, or comparisons of the story to other books by the same author, or other stories on a similar theme. Written reviews can be presented orally, posted on a Web site or bulletin board or turned into a videotaped commercial for the book. Scholastic's "Write a Book Review with Rodman Philbrick" describes a five-step plan for writing a review and an accompanying teaching guide.[2]

- **Electronic Book Reports** can be created using KidPix, Hyperstudio, Digital Chisel or PowerPoint. These can be simple in format, focusing on key elements of a book. More complex reports include definitions for unique or unfamiliar words, background information about the author and illustrator or a map showing where the story takes place. Graphical representations of data from surveys (such as the reader's favorite part of the story or how the story made the reader feel) and a list of other books by the same author or on a similar theme may be added.[3]

- **Newspapers** reflecting characters and events in a book can be written and published by groups or individual students. Each newspaper should include news and feature stories, advertisements, an editorial and other special sections patterned after a local newspaper. To introduce a model for creating a newspaper, read *The Furry News: How to Make a Newspaper* by Loreen Leedy. This activity provides an opportunity for students to practice using a desktop publishing program.

- **Play Writing** combines reading, writing, set design creation and acting. After reading a battle book, one gifted and talented class turned the book into a play. They spent almost a semester on the project, writing a script, memorizing parts and working on props, stage production and theater techniques. The play was performed for the community in the town civic center and videotaped for future enjoyment. Play production on a smaller scale can be just as effective. Plays re-enacting favorite parts of stories can be presented by battle book teams on school or district contest days.

- **Reading Journals** provide students with a way to keep track of the books they read, and a place to record questions, comments, thoughts, important details or any other information about each book. The journals can be used to refresh the reader's memory of key facts about a book at any time during the reading contest program. They are especially useful to "brush up" on the books before a final battle or bee. An example of a response to literature journal, "A Journal for Corduroy: Responding to Literature," can be viewed at www.readwritethink.org/lessons/lesson_view.asp?id=30.

- **Pattern Writing** is introduced by giving students a writing model or template from which they create their own poems or stories by substituting their own words for the ones in the model. *Brown Bear, Brown Bear, What Do You See?* by Bill Martin, *If You Give a Pig a Pancake* by Laura Numeroff, *A House Is a House for Me* by Mary Ann Hoberman and *There Was an Old Lady Who Swallowed a Fly* by Simms Taback are a few examples of pattern books.[4]

- **Writing to Authors and Illustrators** whose books appear on a book contest list enables students to practice reading, writing, spelling and handwriting or word processing skills with a purpose. Students should do some prewriting research about the author or illustrator and read at least two books by the author or illustrator. Because a wealth of information about authors and illustrators is now easily accessible on the Internet, questions asked should be unique. Common ones are probably answered on the author or illustrator Web site. Responses from authors or illustrators can be displayed in the library. If more than one student wants to write to the same person, a collaborative letter would probably be more effective. In the lower elementary grades a letter from the entire class can be sent. In one third/fourth-grade classroom the letters received were used to study geography by learning more about the places where the authors and illustrators live.

Students also figured out how much money authors and illustrators spent to send their letters, books and gifts to the school. *The Address Book of Children's Authors and Illustrators, Second Edition*[5] includes addresses for more than 100 authors and illustrators as well as suggestions for completing writing projects such as valid reasons for writing, clichéd questions, examples of poor and valid questions and a sample letter. Generally, an author or illustrator Web site will have an address for responses.

Remember: Not all authors have the time or the inclination to respond to readers. It takes time away from their real job—writing. Most appreciate the heartfelt letters that come when a child is touched by a particular book but may ignore the classroom letters where children are only going through the motions. New authors are usually the most receptive. More popular authors can be overwhelmed.

Research Enhancements

- **Fact and Opinion** or determining what actually happened vs. what the author has invented can sometimes be hard to distinguish. When facts found in historical or realistic fiction, science books or biographies are compared with information found in encyclopedias or Web sites the results can be both surprising and enlightening. Before any research on a selected excerpt begins, students can predict whether they think the author's written word is true or made up.

- **Time Lines** can be created to highlight important historical events before, during and after the time period covered in a fiction or nonfiction book. Timelines should include the title, author and illustrator and a brief synopsis of the book as well as a date, an accompanying description and a visual for each key event. Another timeline can be created for all of the titles on a booklist that are set in historical times. This visual representation of the time and place for a variety of stories can help students remember events in books in a different way. An example of a simple six-item timeline is available at Teach-Nology.[6]

- **Award Winning Books** are deemed worthy of recognition and honored based on certain criteria. Have students find out what criteria are used to nominate and award a book with the Newbery Medal, Caldecott Medal or special state awards. Next ask students to select an award winning book and explain why they think that book received the award based on the criteria or why they think the book should **not** have received the award. The Kids' Choice Awards Lesson plan, web.syr.edu/~crzufelt/medallp.html, outlines a process for students to determine what makes an award winning book, create their own personal book award and honor a book deserving of that award.

- **Historical Events** mentioned in books can be studied in-depth with research that culminates in an oral, written or graphic presentation. These presentations can include a summary of the historical event, the time period and location of the event, the important people involved in the event, the cause of the event and the importance of the event to the people involved and the world. Students can also identify which events are accurately or inaccurately described in the book.

- **A Wall of Unusual or Difficult Words** can display word cards with a sentence from a book that includes a challenging word written on the top of the card and a definition and synonyms for the word written below the sentence. The challenging word should be highlighted or circled. Students use a dictionary and thesaurus to find the meaning and alternate words for the challenging word. The third part of the card includes a new sentence substituting the definition or synonym for the word in the original sentence.

- **Author and Illustrator Studies** can culminate in the writing of simple biographies or more complex multimedia projects. All projects require students to find out information about the author or illustrator, analyze and synthesize the information and present the information to others. A more complex presentation would be for a student to demonstrate how the author and illustrator's backgrounds or personalities are represented in their work. For example: Do any characters in the story look or act like the author or illustrator? Does the story take place where the author or illustrator lives? Did the author or illustrator experience an event in his/her life that also takes place in the story? Do any of the characters look like the illustrator? Does the illustrator hide clues in the pictures that have something to do with the author or illustrator's life?

Author and illustrator Jan Brett sends newsletters to schools about her new books. These give insights into how she creates her books and who her models are. She will send a free teacher's pack to teachers or librarians. Write to her at P.O. Box 366 Norwell, MA 02061, or check her Web page at www.janbrett.com for newsletters and craft activities to go with favorite titles.

Other resources to help with this activity are: *The Big Book of Picture Book Authors & Illustrators* by James Preller (Scholastic Professional Books, 2001); *The Author Studies Handbook* by Laura Kotch and Leslie Zackman (Scholastic, 1995); *Meet the Authors & Illustrators Volume 1* (Grades K–6) by Deborah Kovacs and James Preller (Scholastic, 1991).

- **Authors and Illustrators: Where Do they Live?** combines research and mapping skills. Students find out where favorite authors and illustrators live, then mark the places on a map of the world (or United States). Flags with pins or dots with string leading to a small card can be used to mark the location. The author or illustrator name is written on the flag or card. Once all the markers are in place, students can look for patterns. For example: Which state has the most authors and illustrators? Which region of the United States has the most authors and illustrators?

- **Curiosity Kills the Cat** encourages students to look up information related to things they read about in stories. For example: After reading *Blueberries for Sal* by Robert McCloskey, a student might explore various berries that are picked for canning. After reading William Steig's *Dr. DeSoto*, a student might find out what education is needed to become a dentist or what tools a dentist uses to fix teeth. After reading Karen Ackerman's *Song and Dance Man*, a child can find out about vaudeville life. After reading *Cam Jansen and the Mystery of the Stolen Diamonds* by David Adler, a student can find out more about a photographic memory.

These activities lend themselves well to team teaching. Collaborate with teachers to correlate activities with the various language arts, science, social studies and information literacy standards and benchmarks.

Endnotes
1. Shimjima, Anne. Adapted from a more complex activity. Braeside School IMC, Highland Park, Illinois.
2. teacher.scholastic.com/writewit/bookrev/index.htm.
3. Examples of PowerPoint book reports can be found at the Harris Elementary Schools, Eugene, Oregon, Room 6 Projects at schools.4j.lane.edu/harris/programs/Room6/Slideshows/PPindex.html or Books Alive at www.ncsu.edu/midlink/bkfair/books.alive.html.
4. "Pattern Writing from Books and Poems: Learning to Write from the Masters." www.youthlearn.org/learning/activities/language/pattern2.html. Includes a pattern book writing lesson for *The Important Book* by Margaret Wise Brown.
5. School Specialty Children's Publishing, 1994.
6. teachers.teach-nology.com/web_tools/materials/timeline/.

Activities for Fun and Learning 7

"I think Battle of the Books is a great challenge. You try your hardest and be happy because it is not about winning. It is about having fun and seeing how well you get to know your books."

Hannah Natwick, Tanalian School, Port Alsworth, Alaska

Library Media Center and Classroom Activities

- **Author or Illustrator Phone Conversations** can be arranged with willing authors or illustrators. The librarian or classroom teacher should contact the author or illustrator by letter with a request to "meet" with the person via telephone at the author or illustrator's convenience. If the author or illustrator responds with a "yea," the next step is a phone call or e-mail to determine a day and time for the "chat." Be sure to get the contact phone number and place the call on time. Even a 15-minute conversation with an author or illustrator can get students excited about reading books by that person. Brainstorming questions well in advance of the conversation enables duplicate or similar questions to be eliminated or combined. Prior to the phone call, students asking the questions should practice stating their question loud and clear. To broadcast the telephone conversations use a speakerphone or audio conferencing equipment. Be sure to follow up with thank-you letters from the students. If possible, and if the author/illustrator allows, tape the conversation. If this isn't possible, have a recorder write the author responses to questions so they can be typed up and posted in the library or on a Web page.

- **Book Chains** enable students to keep track of books read. For each completed book, a student writes the title and author on a strip of paper that is looped through the previous link and glued to make a new circular link. The first link should include the student's name, grade or room number. Chains can be displayed in the library, classroom or hallway.

- **Book Sales and Giveaways** get books on the reading list into the hands of students. Contest books can be made available for sale during school book fairs or RIF book distributions. Used copies of books, donated or purchased at used bookstores, can be given to students as prizes for completing reading activities in the classroom or library.

- **Bulletin Boards** highlighting titles on a book contest list serve as visual reminders of book titles, authors, illustrators or genres. Pictures and information about authors and illustrators provide interesting background information about a book. A piece of poster paper for each genre with a definition of the genre can be posted on a bulletin board. Students can add the titles of books for a particular genre. A large interactive bulletin board that includes book titles and markers with student names can be used by students to show which books they have read.

- **Flannel Board Characters** enable students to tell the stories in their own words. Students can make the characters by tracing or drawing images on Pellon®, then coloring the images with crayon, fabric paint or markers. Pellon® sticks well to a commercially or locally made flannel board or a large square of flannel attached to a wall or easel. Each set of characters and any other accompanying images can be stored in clearly labeled envelopes or Ziplock bags.

- **Food Feasts** provide a way to reinforce food details from various books. Have a brainstorming session with students to identify all the different foods mentioned in the books, then have the students sign up to bring a dish to the feast. For example, make green eggs and ham to represent the Dr. Seuss book, or serve olives to represent *The Thief* by Megan Whelan Turner. Books including food from other countries such as vegemite or unusual foods like fried worms might present a challenge, but clever substitutes can be made. Recipes to match books can often be found in magazines or in the cookbook section of the library. A list of cookbooks based on children's books is compiled and updated by Kay Vandergrift at www.scils.rutgers.edu/~kvander/ChildrenLit/cookbooks.html.

- **What Book Am I?** is played by hiding a book in a canvas bag that is hung next to a large piece of poster board. Students write questions that can be answered with a "yes" or "no" on the board. The librarian or teacher writes the answer and students try to guess the name of the hidden book. Students continue to ask questions until they have the correct title.

- **Songs About Books** can be made up by using a well-known tune and substituting the book character names or events from a story. Students who are musically inclined can compose and write original tunes and lyrics. "The Bear Went over the Mountain" or "99 Bottles of Pop on the Wall" work well for this activity. Each verse can be based on a different scene from a book.

- **Stuffed Animals** or other objects representing a character or event can be displayed to represent the titles on a book contest list. The librarian might purchase a few of the more popular ones like Arthur or Clifford from library promotional catalogs. Patterns for some famous characters can be found in sewing catalogs and craft books.[1] Students, teachers and parents can be invited to contribute to the display. Each object should be accompanied with a card noting the title and author of the book.

- **Treasure Hunts and Scavenger Hunts** utilize literacy clues about a particular book that are hidden throughout the library. Students find the clues and place them in a clue box that is on display in the library. Students sort through the clues and guess the name of the book. As the week goes on, more clues are added to the box.

- **Video or DVD** versions of books are a good way to get students interested in reading a book. It is important to remind students that the movie format of a book often is different from the book version. If a video or DVD is shown after students have read a book, a lively discussion can follow comparing the written and visual versions. Similarities and differences can be recorded. (Be aware of copyright and fair use rules before using a taped version.)

- **T-shirts, Bandannas, Wall Hangings and Other Fabric Items** can be decorated with images of characters, places or events in a particular book. Finished items should also include the title and author of the book. Scenes can be drawn on fabric squares with color markers or special iron-on computer transfers.

- **Memorable Quotes and Sayings** from books can be read aloud so students can guess from which book the quote or saying was taken and who said it. Longer excerpts from books can be read aloud to see if students can identify from which book they came. Students can be asked to guess the character after excerpts describing how a character looks, acts or feels is read.

- **Read Aloud Books.** Once a book is chosen, make a poster for the school to indicate which book will be read and the time of the reading. If there is a concern about having too many students attend, tickets can be given in advance to a set number of participants.

Parent Involvement and Take-Home Activities

- **Coloring Pages** for characters or other key elements of a story can be located on the Internet by using the key words "coloring page" followed by the name of a character or related image. For example, if you are looking for a coloring page for *George and Martha Rise and Shine* by James Marshall, you would type in "coloring page" "George and Martha" or "coloring page" "hippopotamus."

- **Do Not Disturb Me, I'm Reading a Battle Book** doorknob hanger can be given to students to display while they are engaged in reading a title on the book contest list.

- **Bookmarks** including titles highlighting books by a particular author, illustrator or theme can be designed by students. The Alaska Association of School Librarians posts each grade level booklist on its Web site. These can be used as study guides for learning book titles and authors or as a checklist for students to keep track of books they have read. Students can also design bookmarks to represent a particular book.

- **Books as Presents** also get titles on a book contest list into the hands of students. Parents can be encouraged to buy these books for their children. Students can be encouraged to buy these books for their friends and to include a note explaining why they chose the book as a gift.

Book Report Variations

- **Dioramas** or other 3-D representations of stories can be made from a wide variety of arts and crafts materials. The title and author of the book should appear clearly on a one-dimensional map or drawing showing each item in the diorama. An accompanying description of each item written on a note card should be included with the project. Display a copy of the book next to the diorama. Examples of dioramas can be found at Easy Dioramas, www.edu-orchard.net/PROFESS/LESSON/ARTS/KR/elem28.html or at Enchanted Learning, www.enchantedlearning.com/crafts/diorama/book/.

- **Postcards** created by students can be used to illustrate the theme or key parts of a story. The front of the postcard should include a visual image that captures the essence of the story. A one- or two-sentence summary of the story and the title, author and illustrator should appear on the back of the postcard. An appropriate stamp can also be designed. Postcards can be created using a word processing or graphics program and printed out for student use. Cards can also be sold as a fundraising activity.

- **Story Mobiles and Collages** enable students to share a book visually. To create a mobile, students draw and cut out pictures of characters and symbols that represent the story. These are attached to a hanger or rod with wire or string. The main part of the mobile should include the title and author of the book. All other illustrations hang from this main section. To create a collage students draw or cut out pictures from old magazines and newspapers that relate to the story. The images are then pasted to a large piece of paper. The title of the book and the author's name should appear on the collage.

- **Book Maps** identify the settings for titles on a book contest list and can be completed as a group project or by individuals. A map of the world can be posted on a bulletin board, and pins with flags including the title of the book can be placed on the map to show where each story takes place. Or students can label and draw lines to places on a smaller map that they can keep as a reminder of the various story settings. Book maps can also be created for an individual book to show where all parts of the story took place. An example of a book map for *Winnie the Pooh* by A. A. Milne can be found at www.lavasurfer.com/pooh-guide.html.

- **Book Posters** including the title, author, illustrator, characters and key events from a story can be created by groups of students or individuals as they read through a book. On the first day the book's title, author, illustrator and characters are added. On subsequent days additional characters and important scenes are included in the poster. As an alternative to using poster board, small scale "posters" can be created using a word processing or desktop publishing program.

Games, Puzzles and Other Amusements

- **Literary Hangman** is based on author, title, events, characters or setting details from a book. Draw a hangman (one per student) on a chalkboard. Put one underline mark for each letter of the answer. One student at a time guesses a letter. They keep going until they miss. If they miss they get the head of a hangman and the next student gets a turn. Keep playing until the correct answer is given. This activity can also be played with partners or smaller groups. The Southwest Michigan Schoolcraft Battle of the Books Web site[2] includes links to online Hangman, Concentration and Phrase Match games for books.

- **Card Games** can be created by designing cards that illustrate book characters, settings or events from a book and corresponding title and author cards. These can be used to play Snap or Concentration. Summary cards can also be used. The old game of Authors can be adapted for books on a reading contest list. After children read a book by one author, have them find three other books by the author and make a set of four cards for that person. For books with at least four characters, cards for each of the characters in a book can be created to play Go Fish. Old Maid is another good card game to use for books with many characters.

- **Games** can be created for most books. Game boards can represent plot points in a story. Chutes and Ladders and Parcheesi are good models for books with an in-depth plot. Battle Book Pictionary can include cards for each title on the book list. Book clues about very specific details can be used in a game of Trivial Pursuit. Squares on Battle Bingo cards can include book titles and authors. "In which book…" questions are read aloud and squares that have titles or authors that answer the question are covered with markers.

- **Puzzles** using character names, places and key concepts from books can be generated from software programs or Web sites. Word searches and crossword puzzles created by students provide an opportunity to identify details found in the stories they read.[3]

- **Stickers** that include the title and author of books on the book contest list can be printed out on address labels. Students can design their own book stickers with a visual clue that represents the story. Each student can make a set of stickers, one for each title on the book list, or individuals can be assigned a book and make enough stickers for everyone in the class. Stickers can be placed on personal notebooks or background paper to be taped to lockers or on a wall at home. It is helpful to use one of the standard word processing label templates for this activity.

- **Trading Cards or Flash Cards** can be created by students for each of the titles on the book contest list. Trading cards can represent the entire book or individual characters or events from the story. Each card should include the title and author of the book. Cards can also include brief book summaries. Decorated paint sticks or Popsicle sticks can also be used to help students remember titles and authors of books. One side of the stick states the title of the book, the other side the name of the author.

- **Riddles** that ask questions about characters, places or entire stories encourage readers to focus on details that are unique to a particular character, setting or story. For example: "I like to work on patient's teeth. My wife assists me in the dental office. I don't like to treat dangerous animals. I once outsmarted a fox. Who am I?" (Answer: *Dr. DeSoto.*) An example of a place riddle is: "If you go to this place you will find where the Woozle wasn't, a trap for Heffalumps and a Hunny bee tree. You will also find six pine trees, a floody place and a woolery. Where are you?" (Answer: *The 100 Aker Wood, Winnie the Pooh* by A. A. Milne.) An example of a book riddle is: "The father in the story makes lemon pudding. Seeds are ordered out of a catalog. Something happens because of figs. A character loses a loose tooth. What book am I?" (Answer: *The Stories Julian Tells* by Ann Cameron.) Another version of this activity is to begin with "I'm thinking of a book that…" Facts or details from a book are stated until someone comes up with the answer. Sticky notes with riddle clues can be affixed to a calendar with large squares. Post a new clue each day of the week until someone guesses the riddle.

- **Jigsaw Puzzles** for titles on a book contest list can be made from unused dust covers or student-designed scenes from a book. Laminate the images to cardboard, then cut them up into puzzle pieces for students to put together. It is a good idea to label each puzzle piece with the name of the book. Puzzle pieces can be stored in an envelope or Ziplock bag.

- **Go Fishing** for questions on paper fish by affixing a magnet on the back of question cards and a magnet on the end of a fishing pole (a stick with string). Students fish for a question and, if they answer the question correctly, they get a sticker or a coupon to trade for a small prize.

- **Paper Dolls** for characters in a story can be dressed in student-designed wardrobes suitable for different events in the book. The paper doll book *Cutting Up with Ramona! Paper Cutout Fun for Boys and Girls* (Dell Publishing, 1983) works well for this activity.

- **Mnemonics** can be made up to help students remember book titles and corresponding author names, especially official author names that include a middle name or initial. For example: Eric Kimmel's middle initial is A and Anansi begins with the letter A. Curious George makes me laugh with a HA! as in H. A. Rey. If you have a key you can Escape to Witch Mountain with Alexander Key.

All-School Activities

- **Teen Reading Practice.** Celebrate Dr. Seuss's birthday by inviting high school students to come to the elementary school and practice their skills by reading to young children. This is a useful parenting skill for future parents—and those who may already have that responsibility—and it could be extended at any time throughout the school year.

- **Book Parades** scheduled for a special literacy week such as Children's Book Week or National Library week involve the entire school in a literary event. Participants dress up as favorite book characters or pull floats on wagons to represent a favorite book.

- **In Which Book? Day or Week** is a fun way to get the entire school involved in Battle of the Books. Each staff person receives a set of battle questions to ask students anytime throughout the school day or week. For example, the PE, art or music teacher can ask battle questions at the start or end of a class period. Recess monitors can ask battle questions on the playground. Cooks and lunchroom supervisors can ask questions during lunchtime. The bus driver can ask questions as students board the bus. The school nurse can ask a question as a student receives a Band-Aid. The principal can ask questions before or after the morning intercom announcement. In one school the custodian had a bulletin board in the lunchroom where he posted jokes and witty sayings. Every so often he would include a question on a battle book. The students loved it.

- **Stumper Questions** about books can be accessed from the library Web page, read over the school's PA system or posted in or outside the library. Stumpers can include difficult or challenging questions or questions that can be answered with more than one title. For example: In which books do the stories take place in the winter? (*Snowy Day, Owl Moon, Froggy Gets Dressed.*) In which books do characters eat pancakes? (*Cloudy With a Chance of Meatballs, If You Give a Pig a Pancake, Wolf's Chicken Stew.*) In which books do characters use a compass? (*Flight, The Big Balloon Race, Amos and Boris.*)

- **Vote For a Favorite Book.** "Of all the Battle books you read this year, which one did you like the best and why?" Students vote for their favorite book by responding to a paper ballot, verbal poll or an interactive ballot posted on a Web page. Answers can be tallied and then acknowledged with a locally designed sticker.

- **Caught in the Act.** Digital photos can be taken of students reading contest books and posted on a Web site or enlarged and displayed on a bulletin board.

- **Murals and Door Decorations** representing books on a book contest list can liven up the library, classrooms or hallways. Students can volunteer to design door decorations to be displayed during a special event week such as Children's Book Week or National Library Week. If the titles are left off, these can be used as a contest for other classes to guess the title of the book the door represents. In the Arctic Light School in Ft. Wainwright, Alaska, judges—including support staff, students and parents—give each door a special title such as "Most Lifelike Characters" or "Best Title Representation." Large murals can serve as a stage prop for booktalks. Cut holes where a character's face would be so that students can put their own heads through the hole as they talk about a book or character.

- **Battle Book Swaps** can take place anytime during or at the conclusion of a battle season. They provide an opportunity for students to trade books on the battle list with other students. Students receive a ticket for every battle book they donate to the swap, and on swap day they can exchange their tickets for other books. It helps to have extra books available. Extra multi-copy library books discarded from the collection or books purchased from a used bookstore can be added to the selection pool.

- **Book Club Discussions** involving adults and students can be based on books on a book contest list. Both students and adults read a particular book, then get together to discuss the story. A librarian or teacher can provide some jump-start questions or a focus for the discussion. Discussion leaders can rotate among the participants including student leaders. *The Mother-Daughter Book Club: How Ten Busy Mothers and Daughters Came Together to Talk, Laugh and Learn Through Their Love of Reading*[4] offers suggestions for organizing and implementing a club.

Vote for your favorite book using a paper ballot, verbal poll or interactive ballot posted on a Web page by responding to "Of all the battle books you read this year, which one was your favorite and why?" Once the responses are tallied, winning titles can be acknowledged with locally designed stickers. Distribute the list of winners to classrooms, the district office and the local media.

Endnotes

1. Girard, Sherry. *Twenty Irresistible Reading-Response Projects Based on Favorite Picture Books: Adorable Reproducible Patterns with Engaging Writing Prompts.* Scholastic Professional Books, 2002.
2. daily-tangents.com/Book2002/games.
3. Online Word Search Maker and Online Puzzle Maker. www.puzzle-maker.com.
4. Dodson, Shireen. *The Mother-Daughter Book Club: How Ten Busy Mothers and Daughters Came Together to Talk, Laugh and Learn Through Their Love of Reading.* Perennial, 1997.

Public Relations

"The time and effort you commit to a Battle of the Books program will be well rewarded with many positive comments from librarians, teachers, administrators, parents and other community members who notice major changes in students' reading habits and their motivation to read good books."

The Sourdough (the newsletter of the Alaska Library Association), June 1982

Your public includes all who are affected by the school library program. Obviously children come first, followed by teachers, parents, administrators and the wider community. Although there's been much discussion lately regarding the importance of reading, surprisingly little focus is placed on the school library as a support and reinforcement for reading instruction.

Book contests, like sports events, are exciting to the participants, the parents and the community. Our contest puts readers and well-chosen books in the spotlight. Sponsored by the school library, they can bring attention to the school librarian's role as part of the reading instructional team. As the emphasis on tests increased in her classes, one Hawaiian teacher saw a decline in students reading for fun. The teacher had heard of the battle held in another school. She recognized the benefits of pleasure reading and decided to begin a classroom edition of the Battle of the Books program. This promoted reading and introduced a variety of genres to her students. The activity was a hit. Students were soon reading and discussing books in class, in the library, in the lunchroom and over the phone at home. Good public relations? The best!

Teachers

As soon as you decide to begin this program, you must inform and involve your staff. If teachers aren't enthusiastic about the program or its goals, it will be difficult for students in their classes to participate. Each teacher in the school usually feels his or her subject matter is important and the time allotted is not enough to do it justice. How can they give up classroom time to engage in reading contest activities?

Be willing to go to a classroom and give booktalks for titles on the list. Volunteer to read one of the books to students in the classroom or library. Offer to lead book activities with the students—chapters 5, 6 and 7 contain many ideas for these.

Support usually increases once a few teachers participate in a book contest. Talk about it during the fall orientation meeting for new teachers. Solicit their input on creating summer reading lists. Classroom teachers know that students need to keep reading over the summer in order to keep their skills sharp.

Administrators

Involvement in and knowledge about a book contest brings support from the principal and other school district administrators. Principals are your first line of school public relations cheerleaders. Their support is crucial to an effective program. Principals can get involved as scorekeepers, timers or the asker of questions. They can offer support by congratulating the participants on their reading efforts. One principal dressed up like the Cat in the Hat while reading the questions. This not only helped decrease the tension among the participants, but provided great photos for the local media. This very visible support underscores the relationship and importance of the activity to student academic achievements.

Although it takes time, make sure other district administrators and school board members know about your school book contest. At the end of the battle season, one Alaskan librarian prepares a four-page brochure highlighting the winners, favorite books (voted on by students) and comments from teachers and students about the program. The brochures are included in the district's newsletter that goes to all parents and school members.

In an Illinois district, the principal sends copies of outstanding classroom projects to the superintendent to be included in the board member packets. Information about Battle of the Books piqued the interest of several board members who came to watch. If the school board meets in the school library, make sure there are plenty of posters around. These will attract the interest of board members and community attendees.

Are you working with just one classroom or are you planning for a school-wide or district program? A district-wide or state-wide program requires support from a wide variety of people, and commands a broad, interested audience. Besides writing up the idea for school and/or public library newsletters, reach out to other types of educators. Send an article to the educational and professional journals read by the principal, the reading consultant and English teachers.

Parents

Parents are your first line of support outside the school setting. Some school libraries are open before the school day starts when parents can drop in to borrow books and read with their children. This is a wonderful time for informing them about book contests on a one-to-one basis. Another opportunity to share titles on book contest lists is when they are part of a parent-child book club. Some public libraries and bookstores have special Battle of the Books displays that create interest in parents and other adults.

Local parent-teacher association meetings are another place to highlight your program. Conduct a mock battle at a meeting so parents can see for themselves how it works. Schedule fun battles, where parents and teacher teams battle and students do the questioning. This could also be a neat addition to a school Grandparents' Day. Make the title lists and contest rules available to parents via booklets, bookmarks or print or e-mail newsletters.

Encourage parents to donate or secure extra copies of the titles or coach teams in preparation for upcoming battles. They might choose one of the books to read aloud at home as a family. The more involved the parents, the more students will find value in participating.

When the book contests are over, recognize the contestants by congratulating them for their achievements and sportsmanship. Make up a flier with action photographs highlighting the winners. Include their favorite books and any comments from teachers and students about the program. You know these will circulate among the family of every highlighted child! Send one to the local newspapers and television stations.

Encourage parents and students to read titles on book contest lists during the summer months. Promote next years' battles by including a copy of the new reading list with the last report card. One school librarian creates paper bags to hold paperback copies of the books for students to take home for summer reading. A book fair before the end of the school year or during summer school enables readers to purchase their own copies of the books. Most vendors are quite willing to bring in suggested titles.

A Hawaiian school conducts two battles a year. One is in the fall before winter break and one is in the spring. Teachers and students often request reading lists for upcoming battles as soon as the current ones are finished. Have them ready ahead of time to capitalize on the interest generated.

A parent organization might contact community businesses for prizes or to showcase posters of the battle titles. They may offer the dollars needed to obtain multiple copies of the books.

School newsletters, parent newsletters and local newspapers featuring school activities are the first level of media promotion. Perhaps parents can help in contacting the local media as well.

Community

Parents can act as ambassadors to other community groups. Nonprofit community organizations are often more than willing to provide support. The local women's group of Altrusa International, for example, teams up with the Boys and Girls Club to sponsor a Battle of the Books program in Douglas County, Oregon. It's part of their literacy outreach.

If local private schools are also conducting battle programs, invite them to participate in the public school battles. Hold them outside the school in a public place where people throughout the community can see what the program is like. A district public library in Illinois brings together parochial and public school teams for a regional battle. The public library public relations officer handles the nitty gritty of publicity in local papers and news shows. Hawaii's Nene Award for the favorite book of the year inspires media coverage from island to island. These same sources are often willing to highlight local events.

Community involvement may stem from a state's focus on improving student reading skills or a broader desire to help local schools in some visible way. Pizza Hut promotions and MS Readathons are two examples of commercial programs designed to support school reading programs. Local businesses might offer prizes for contests or volunteer to treat the winners to pizza or ice cream for their efforts.

Reach out to other local librarians for access to the books and support in reading them. Local bookstores are generally willing to order extra copies of the titles on your booklist, put up posters, offer prizes or even mention the contest in their ads and patron newsletters. The soft drink companies providing large banners for athletic events may be willing to provide equal support to educational and intellectual events such as Battle of the Books.

District Publicity and Web Pages

Who can resist students who are doing something special? Digital photos can be taken of students reading contest books and posted on a Web site or enlarged and displayed on a bulletin board near the district office. School yearbooks should include pictures of students in action during book contests. Be sure to let the yearbook staff know your calendar of activities in advance so plans can be made to take appropriate photos.

Publicity photos for newsletters or newspaper articles, such as a series on "Reading: Caught in the Act" can highlight the upcoming battle and show your school in a positive light. If winning teams receive trophies, perhaps a district one could be displayed in a trophy case near the district office. This acknowledges the importance of reading and the Battle of the Books program along with other district activities.

Many school districts create Battle of the Books Web pages complete with book links, information about the books, dates of upcoming battles, etc.

Media

Ask your local paper, radio or television station to send a reporter to learn the details of the program and highlight it occasionally during the school year. See if they will print sample "stumper" questions occasionally. Perhaps a local radio station would broadcast a battle live on the air? This is the way Battle of the Books was first conducted in the early 1930s. Invite local TV stations to cover the district battles. Ask one of the "stars" to ask questions, be a timer or talk about his or her favorite books to students.

The media might even initiate the reading excitement. There was—and is—much ado whenever a new Harry Potter book comes out. The Dr. Seuss birthday party in March often brings a community reading focus to his works—from the grocery store featuring sandwich bags with his artwork, to public libraries and bookstores featuring special events. Television series such as *Lizzie McGuire* or *PowerPuff Girls* create a demand for these particular books. Incorporate a few of these titles on your book contest list.

The end result and goal is to have students reading more books and becoming avid readers.

<blockquote>
The more you read, the more you know.
The more you know, the smarter you grow.
The smarter you grow, the stronger your voice,
When speaking your mind or making your choice.

Author Unknown
</blockquote>

Battle Books and Questions 9

Kindergarten through Third Grade Books

17 Kings and 42 Elephants

Margaret Mahy. Illustrator: Patricia MacCarthy. Dial, 1972. ISBN: 0803704585.
URL: www.friend.ly.net/scoop/biographies/mahymargaret/index.html (author)
Subjects: stories in rhyme; animals; humorous fiction

Questions

1. In which book do you read about umbrellaphants and rockodiles?

2. In which book do white-toothed crocodiles romp in a river?

3. In which book do jungle animals go on a journey on a wet and wild night?

4. In which book do flamingos chant "Ding Dong Bellicans!"?

5. In which book are there trillicans and gorillicans?

Abe Lincoln's Hat

Martha Brenner. Illustrator: Donald Cook. Random House, 1994. ISBN: 0679949771.
URLs: www.eduplace.com/tview/pages/a/Abe_Lincoln_s_Hat_Martha_Brenner.html (guide)
  www.enchantedlearning.com/crafts/presidentsday/lincolnhat/ (craft)
Subjects: biography; humorous fiction

Questions

1. In which book do the clothes a man wears help people remember him?

2. In which book do you learn that the job of lawyers is to help people settle arguments?

3. In which book do characters stay in poor country inns?

4. In which book is a character known for telling good jokes and stories?

5. In which book does a character travel on a slow, skinny horse named Old Buck?

Adventure on Klickitat Island

Hilary Horder Hippely. Illustrator: Barbara Upton. Dutton, 1998. ISBN: 0525452931
Subject: stories in rhyme

Questions

1. In which book does a character run to the sea carrying a blankie?
2. In which book do characters row an old dinghy in big waves?
3. In which book do sad and bedraggled deer, birds and otters huddle in a clearing?
4. In which book do characters build a shelter out of sticks, twigs, driftwood, clamshells, seaweed, boulders and kelp?
5. In which book do characters stay safe, warm and cozy in a fort on a very stormy night?

Ahyoka and the Talking Leaves

Peter and Connie Roop. Illustrator: Yoshi Miyake. Lothrop, Lee & Shepard, 1992. ISBN: 0688106978.
URLs: www.gbso.net/skyhawk/cher-alf.htm (cherokee alphabet)
   www.authorsillustrators.com/roop/roop.htm (authors)
Subjects: biography; Native Americans

Questions

1. In which book does a character's name mean "She Who Brought Happiness"?
2. In which book is red thread used to sew moccasins?
3. In which book is a national park named after the main character?
4. In which book is the story about the invention of the Cherokee alphabet?
5. In which book does a character create a written language from a spoken language?

Airmail to the Moon

Tom Birdseye. Illustrator: Stephen Gammell. Holiday House, 1988. ISBN: 044084715.
URL: www.tombirdseye.com/sitefrm.html (book information)
Subjects: family life; teeth

Questions

1. In which book does a character think a lost tooth has been stolen?
2. In which book does a character say the tooth fairy makes doorknobs out of teeth?
3. In which book is a character as embarrassed as a "possum up a plum tree and a zebra without stripes"?
4. In which book does a character say she's going to "open a can of gotcha"?
5. In which book does a loose tooth fall out in a dish of spaghetti?

Amos and Boris

William Steig. Farrar, Straus and Giroux, 1971. ISBN: 0374302782.
URLs: www.williamsteig.com/rg-amosandboris.htm (reading guide)
   www.williamsteig.com/williamsteig.htm (author)
Award: ALA Notable Book
Subjects: animals; friendship

Questions

1. In which book does the story take place on the Ivory Coast of Africa?
2. In which book do a mouse and a whale help each other and become good friends?
3. In which book does a character fall off a boat called The Rodent?
4. In which book is a character tossed ashore by a tidal wave and stranded on a beach?
5. In which book does a character use a gyroscope and a sextant?

Anansi and the Moss-Covered Rock

Eric A. Kimmel. Illustrator: Janet Stevens. Holiday House, 1988. ISBN: 082340689X.
URLs: www.ericakimmel.com/includes/Anansi_Rock.pdf (guide)
  www.ericakimmel.com/ (author)
  www.janetstevens.com/ (illustrator)
Subjects: folklore—Africa; Africa

Questions

1. In which book does a character go walking, walking, walking through the forest?
2. In which book does a character play a trick on a lion, an elephant, a rhinoceros, a hippopotamus, a giraffe and a zebra?
3. In which book does a little bush deer finally trick the trickster?
4. In which book are yams and bananas stolen and returned?
5. In which book does a character love coconuts?

Anansi the Spider: A Tale from Ashanti

Gerald McDermott. Holt, Rinehart and Winston, 1972. ISBN: 0030802342.
Award: Caldecott Honor Book
Subjects: folklore—Africa; Africa

Questions

1. In which book does the story take place in Ghana?
2. In which book does a character have six sons?
3. In which book is the story based on an Ashanti tale?
4. In which book does Nyame help solve a problem?
5. In which book does a character have to decide which son deserves the prize?

Annie and the Old One

Miska Miles. Illustrator: Peter Parnall. Little, Brown and Company, 1971. ISBN: 0316571172.
URL: www.sdcoe.k12.ca.us/score/annie/annietg.html (guide)
Award: Newbery Honor Book
Subjects: death; Native Americans

Questions

1. In which book do the characters live in the Navajo world?

2. In which book does a character like to listen to grandmother tell stories of times long ago?

3. In which book is a character given a weaving stick?

4. In which book does a character try to keep someone from weaving?

5. In which book does a character let the sheep out of the night pen?

Anno's Mysterious Multiplying Jar

Masaichiro and Mitsumasa Anno. Philomel Books, 1983. ISBN: 0399209514.
Subject: mathematics

Questions

1. In which book does rippling water become a wide, deep sea?

2. In which book do two countries share an island?

3. In which book are there villages in walled kingdoms on mountains?

4. In which book does each of the houses have seven rooms?

5. In which book are there nine boxes within each cupboard?

Arthur's Birthday

Marc Brown. Little, Brown And Company, 1989. ISBN: 0316110736.
URLs: pbskids.org/arthur/ (Arthur)
www.enchantedlearning.com/subjects/mammals/aardvark/ (activity)
Subject: birthdays

Questions

1. In which book does Grandma make a chocolate cake for a special occasion?

2. In which book are two parties planned for the same Saturday afternoon?

3. In which book do two characters write notes while sitting in a tree house?

4. In which book does a character want to play spin-the-bottle?

5. In which book is a present so big it can't be carried?

Babushka's Doll

Patricia Polacco. Simon & Schuster, 1990. ISBN: 0671683438.
URLs: www.eduplace.com/tview/pages/b/Babushka_s_Doll_Patricia_Polacco.html (guide)
www.patriciapolacco.com/fun/quizes/babushkadoll.html (activity)
www.patriciapolacco.com/author/index.html
Subjects: toys; human behavior

Questions

1. In which book does a character have trouble understanding why she has to wait for things to happen?

2. In which book is a character taken for a ride in a goat cart?

3. In which book does a character make a big mess with tea, soup and noodles?

4. In which book does a character complain about a dress that is dirty, then all wrinkled?

5. In which book is the story about a character who wants everything right now?

The Bear's Toothache

David McPhail. Little, Brown and Company, 1972. ISBN: 0316563250.
URLs: www.cr.k12.ia.us/harr/DavidMc.html (author)
  www.eduplace.com/tview/pages/b/The_Bears_Toothache__David_Mc_Phail.html (guide)
Subjects: teeth; humorous fiction

Questions

1. In which book does a character chew on a steak to loosen a tooth?

2. In which book does a character accidentally break a lamp with a pillow?

3. In which book is a cowboy rope used to pull on a tooth?

4. In which book do you see a picture of a character using a flashlight to examine the inside of a mouth?

5. In which book does a character jump out of a window on purpose?

Ben Franklin and the Magic Squares

Frank Murphy. Illustrator: Richard Walz. Random House, 2001. ISBN: 0375806210.
URLs: www.edu4kids.com/msq/ (activity)
  www.eduplace.com/tview/pages/b/Ben_Franklin_and_the_Magic_Squares_Frank_Murphy.html
Subjects: biography; mathematics

Questions

1. In which book does a character add numbers that always equal 15?

2. In which book do you find out who wrote Poor Richard's Almanac?

3. In which book does a character have a pet squirrel?

4. In which book is the main character a thinker, a writer and an inventor?

5. In which book does a character find out that lightning is made of electricity?

The Big Balloon Race

Eleanor Coerr. Illustrator: Carolyn Croll. Harper & Row, 1981. ISBN: 0060213523.
URL: www.eduplace.com/tview/pages/b/The_Big_Balloon_Race_Eleanor_Coerr.html (guide)
Subject: flight

Questions

1. In which book is the main character an aeronaut?

2. In which book does a pigeon go on every flight?

3. In which book does a character accidentally fall asleep in the Lucky Star?

4. In which book does a character use an altimeter, map and compass?

5. In which book is the Odds and Ends box tossed out of a basket?

The Biggest Bear

Lynd Ward. Houghton Mifflin, 1952. ISBN: 0395148065.
Award: Caldecott Medal
Subjects: animals; bears

Questions

1. In which book do apple trees grow in Orchard's orchard?

2. In which book is a character humiliated because there is no skin nailed to a barn?

3. In which book does a character feed an animal a piece of maple sugar?

4. In which book is a character called a trial and tribulation to the whole valley?

5. In which book are two characters caught in a baited trap?

Bigmama's

Donald Crews. Greenwillow Books, 1991. ISBN: 0688099505.
Subjects: family life; country life

Questions

1. In which book do characters travel to a place called Cottondale?

2. In which book do characters ride on the Southern Railway?

3. In which book do characters look for eggs under a tractor?

4. In which book does a family spend the summer at their grandparents' house?

5. In which book is there a pot for making syrup from sugar cane juice?

Boxes for Katje

Candace Fleming. Illustrator: Stacey Dressen-McQueen. Farrar, Straus and Giroux, 2003. ISBN: 0374309221.
Subject: historical fiction—World War, 1939–1945

Questions

1. In which book does the story take place in a Dutch town after World War II is over?

2. In which book does a character send soap, socks and chocolate to someone she doesn't know?

3. In which book does a character share gifts from America with the neighbors?

4. In which book does a whole town send a thank-you gift of tulip bulbs?

5. In which book are people so poor they don't have socks to wear?

Bringing the Rain to Kapiti Plain: A Nandi Tale

Verna Aardema. Illustrator: Beatriz Vidal. Dial, 1981. ISBN: 0803708092.
URLs: coe.fgcu.edu/students/detschaschell/aardemapg1.html (author)
www.eduplace.com/tview/pages/b/Bringing_the_Rain_to_Kapiti_Plain_Verna_Aardema.html (guide)
teacherlink.ed.usu.edu/tlresources/units/byrnes-africa/monhan/ (activity)
Subjects: stories in rhyme; folklore—Africa; Africa

Questions

1. In which book do acacia trees grow?
2. In which book is the story based on a Nandi tale?
3. In which book does a feather help change the weather?
4. In which book does Ki-pat help end a terrible thing?
5. In which book do the animals have to migrate?

Buffalo Bill and the Pony Express

Eleanor Coerr. Illustrator: Don Bolognese. HarperCollins, 1995. ISBN: 0060233737.
URLs: www.eduplace.com/rdg/gen_act/travel/pony.html (activity)
www.buffalobill.org/history.htm (background information)
Subject: biography

Questions

1. In which book does a character take a job for $25 a week?
2. In which book is a character asked if he can ride, follow trails, swim and shoot?
3. In which book does a character promise to deliver the mail on time no matter what?
4. In which book does a character carry a shiny horn, two pistols and a knife?
5. In which book is a straw man used to trick Terrible Tod and a gang of outlaws?

Butterfly Buddies

Judy Cox. Illustrator: Blanche Sims. 2001. ISBN: 0823416542.
URL: www.enchantedlearning.com/subjects/butterfly/activities/printouts/lifecycle.shtml (activities)
Subjects: school stories; humorous fiction

Questions

1. In which book does a character glue bottle caps onto a pair of shoes to make them click like tap shoes?
2. In which book does a third grader speak French and wear lipstick?
3. In which book does a class hatch painted lady caterpillars?
4. In which book does a character wear yard sale glasses in order to be twins with a teacher and best friend?
5. In which book is there an ear wiggling character?

The Case of the Climbing Cat

Cynthia Rylant. Illustrator: G. Brian Karas. HarperCollins, 2000. ISBN: 0688163106.
URL: www.cynthiarylant.com
Subjects: mystery fiction; detective stories

Questions

1. In which book is Bunny the brains and Jack the snoop?

2. In which book does a character like to sit on a balcony?

3. In which book do characters live in a high-rise apartment building?

4. In which book are a feather and a ticket stub clues to solving a mystery?

5. In which book is a pair of binoculars missing?

Catching the Wind

Joanne Ryder. Illustrator: Michael Rothman. William Morrow and Company, 1989. ISBN: 0688071708.
Subjects: animals; birds

Questions

1. In which book does a character turn into a goose for a day?

2. In which book does a character join a flock of wild geese?

3. In which book does a character have a smooth dark bill, a long, long throat and webbed toes?

4. In which book does a character brush and oil its feathers?

5. In which book do characters fly across the sky in a V formation?

Chicka Chicka Boom Boom

Bill Martin. Illustrator: Lois Ehlert. Simon & Schuster, 1989. ISBN: 061767949X.
URLs: www.eduplace.com/tview/pages/c/chicka_chicka_boom_boom_bill_martin__jr_.html (guide)
  www.friend.ly.net/users/biographies/martinbill/index.html (author)
  www.friend.ly.net/users/biographies/ehlertlois/index.html (illustrator)
Subjects: stories in rhyme; alphabet

Questions

1. In which book does a coconut tree fall over?

2. In which book does the letter "f" wear a Band-Aid?

3. In which book is there a black-eyed "P"?

4. In which book does one character have a skinned knee and another a stubbed toe?

5. In which book do you read the words "Skit skat skoodle doot. Flip flop flee"?

The Chick and the Duckling

Mirra Ginsburg. Illustrators: Jose Aruego and Ariane Dewey. Simon & Schuster, 1972. ISBN: 0021790086.

URLs: www.eduplace.com/kids/hmr/mtai/ginsburg.html (author)
www.eduplace.com/kids/hmr/mtai/aruego_dewey.html (illustrator)
Subjects: animals; birds

Questions

1. In which book do characters come out of a shell?
2. In which book do you see a picture of a broken eggshell?
3. In which book do characters dig holes to find worms?
4. In which book do characters catch butterflies?
5. In which book does one character do everything the other character does except go swimming one more time?

Clara and the Bookwagon

Nancy Smiler Levinson. Illustrator: Carolyn Croll. HarperCollins, 1988. ISBN: 0060238372.
URL: nancysmilerlevinson.com/biography.htm (author)
Subjects: historical fiction; books and reading

Questions

1. In which book does the story take place on a small farm in Maryland?
2. In which book does a character dream while rocking in a chair that Papa carved?
3. In which book is Mr. Holzer's store also a book station?
4. In which book does a character bring books to people who live in the country?
5. In which book does a character want a peppermint stick for a treat?

Click, Clack, Moo Cows that Type

Doreen Cronin. Illustrator: Betsy Lewin. Simon & Schuster, 2000. ISBN: 0689832133.
URLs: pbskids.org/lions/cornerstones/click/ (guide)
www.folusa.org/html/ClickClackMoo.pdf (guide)
www.betsylewin.com/ (illustrator)
Award: Caldecott Honor Book
Subjects: animals; humorous fiction

Questions

1. In which book does Farmer Brown get notes about a cold barn?
2. In which book do characters want some electric blankets?
3. In which book do animals go on strike and refuse to give milk or lay eggs?
4. In which book is a duck said to be a neutral party?
5. In which book do characters request a diving board for a pond?

Cloudy with a Chance of Meatballs

Judi Barrett. Illustrator: Ron Barrett. Atheneum, 1978. ISBN: 0689306474.
URLs: www.sdcoe.k12.ca.us/score/Cloudy/cloudytg.htm (guide)
www.eduplace.com/tview/pages/c/Cloudy_with_a_Chance_of_Meatballs_Judi_Barrett.html
Subjects: weather; humorous fiction

Questions

1. In which book does the story take place in the town of Chewandswallow?
2. In which book does the weather provide all the food?
3. In which book does the Sanitation Department have a big clean-up job after every meal?
4. In which book are rafts made out of stale bread and peanut butter?
5. In which book does the sun look like a giant pat of butter?

Commander Toad and the Planet of the Grapes

Jane Yolen. Illustrator: Bruce Degen. Coward McCann, 1982. ISBN: 0698205405.
URL: www.janeyolen.com/janebio.html (author)
Subject: science fiction

Questions

1. In which book is the Captain of the ship brave and bright and bright and brave?
2. In which book is the mother ship called Star Warts?
3. In which book do characters travel in a sky skimmer?
4. In which book do characters like to play chess, checkers and leapfrog-and-toad?
5. In which book does a doctor wear a grass-green wig?

The Courage of Sarah Noble

Alice Dalgliesh. Illustrator: Leonard Weisgard. Atheneum, 1954. ISBN: 0684188309.
URLs: www.eduplace.com/tview/pages/c/The_Courage_of_Sarah_Noble_Alice_Dalgliesh.html
www.sdcoe.k12.ca.us/score/courage/couragetg.html (guide)
Award: Newbery Medal
Subject: historical fiction—frontier and pioneer life; character

Questions

1. In which book does a character hear the sounds of an owl, a fox and a wolf and become too frightened to sleep?
2. In which book does a father say, "In our home all will be treated with kindness. The Indians too and they will not harm us"?
3. In which book is a father worried about the safety of his eight-year-old daughter when he leaves her with another family?
4. In which book does a character read aloud from the Bible to children who do not understand English?
5. In which book does a character pray to the Great Spirit for the safety of family, friends and a horse?

Crinkleroot's Guide to Walking in Wild Places

Jim Arnosky. Macmillan Publishing Co., 1990. ISBN: 0027058425.
URL: www.jimarnosky.com/ (author)
Subject: nature study

Questions

1. In which book do you find out how to remove a tick from your clothes or skin?
2. In which book do you learn about different kinds of ferns?
3. In which book do minnows tickle a character's toes?
4. In which book does a character look at a miniature forest growing in a crack in a large rock?
5. In which book do you read about poison ivy, poison oak and poison sumac?

The Day Jimmy's Boa Ate the Wash

Trinka Hakes Noble. Illustrator: Steven Kellogg. Dial, 1980. ISBN: 0140546235.
URLs: t3.preservice.org/T0300794/ (guide)
www.stevenkellogg.com/page2.html (illustrator)
Subjects: imagination; humorous fiction

Questions

1. In which book does a character go on a class trip to a farm?
2. In which book do pigs get on a school bus?
3. In which book do characters throw corn and eggs at each other?
4. In which book does a hen lay an egg on someone's head?
5. In which book does a pet pig replace a pet snake?

Dinner at the Panda Palace

Stephanie Calmenson. Illustrator: Nadine Bernard Westcott. HarperCollins, 1991. ISBN: 0060210109.
URLs: www.stephaniecalmenson.com/author.phtml (author)
www.nationalgeographic.com/kids/creature_feature/0011/pandas.html (activities)
Subjects: animals; stories in rhyme; counting

Questions

1. In which book does an elephant spend the day on the road selling peanuts?
2. In which book do peacocks ask about reservations at a restaurant?
3. In which book do penguins wearing hats and jewels waddle inside to eat?
4. In which book do the Honey Bear All-Stars carry gloves, balls and bats?
5. In which book do waiters have to feed fifty-five diners?

Doctor De Soto

William Steig. Farrar, Straus and Giroux, 1982. ISBN: 0374318034.
URLs: www.eduplace.com/tview/pages/d/Doctor_De_Soto_William_Steig.html (guide)
www.williamsteig.com/rg-doctordesoto.htm (guide)
www.williamsteig.com/williamsteig.htm (author)
Award: Newbery Honor Book
Subjects: teeth; humorous fiction; mice; animals; dentists

Questions

1. In which book do a dentist and his wife work together?
2. In which book does a character refuse to treat animals dangerous to mice?
3. In which book does a character have a rotten bicuspid and bad breath?
4. In which book does a character wear a flannel bandage around his jaw?
5. In which book do characters outsmart their patient?

Do Not Open

Brinton Turkle. Dutton, 1981. ISBN: 0525442243.
URL: www.eduplace.com/tview/pages/d/Do_Not_Open_Brinton_Turkle.html (guide)
Subjects: cats; animals; humorous fiction

Questions

1. In which book is Captain Kidd a cat?
2. In which book does a character like to find things on the beach after a storm?
3. In which book does a character find a deep purple bottle?
4. In which book does a character want a banjo clock to run properly?
5. In which book is a big, ugly creature tricked into becoming a mouse?

The Doorbell Rang

Pat Hutchins. William Morrow and Co., 1986. ISBN: 0688052517.
URLs: www.eduplace.com/tview/pages/d/The_Doorbell_Rang_Pat_Hutchins.html (guide)
www.harperchildrens.com/teacher/catalog/author_xml.asp?authorID=17047 (author)
Subject: counting

Questions

1. In which book does Ma bake twelve cookies for her two children?
2. In which book do characters think Grandma makes the best cookies?
3. In which book does a character try to mop the kitchen floor clean each time new visitors track it up?
4. In which book does the kitchen keep getting filled up with more and more people?
5. In which book do characters have less and less to eat as more people come to their house?

Drummer Hoff

Barbara Emberley. Illustrator: Ed Emberley. Prentice Hall, 1967. ISBN: 0132208229.
URL: www.readin.org/authors/author_pages/Emberley/emberley.htm (author)
Award: Caldecott Medal
Subjects: stories in rhyme; peace; historical fiction; war

Questions

1. In which book is a character in charge of firing a cannon off?
2. In which book is a carriage needed to hold a barrel?
3. In which book does a General give an order?
4. In which book is a rammer used?
5. In which book do you see a picture of a character holding a barrel of gunpowder?

Each Peach Pear Plum

Janet and Allan Ahlberg. Viking, 1979. ISBN: 0670287059.
URL: www.mystworld.com/youngwriter/authors/allanahlberg.html (author)
Subject: stories in rhyme

Questions

1. In which book do you play an I Spy game?
2. In which book do you see a picture of Tom Thumb and Mother Hubbard?
3. In which book do you see a picture of the Three Bears looking through a window?
4. In which book are Bo-Peep and Jack and Jill characters?
5. In which book do all the characters eat a pie that is sitting in the sun?

Edgar Badger's Fishing Day

Monica Kulling. Illustrator: Neecy Twinem. Mondo, 1999. ISBN: 157255603X.
Subjects: friendship; fishing

Questions

1. In which book do characters rent a speedboat?
2. In which book is a character disappointed when the big one gets away?
3. In which book are earwigs, worms, grubs and acorns eaten?
4. In which book do two friends spend a day on Pine Lake?
5. In which book are a salamander and a porcupine invited for dinner?

The Elephant's Child

Rudyard Kipling. Illustrator: Lorinda Bryan Cauley. Harcourt Brace, 1983. ISBN: 0152253858.
Subjects: animals; humorous fiction

Questions

1. In which book does a character have a "satiable curiosity"?
2. In which book does a character get spanked for asking questions?
3. In which book does a character want to know what the Crocodile has for dinner?
4. In which book does a character go to the great grey-green, greasy Limpopo River?
5. In which book does a character say, "Come hither, Little One"?

The Erie Canal Pirates

Eric A. Kimmel. Illustrator: Andrew Glass. Holiday House, 2002. ISBN: 0823416577.
URLs: www.erickimmel.com/biog.htm
www.erickimmel.com/includes/Erie_Canal.pdf (guide)
Subject: songs

Questions

1. In which book is a character known as the "Terror of Buffalo"?

2. In which book is a shot fired that can be heard from Saratoga to Montreal?

3. In which book does a ship sail up Niagara Falls?

4. In which book do pirate ghosts walk on the shores of Tonawanda?

5. In which book does a mule named Frank have to defend hay from another mule?

First Grade Takes a Test

Miriam Cohen. Illustrator: Lillian Hoban. Greenwillow Books, 1980. ISBN: 0688802656.
URL: www.lillianhoban.com/biography.htm (illustrator)
Subject: school stories

Questions

1. In which book is a student excited to find out how smart she is?

2. In which book are students told to read the questions and fill in the box next to the right answers?

3. In which book do characters have to figure out what rabbits eat and what firemen do?

4. In which book does a character wonder what being tall has to do with getting a baloney sandwich?

5. In which book does a character decide she doesn't want to be in a special class?

A Fish in His Pocket

Denys Cazet. Orchard Books, 1987. ISBN: 0531057135.
URL: www.harperchildrens.com/authorintro/index.asp?authorid=20824 (author)
Subject: school stories

Questions

1. In which book does a character break the ice on Long Meadow Pond?

2. In which book does an arithmetic book fall into a pond?

3. In which book is a paper boat named Take Care?

4. In which book does the story take place on a day in the month of November?

5. In which book does a character shout, "I know!" during quiet time?

Flat Stanley

Jeff Brown. Illustrator: Tomi Ungerer. HarperCollins, 1964. ISBN: 0060206810.
URLs: www.eduplace.com/tview/pages/f/Flat_Stanley_Jeff_Brown.html (guide)
  flatstanley.enoreo.on.ca/index.htm (activities)
  flatstanley.enoreo.on.ca/jeff_brown.html (author)
Subjects: humorous fiction; travel

Questions

1. In which book does an enormous bulletin board fall on top of a character?
2. In which book is a character mailed to California in a brown paper envelope?
3. In which book does a character stand inside a picture frame?
4. In which book is an old bicycle pump used to blow up a character?
5. In which book does a character get to fly his brother like a kite?

Flight: The Journey of Charles Lindbergh

Robert Burleigh. Illustrator: Mike Wimmer. Philomel Books, 1991. ISBN: 0399222723.
URL: www.charleslindbergh.com/history/paris.asp
Subjects: biography; flight; travel

Questions

1. In which book is the main character known as the Lone Eagle?
2. In which book is something named *The Spirit of St. Louis*?
3. In which book does a character plan a trip from New York to Paris?
4. In which book does a character stay awake for more than 60 hours?
5. In which book is a character famous for traveling across the Atlantic Ocean?

Flossie and the Fox

Patricia C. McKissack. Illustrator: Rachel Isadora. Dial, 1986. ISBN: 0803702507.
URLs: www.eduplace.com/tview/pages/f/Flossie_and_the_Fox_Patricia_McKissack.html (guide)
  www.childrenslit.com/f_mckissack.html (author)
  www.harperchildrens.com/authorintro/index.asp?authorid=17066 (illustrator)
Subject: animals

Questions

1. In which book does a character walk through the piney woods carrying a basket of eggs?
2. In which book does a character have a hard time proving he is who he says he is?
3. In which book do you see a picture of a character sorting peaches?
4. In which book is a character worried about losing his confidence?
5. In which book does a character think he can outrun one of J. W. McCutchin's mutts?

The Fossil Girl: Mary Anning's Dinosaur Discovery

Catherine Brighton. Millbrook Press, 1999. ISBN: 0761314687.
URL: www.ucmp.berkeley.edu/history/anning.html (history)
Subjects: biography; dinosaurs

Questions

1. In which book does the story take place in Lyme Regis, Dorset, England, in 1810?

2. In which book do characters collect and sell curiosities?

3. In which book is a special tower built so a character can work on something in the side of a cliff?

4. In which book does a character find and study the remains of a creature that lived a long time ago?

5. In which book does a character look for information in a book called *Strange Creatures of the World*?

Franklin in the Dark

Paulette Bourgeois. Illustrator: Brenda Clark. Scholastic, 1986. ISBN: 0590445065.
URL: www.franklin.ecsd.net/author_paulette_bourgeois.htm (author)
Subjects: animals; fear

Questions

1. In which book is a character afraid of crawling into a small shell?

2. In which book does a duck wear water wings?

3. In which book does a lion wear earmuffs?

4. In which book are characters afraid of deep water, loud noises and freezing?

5. In which book does a character solve a problem by turning on a nightlight?

Frog and Toad Are Friends

Arnold Lobel. HarperCollins, 1970. ISBN: 0060239581.
URLs: www.sdcoe.k12.ca.us/score/frog/frogtg.html (guide)
  www.eduplace.com/tview/pages/f/Frog_and_Toad_Are_Friends_Arnold_Lobel.html (guide)
  www.eduplace.com/kids/hmr/mtai/lobel.html (author)
Award: Caldecott Honor Book
Subject: friendship

Questions

1. In which book does a character want to be awakened at half past May?

2. In which book does a character have a very hard time thinking up a story to tell?

3. In which book do characters look for a button missing from a jacket?

4. In which book does a character **not** want to be seen wearing a bathing suit?

5. In which book does an empty mailbox make a character feel unhappy?

Froggy Gets Dressed

Jonathan London. Illustrator: Frank Remkiewicz. Penguin Books, 1992. ISBN: 0670842494.
URL: www.eduplace.com/kids/hmr/mtai/london.html (author)
Subject: winter

Questions

1. In which book does a character yell "Wh-a-a-a-t?" when his mother calls him?

2. In which book does a character walk with a flop, flop, flop sound?

3. In which book does a character forget to put on underwear?

4. In which book does a character's green face turn red?

5. In which book does a character keep putting clothes on and taking clothes off making zoop, zup, zat, zwit, zum, zip, znap sounds?

The Furry News: How to Make a Newspaper

Loreen Leedy. Holiday House, 1990. ISBN: 0823407934.
URL: www.loreenleedy.com/pages/04author.html (author)
Subject: newspapers

Questions

1. In which book does a character volunteer to be the publisher?

2. In which book do reporters receive assignments and get instructions on how to write a story?

3. In which book is an editorial written?

4. In which book do characters sell space for advertisements?

5. In which book is there a three o'clock deadline for getting the job done?

Galimoto

Karen Lynn Williams. Illustrator: Catherine Stock. Lothrop Lee and Shepard Books, 1990. ISBN: 0688087892.
URLs: teacherlink.ed.usu.edu/tlresources/units/byrnes-africa/chrhal/galimoto.GIF
   www.catherinestock.com/aboutcatherine.html (author)
Subjects: toys; Africa

Questions

1. In which book does a character keep special things in a shoebox?

2. In which book does a character need wire to make something special?

3. In which book does a character help someone catch a large ant?

4. In which book do women carry heavy baskets of maize to the grinder at the flour-mill?

5. In which book does a character make a toy that looks like a pickup truck?

The Gardener

Sarah Stewart. Illustrator: David Small. Farrar, Strauss and Giroux, 1998. ISBN: 0374325170.
URL: www.randomhouse.com/kids/author/results_spotlight.pperl?authorid=28746 (illustrator)
Award: Caldecott Medal
Subjects: New York City; Great Depression; gardening; family life

Questions

1. In which book does a character travel all alone by train to live with an uncle in New York City?

2. In which book does a character look for a stranger who has her mother's face and a mustache?

3. In which book does a garden grow on the roof of an apartment building?

4. In which book do neighbors share flowers and plant window boxes?

5. In which book does a character teach Latin in exchange for learning how to bake?

George Washington's Mother

Jean Fritz. Illustrator: DyAnne DiSalvo-Ryan. Grosset & Dunlap, 1992. ISBN: 0448403846.
URL: www.eduplace.com/kids/hmr/mtai/fritz.html (author)
Subject: biography

Questions

1. In which book is a character made the top general of the American army?

2. In which book is a character known as the father of our country?

3. In which book do characters live at a place called Mount Vernon?

4. In which book does a character wear a cape and a three-cornered hat?

5. In which book does part of the story take place when Virginia was an English Colony?

The Girl Who Loved Wild Horses

Paul Goble. Bradbury Press, 1978. ISBN: 0878881212.
URLs: www.murrieta.k12.ca.us/tct/reading/grade3/core%5Flit/girl%5Fwho%5Floved%5Fwild%5Fhorses/ (activities)
  monet.unk.edu/mona/exhibit/artists/goble/gobleexh.html (author)
Award: Caldecott Medal
Subjects: folklore—Native American; horses; Native Americans; animals

Questions

1. In which book do characters follow the buffalo?

2. In which book do thunder and lightning cause animals to gallop faster and faster?

3. In which book does a character prefer to live with a wild spotted stallion?

4. In which book is a colt given to the main character's parents?

5. In which book are animals given blankets, decorated saddles, eagle feathers and ribbons?

Gold Fever

Verla Kay. Illustrator: S. D. Schindler. Putnam, 1999. ISBN: 039923027.
URLs: www.verlakay.com/ (author)
   www.penguinputnam.com/nf/Author/AuthorPage/0,,0_1000039496,00.html?sym=BIO
   www.cr.nps.gov/nr/twhp/wwwlps/lessons/55klondike/55klondike.htm (activities)
Subjects: historical fiction; gold mines and mining

Questions

1. In which book does a farmer decide to get rich by going west?

2. In which book do you see pictures of two men escaping from a bear and a bobcat by climbing trees?

3. In which book does a miner see rattlesnakes hiding in a rocky crevice?

4. In which book does a character find out that mining is hard and dirty work?

5. In which book do the grumpy miners have a fireside brawl?

The Golly Sisters Ride Again

Betsy Byars. Illustrator: Sue Truesdell. HarperCollins, 1994. ISBN: 0060215631.
URL: www.betsybyars.com/ (author)
Subjects: historical fiction—frontier and pioneer life; humorous fiction

Questions

1. In which book is it bad news that a goat is in the audience?

2. In which book do characters listen to a talking rock?

3. In which book does a character write a play about a princess and a troll?

4. In which book do characters need a holiday from dancing and singing?

5. In which book do two characters remember when they were little and afraid of thunder and lightning?

Grandfather Twilight

Barbara Berger. Putnam, 1984. ISBN: 0399209964.
URL: bhberger.com/children/frameset_children.htm (author)
Subject: night

Questions

1. In which book does a character close a book, comb his beard and put on a jacket at the end of every day?

2. In which book is there an endless strand of pearls?

3. In which book does a character go for a walk holding a pearl in one hand and a cane in the other hand?

4. In which book does a character use a key to open a chest?

5. In which book does a character toss something to the silence of the sea?

Green Eggs and Ham

Dr. Seuss. Random House, 1960. ISBN: 0394800168.
URLs: www.eduplace.com/tview/pages/g/Green_Eggs_and_Ham_Dr__Seuss.html (guide)
www.seussville.com/ (author)
Subjects: stories in rhyme; humorous fiction

Questions

1. In which book do you see a picture of a sign that reads "Sam I am"?

2. In which book does a character **not** want to eat something in a box or with a fox?

3. In which book is a character offered something in a car, on a train or on a boat?

4. In which book does a character finally try something he didn't think he would like to eat?

5. In which book does a character finally decide to eat something anywhere?

Gregory the Terrible Eater

Mitchell Sharmat. Illustrators: Jose Aruego and Ariane Dewey. Four Winds Press, 1985. ISBN: 0027822508.
URLs: teacherlink.ed.usu.edu/tlresources/units/MonsonUnits/AmyHal/Nutrition.html
www.eduplace.com/tview/pages/g/Gregory_the_Terrible_Eater_Mitchell_Sharmat.html
www.eduplace.com/kids/hmr/mtai/aruego_dewey.html
Subjects: humorous fiction; human behavior

Questions

1. In which book does a character like to kick his legs into the air and butt his head against walls?

2. In which book do characters eat tin cans, clothes and old shoes?

3. In which book does a character think fruits and vegetables are revolting foods?

4. In which book does a character get a stomachache from eating too much?

5. In which book is a character given spaghetti and a shoelace with tomato sauce for dinner?

Harold and Chester in Hot Fudge

James Howe. Illustrator: Leslie H. Morrill. William Morrow and Company, 1990. ISBN: 0688082378.
URL: teacher.scholastic.com/authorsandbooks/
Subject: humorous fiction

Questions

1. In which book is the story told by a dog who has written other books about his family?

2. In which book do characters fall asleep full of good stories and good chocolate?

3. In which book does a character think pets are really a cheap burglar alarm system?

4. In which book is a character believed to be a vampire?

5. In which book does a character fall asleep while protecting a house from robbers?

Heckedy Peg

Audrey Wood. Illustrator: Don Wood. Harcourt Brace, 1987. ISBN: 0152336788.
URLs: www.audreywood.com/mac_site/auds_jumpstation/aud_jumpstation.htm (author)
www.audreywood.com/mac_site/don_stuff/don_page/don_page.htm (illustrator)
Subject: fairy tales

Questions

1. In which book are characters named after the days of the week?

2. In which book are the children told not to let in a stranger?

3. In which book are children turned into food?

4. In which book does a character jump off a bridge never to be seen again?

5. In which book is there a character with a missing leg?

Henry and Mudge in the Sparkle Days

Cynthia Rylant. Illustrator: Suçie Stevenson. Simon & Schuster, 1988. ISBN: 0689810180.
URL: www.cynthiarylant.com/growing.htm (author)
Subjects: winter; humorous fiction; pets

Questions

1. In which book does a character dress up for a special candlelight dinner?

2. In which book does snow make someone sneeze?

3. In which book does Dad bake the turkey?

4. In which book does a character wish for peace on Earth?

5. In which book does a character wish for a certain basketball team to win?

Hey, Al

Arthur Yorinks. Illustrator: Richard Egielski. Farrar, Straus and Giroux, 1986. ISBN: 0374330603.
URL: www.rif.org/art/illustrators/egielski.mspx (illustrator)
Award: Caldecott Medal
Subjects: fantasy; humorous fiction

Questions

1. In which book is the main character a janitor?

2. In which book do characters travel to an island in the sky?

3. In which book is the moral of the story "Paradise lost is sometimes Heaven found"?

4. In which book are a man and a dog carried away by a bird?

5. In which book does a character say, "I'd rather mop floors"?

Battle Books and Questions

A House Is a House for Me

Mary Ann Hoberman. Illustrator: Betty Fraser. Viking, 1978. ISBN: 0670380164.
URL: www.maryannhoberman.com/ (author)
Subject: stories in rhyme

Questions

1. In which book is the story about all kinds of houses?

2. In which book do you find out who lives in a coop, a sty, a fold and a hutch?

3. In which book do you learn about the shelter for an ear of corn, a hickory nut and a pea?

4. In which book do you see a picture of a boy playing the song "My Dog Has Fleas" on a flute?

5. In which book do you find out where Eskimos and Cree, Hopi and Mohee Indians live?

How I Became a Pirate

Melinda Long. Illustrator: David Shannon. Harcourt, 2003. ISBN: 0152018484.
URL: www.harcourtbooks.com/authorinterviews/bookinterview_shannon.asp (author/illustrator)
Subjects: imagination; pirates

Questions

1. In which book does the main character like to play soccer?

2. In which book is a character valued for his skills as a digger?

3. In which book is a character asked to bury a chest of gold and jewels?

4. In which book do most of the characters have green teeth or no teeth at all?

5. In which book does the Captain wear a braided beard?

How My Parents Learned to Eat

Ina R. Friedman. Illustrator: Allen Say. Houghton Mifflin, 1984. ISBN: 0395353793.
URLs: www.sdcoe.k12.ca.us/score/food/foodtg.html (guide)
www.eduplace.com/tview/pages/h/How_My_Parents_Learned_to_Eat_Ina_R__Friedman__illustrated_by_Allen_Say.html (guide)
www.eduplace.com/author/say/ (illustrator)
Subjects: culture; family life; eating customs

Questions

1. In which book is the story about a Japanese schoolgirl and an American sailor?

2. In which book do characters eat with knives, forks and chopsticks?

3. In which book do characters eat sukiyaki and tofu?

4. In which book does a character get help from Great Uncle?

5. In which book do characters go to a Japanese restaurant?

Hubert's Hair-Raising Adventure

Bill Peet. Houghton Mifflin, 1987. ISBN: 0395282675.
URL: library.thinkquest.org/j0111400/biography.htm (author)
Subjects: stories in rhyme; humorous fiction

Questions

1. In which book does a character walk along Zamboozi Creek?

2. In which book does a character laugh so hard he cries tears?

3. In which book is the elephant the only character brave and clever enough to get what is needed to solve a problem?

4. In which book is a character described as being haughty, vain and conceited?

5. In which book is old Hornbill called the neighborhood gossip?

If You Give a Pig a Pancake

Laura Numeroff. Illustrator: Felicia Bond. HarperCollins, 1998. ISBN: 0060266864.
URLs: www.lauranumeroff.com/bio/index.htm (author)
  www.kiddyhouse.com/Teachers/Literature/LPig.html (activities)
  www.lauranumeroff.com/kids_fun/index.htm (activities)
Subject: repetitive story

Questions

1. In which book is a character given maple syrup?

2. In which book does a character want bubbles for a bath?

3. In which book does a character want to send a picture to her friends?

4. In which book does a character dance to piano music?

5. In which book does a character want wallpaper and glue to decorate a tree house?

Imogene's Antlers

David Small. Crown Publishers, 1985. ISBN: 0517555646.
URLs: www.pippinproperties.com/authill/small/index.htm (author)
  pbskids.org/readingrainbow/family/activities/activity33.html (activity)
Subject: imagination

Questions

1. In which book does a character wake up on a Thursday with something strange growing out of her head?

2. In which book does a mother faint every time she sees her daughter?

3. In which book does a character think his sister has turned into a rare miniature elk?

4. In which book do characters eat donuts?

5. In which book does a milliner create a very special hat?

In the Dinosaur's Paw

Patricia Reilly Giff. Illustrator: Blanche Sims. Dell Publishing, 1985. ISBN: 0440441501.
URL: www.cbcbooks.org/html/patricia_reilly_giff.html (author)
Subject: school stories

Questions

1. In which book do characters read about King Midas?

2. In which book does a class celebrate National Handwriting Day?

3. In which book does a character often say "Ruff-a-roo"?

4. In which book does much of the story take place in room 113?

5. In which book do the characters race down the hall to "special help reading"?

Is Your Mama a Llama?

Deborah Guarino. Illustrator: Steven Kellogg. Scholastic, 1989. ISBN: 0590447254.
URL: www.stevenkellogg.com/page2.html (illustrator)
Subjects: stories in rhyme; humorous fiction

Questions

1. In which book does a character talk to a bat, a swan, a cow, a seal and a kangaroo?

2. In which book are animals asked about their mothers?

3. In which book does a character ask the same question to several different friends?

4. In which book does the main character have big ears, long lashes and fur?

5. In which book are the friends named Dave, Fred, Jane, Clyde, Rhonda and Lyn?

James Marshall's Mother Goose

James Marshall. Farrar, Straus and Giroux, 1979. ISBN: 0374336539.
URLs: www.hbook.com/exhibit/marshallradio.html (author)
   www.enchantedlearning.com/rhymes/coloring/ (activity)
Subject: nursery rhymes

Questions

1. In which book do characters go around a mulberry bush?

2. In which book does a mouse run up a clock?

3. In which book does a character fall asleep under a haystack?

4. In which book does a character break after falling off of a wall?

5. In which book does a merry old king have three fiddlers?

Jesse Bear, What Will You Wear?

Nancy White Carlstrom. Illustrator: Bruce Degen. Macmillan Publishing, 1986. ISBN: 002717350X.
Subject: stories in rhyme

Questions

1. In which book does a character have a red shirt and pants that dance?

2. In which book do you see a picture of a rose between a character's toes?

3. In which book does a character play in a sandbox?

4. In which book is a character stuck in a chair at noon?

5. In which book does a character wear pajamas with feet and a face on the seat?

John Henry

Julius Lester. Illustrator: Jerry Pinkney. Dial Books, 1994. ISBN: 0803716060.
URLs: www.eduplace.com/tview/pages/j/John_Henry_Julius_Lester.html (guide)
  www.eduplace.com/kids/hmr/mtai/lester.html (author)
  www.friend.ly.net/users/jorban/biographies/pinkneyjerry/ (illustrator)
Award: Caldecott Honor Book
Subjects: folklore—United States; railroads

Questions

1. In which book does a baby grow so big his head and shoulders bust through the porch roof?

2. In which book does the meanest man in the state become Frederick the Friendly after losing a race?

3. In which book does a character leave home carrying two 20-pound sledgehammers?

4. In which book does a character pulverize a boulder into pebbles and finish building a road?

5. In which book is there a contest between a steam drill and a man?

The Josefina Story Quilt

Eleanor Coerr. Illustrator: Bruce Degen. HarperCollins, 1986. ISBN: 0060213485.
URL: teacher.scholastic.com/authorsandbooks/
Subject: historical fiction—frontier and pioneer life

Questions

1. In which book does a family travel to California in a covered wagon?

2. In which book does a pet hen get into trouble?

3. In which book does Pa use a long whip to move the oxen?

4. In which book does a character sew a pine tree patch?

5. In which book is an animal too old to lay eggs and too tough to eat?

Joseph Had a Little Overcoat

Simms Taback. Viking, 1999. ISBN: 0670878553.
URL: www.eduplace.com/tview/pages/j/Joseph_Had_a_Little_Overcoat_Simms_Taback.html (guide)
Award: Caldecott Medal
Subjects: clothing; storytelling; folklore—Jewish

Questions

1. In which book is the lesson of the story "you can always make something out of nothing"?

2. In which book does the story come from an old Yiddish folk song?

3. In which book does a man take a worn out jacket and turn it into a vest?

4. In which book does a lost button turn into a story?

5. In which book is the story partly told by the holes in the pages?

Just Another Ordinary Day

Rod Clement. HarperCollins, 1995. ISBN: 0060276665.
Subjects: imagination; humorous fiction; school stories

Questions

1. In which book does a character awake to the sound of an alarm which rings at 6:30 a.m. every school day?

2. In which book does a character ride to school with the oldest person on the block?

3. In which book does a character like science and doing experiments?

4. In which book do you see a picture of a waiter serving cheeseburgers for lunch?

5. In which book does a dad make some very hot curry for dinner?

Keep the Lights Burning, Abbie

Peter and Connie Roop. Illustrator: Peter E. Hanson. Carolrhoda Books, 1985. ISBN: 0876142757.
URLs: www.usalights.com/maine/abbie.htm (history)
 www.author-illustr-source.com/peter_and_connie_roop_____auth.htm (author)
Subject: biography

Questions

1. In which book does a family live on a rock off the coast of Maine?

2. In which book does the father go for supplies in a little boat called *The Puffin*?

3. In which book does a character have to scrape ice off the windows so a light can be seen?

4. In which book is a character afraid her chickens will be washed away during a storm?

5. In which book does a character have to trim wicks, clean the lamps and put oil in them?

The King's Equal

Katherine Patterson. Illustrator: Vladimir Vagan. HarperCollins, 1992. ISBN: 0060224967.
URL: www.terabithia.com/about.html (author)
Subject: fairy tales

Questions

1. In which book does a greedy and arrogant prince rule the country?
2. In which book is a circlet of gold important to the story?
3. In which book does a character want to marry three people?
4. In which book is a dungeon the penalty for characters who can't solve a problem?
5. In which book is a character sent away to live with goats in the mountains?

Knots On a Counting Rope

Bill Martin Jr. and John Archambault. Illustrator: Ted Rand. Henry Holt & Company, 1987. ISBN: 0805005714.
URLs: www.friend.ly.net/users/jorban/biographies/martinbill/index.html (author)
   www.eduplace.com/tview/pages/k/Knots_on_a_Counting_Rope_Bill_Martin_Jr__and_John_Archambault.html (guide)
Subjects: Native Americans; grandparents

Questions

1. In which book do a grandfather and his grandson share a story as they sit around a campfire?
2. In which book does a character find out he was born sick and frail?
3. In which book does a character get strength from blue horses?
4. In which book is a foal named Rainbow?
5. In which book does a character ride a horse bareback in a race?

The Legend of the Bluebonnet

Tomie de Paola. Putnam, 1983. ISBN: 0399209379.
URLs: www.tomie.com/main.html
   www.tomie.com/about_tomie/index.html (author)
Subject: folklore—Native American

Questions

1. In which book do characters talk to the Great Spirits about sending rain?
2. In which book does a character have a warrior doll?
3. In which book is a character called She-Who-Is-Alone?
4. In which book does a character have to sacrifice a valuable possession?
5. In which book do characters live in tepees?

Lewis and Clark: A Prairie Dog for the President

Shirley-Raye Redmond. Illustrator: John Manders. Random House, 2003. ISBN: 0375811206.
URLs: teacher.scholastic.com/products/instructor/lewisandclark.htm (activity)
   www.kidsplanet.org/factsheets/prairie_dog.html
Subjects: biography; Lewis, Meriwether; Clark, William; explorers; West (U.S.)—exploration

Questions

1. In which book is Thomas Jefferson a character in the story?

2. In which book do characters make maps, explore rivers, collect plants and draw wild animals?

3. In which book is an animal flooded out of a hole in the ground?

4. In which book are presents sent to Mr. Peale's museum in Philadelphia?

5. In which book do two explorers reach the Pacific Ocean in the year 1805?

The Library

Sarah Stewart. Illustrator: David Small. Farrar, Straus and Giroux, 1995. ISBN: 0374343888.
URLs: www.eduplace.com/tview/pages/l/The_Library_Sarah_Stewart.html (guide)
  www.parents-choice.org/full_abstract.cfm?art_id=22&the_page=editorials (illustrator)
Subjects: stories in rhyme; books and reading

Questions

1. In which book does a character drag a big, green steamer trunk to school?

2. In which book is the story about someone who owns a lot of books?

3. In which book does a character dream of entering a readers' Olympiad?

4. In which book does a character go to the courthouse to look for a donation form?

5. In which book is a building named after the main character?

The Library Dragon

Carmen Agra Deedy. Illustrator: Michael P. White. Peachtree Publishers, 1994. ISBN: 156145091X.
URLs: www.eduplace.com/tview/pages/l/The_Library_Dragon_Carmen_Agra_Deedy.html (guide)
  www.fcps.edu/fairfaxnetwork/mta2005/authorinsights.html (author)
  dlstewart.com/aboutmichael.htm (illustrator)
Subjects: libraries; school stories

Questions

1. In which book do you see a picture of a claw and nail sharpener?

2. In which book does the school hire a "thick-skinned" librarian?

3. In which book does a character worry about sticky fingered children ruining books?

4. In which book is storytime restored when a near-sighted character reads a book aloud in the library?

5. In which book does the main character lose her scales?

Lilly's Purple Plastic Purse

Kevin Henkes. Greenwillow Books, 1996. ISBN: 0688128971.
URLs: www.kevinhenkes.com/meet/kevin.asp (author)
  www.nancypolette.com/LitGuidesText/LillysPurplePlasticPurse.htm (activities)
Subject: school stories

Questions

1. In which book does a character love the way her boots go clickety, clickety, click?
2. In which book does a character want to be a teacher like Mr. Slinger?
3. In which book do characters like to say the word "Wow"?
4. In which book does a character spend time in the Lightbulb Lab?
5. In which book does a character sit in the uncooperative chair?

The Little Red Hen

Paul Galdone. Seabury Press, 1973. ISBN: 0816430993.
URLs: www.ri.net/schools/Central_Falls/ch/heazak/hen/hen.html (activities)
www.houghtonmifflinbooks.com/catalog/authordetail.cfm?authorID=3709 (author)
Subject: folklore

Questions

1. In which book do a cat, a dog and a mouse like to sleep all day?
2. In which book does a character find some grains of wheat?
3. In which book do some of the characters keep saying "Not I"?
4. In which book does a character say, "Then I will"?
5. In which book does a character eat all of the cake by herself?

The Littles

John Peterson. Illustrator: Roberta Carter Clark. Scholastic, 1967. ISBN: 0590462253.
Subject: fantasy

Questions

1. In which book do characters live in tiny rooms within the walls of a house?
2. In which book is an electric socket really a secret door?
3. In which book do mice threaten the safety of a family?
4. In which book is a sword made from a sewing needle?
5. In which book do characters escape danger by going through a trap door under a radiator?

Lizard's Song

George Shannon. Illustrators: Jose Aruego and Ariane Dewey. Greenwillow Books, 1981. ISBN: 0688803105.
URLs: www.harperchildrens.com/teacher/catalog/author_xml.asp?authorID=12712 (author)
www.eduplace.com/kids/hmr/mtai/aruego_dewey.html (illustrators)
Subjects: repetitive story; songs

Questions

1. In which book does a character like living on a big flat rock?
2. In which book do characters sing "Zoli zoli zoli" over and over again?

3. In which book does a character forget what he learned when he sees ducks and a rabbit?

4. In which book is a character the kind who, when he sees something he likes, he wants it and takes it?

5. In which book do characters sing and dance back to their homes?

Lon Po Po: A Red-Riding Hood Story from China

Ed Young. Philomel Books, 1989. ISBN: 0399216197.
URLs: web.bsu.edu/00smtancock/CyberLessons/LonPoPo/ (guide)
   www2.scholastic.com/teachers/authorsandbooks/authorstudies/authorhome.jhtml?authorID=216&collateralID=5311&displayName=Biography (author)
Award: Caldecott Medal
Subject: folklore—China

Questions

1. In which book do characters climb a gingko tree?

2. In which book are three sisters endangered by a hungry wolf?

3. In which book does a mother tell her children to close the door tight and latch it well?

4. In which book does an animal pretend to be a grandmother?

5. In which book does a character blow out a candle to make the room dark?

The Magic School Bus Lost in the Solar System

Joanna Cole. Illustrator: Bruce Degen. Scholastic, 1990. ISBN: 0590414283.
URLs: www.scholastic.com/magicschoolbus/tour/tour.htm?space (activity)
   www.kidsreads.com/authors/au-cole-joanna.asp (author)
Subjects: solar system; school stories; fantasy

Questions

1. In which book are students disappointed when they find out the planetarium is closed?

2. In which book do you see pictures of reports about spaceships, gravity and the planets?

3. In which book do characters land on a place where there is no air, water or signs of life?

4. In which book is one of the characters called "The Friz"?

5. In which book do the instructions for the autopilot help solve a problem?

Make Way for Ducklings

Robert McCloskey. Viking, 1941. ISBN: 0670451495.
URLs: www.eduplace.com/tview/pages/m/Make_Way_for_Ducklings_Robert_McCloskey.html (guide)
   www.hbook.com/exhibit/mccloskeyradio.html (author)

Award: Caldecott Medal
Subjects: animals; Boston; birds

Questions

1. In which book does the story begin at a place in Boston, Massachusetts?

2. In which book is there a pond in the Public Garden?

3. In which book do birds fly over Beacon Hill and the Charles River?

4. In which book does a policeman help a family cross a busy highway?

5. In which book does a character begin to molt?

Mama Don't Allow

Thacher Hurd. Harper & Row, 1984. ISBN: 0060226897.
URL: pbskids.org/readingrainbow/family/activities/activity30.html (activity)
Subject: songs

Questions

1. In which book does a character play the saxophone?

2. In which book does the Swamp Band play loud music?

3. In which book do characters go to the Alligator Ball?

4. In which book is there a riverboat named the Swamp Queen?

5. In which book do musicians play a lullaby?

The Man Who Walked Between the Towers

Mordicai Gerstein. Roaring Brook Press, 2003. ISBN: 0761317910.
URL: www.mordicaigerstein.com/bio.html (author)
Award: Caldecott Medal
Subject: New York City

Questions

1. In which book do you see pictures of a city, a river and two bridges from a building that's a quarter mile tall?

2. In which book does the hero walk with a balancing bar?

3. In which book do men carry a 450-pound reel of cable up 180 steps?

4. In which book do characters shoot an arrow from one building to another?

5. In which book is a man sentenced to pay for his crime by performing in the park?

Many Moons

James Thurber. Illustrator: Louis Slobodkin. Harcourt Brace, 1970. ISBN: 0156569809.
URL: www.eduplace.com/tview/pages/m/Many_Moons_James_Thurber.html (guide)
Award: Caldecott Medal
Subject: princesses

Questions

1. In which book does a character get sick from eating too many raspberry tarts?

2. In which book does a king get anything he wants from his wise men?

3. In which book do characters read from a long scroll of parchment?

4. In which book does the Court Jester solve the main problem of the story?

5. In which book does a princess explain how something can be in the sky and around her neck at the same time?

Martin's Big Words: The Life of Dr. Martin Luther King Jr.

Doreen Rappaport. Illustrator: Bryan Collier. Hyperion, 2001. ISBN: 0786807148.
URLs: www.bryancollier.com/artist.html (illustrator)
  www.kidsdomain.com/holiday/mlk/ (activities)
Award: Caldecott Honor Book
Subjects: biography; civil rights

Questions

1. In which book does a character teach "love is the key to the problems of the world"?

2. In which book does a man from India pass on ideas about freedom to a man in the United States?

3. In which book does a character say that only love can get rid of hate?

4. In which book does a character believe his work will not stop if he dies because God is with this work?

5. In which book are the words: "love," "peace," "freedom" and "together" important to the story?

Mice Twice

Joseph Low. Simon & Schuster, 1980. ISBN: 0689501579.
Award: Caldecott Honor Book
Subject: animals

Questions

1. In which book does a character think about eating grasshoppers, crickets and a fat sparrow?

2. In which book do two friends eat small pieces of common old rat-trap cheese?

3. In which book does a wasp sting a lion's nose, ear and tongue?

4. In which book does the eight o'clock meal include peanuts, raisins, sugar-frosted cakes, bacon and mint candies?

5. In which book does a crocodile spoil a wolf's plan to eat a dog for dinner?

Milton the Early Riser

Robert Kraus. Illustrators: Jose Aruego and Ariane Dewey. Simon & Schuster, 1972. ISBN: 0671662724.
URL: www.eduplace.com/kids/hmr/mtai/aruego_dewey.html (illustrators)
Subjects: animals; humorous fiction

Questions

1. In which book does a character want to play with Creeps, Whippersnappers and Nincompoops?
2. In which book is a character awake while everyone else is asleep and asleep when everyone else is awake?
3. In which book does a character dance and do tricks with red berries?
4. In which book does a strong wind blow the characters out of their beds?
5. In which book does a character work and work to straighten up a mess of animals?

Ming Lo Moves the Mountain

Arnold Lobel. William Morrow and Company, 1982. ISBN: 0688006108.
URLs: www.eduplace.com/kids/hmr/mtai/lobel.html (author)
   www.eduplace.com/tview/pages/m/Ming_Lo_Moves_the_Mountain_Arnold_Lobel.html (guide)
Subject: houses

Questions

1. In which book are characters unhappy with the location of their house?
2. In which book does a character get advice about a house from the wise man of the village?
3. In which book do falling rocks and stones put holes in the roof of a house?
4. In which book do characters take their house apart stick by stick?
5. In which book do characters do a special dance for many hours with their left and right feet?

Minnie and Moo Save the Earth

Denys Cazet. DK Publishing, 1999. ISBN: 1098765432.
URL: www.embracingthechild.org/acazet.htm (author)
Subject: science fiction

Questions

1. In which book do characters enjoy sitting in a farmer's hot tub?
2. In which book does a character use a flyswatter to whap a mosquito?
3. In which book are characters called the Mother General and the Emperor Pop?
4. In which book do characters eat brie cheese and drink alfalfa fizz?
5. In which book are characters stung with ray guns?

Miss Alaineus: A Vocabulary Disaster

Debra Frasier. Harcourt, 2000. ISBN: 0152021639.
URLs: www.eduplace.com/tview/pages/m/Miss_Alaineus_Debra_Frasier.html (guide)
debrafrasier.com/pages/about/about.html
Subject: school stories; encyclopedias and dictionaries

Questions

1. In which book does a school have a vocabulary parade?

2. In which book is a dictionary definition given for all the characters' names?

3. In which book is a character embarrassed for thinking a word refers to a woman on a spaghetti box?

4. In which book are definitions used as borders on each page?

5. In which book is a character reminded there is "gold in every mistake"?

Miss Bindergarten Gets Ready for Kindergarten

Joseph Slate. Illustrator: Ashley Wolff. Putnam, 1996. ISBN: 0525454462.
URL: www.josephslate.com/questions.html (author)
Subjects: alphabet; school stories; stories that rhyme

Questions

1. In which book does a character in a wheelchair say "Vroo-vroo-vroom!"?

2. In which book do you see a picture of a teacher putting the letters of the alphabet up on the wall?

3. In which book do Quentin and Raffie give each other high-fives?

4. In which book does an iguana put up a fuss on the first day of school?

5. In which book is Sara von Hoff the first one off the school bus?

Miss Nelson Is Missing!

Harry Allard. Illustrator: James Marshall. Houghton Mifflin, 1977. ISBN: 0395252962.
URLs: www.eduplace.com/tview/pages/m/Miss_Nelson_Is_Missing_Harry_Allard.html (guide)
www.hbook.com/exhibit/marshallbio.html (illustrator)
Subjects: school stories; human behavior

Questions

1. In which book do the kids in Room 207 misbehave?

2. In which book do the students and their teacher each have a little secret they will never tell?

3. In which book do students make spitballs and paper planes?

4. In which book does the teacher wear an ugly black dress?

5. In which book do characters talk to Detective McSmogg at the police station?

Miss Rumphius

Barbara Cooney. Viking Penguin, 1982. ISBN: 0670479586.
URLs: www.eduplace.com/tview/pages/m/Miss_Rumphius_Barbara_Cooney.html (guide)
  www.sdcoe.k12.ca.us/score/rumf/rumftg.html (guide)
  www.hbook.com/cooney.shtml (author)
Award: American Book Award
Subjects: plants; character

Questions

1. In which book is the main character known as the little, old Lupine Lady?

2. In which book does a character help her grandfather paint pictures?

3. In which book does a character want to travel to far away places, live by the sea and make the world more beautiful?

4. In which book does a character hurt her back when getting off of a camel?

5. In which book does a character scatter flower seeds over headlands, fields, highways and country lanes?

The Mitten: A Ukrainian Folktale

Jan Brett. Putnam, 1989. ISBN: 039921920X.
URLs: www.eduplace.com/tview/pages/m/The_Mitten_Jan_Brett.html (guide)
  www.sdcoe.k12.ca.us/score/mit/mittg.html (guide)
  www.janbrett.com/newsnotes/mitten_newsnotes2.htm
  www.janbrett.com/biography.htm (author)
Subject: folklore—Ukraine

Questions

1. In which book does a grandmother knit something white for her grandson?

2. In which book do a mole, rabbit and hedgehog share a warm cozy place?

3. In which book do smaller animals decide it's not a good idea to argue with a bear?

4. In which book does a piece of clothing swell, stretch and bulge to many times its size?

5. In which book does the whisker of a mouse cause an enormous sneeze?

Moe the Dog in Tropical Paradise

Diane Stanley. Illustrator: Elise Primavera. Putnam, 1992. ISBN: 0399221271.
URL: www.eduplace.com/kids/hmr/mtai/primavera.html (illustrator)
Subject: friendship

Questions

1. In which book do characters have a week of vacation in the middle of winter?

2. In which book do characters talk to a travel agent about going to Tahiti?

3. In which book does a character look fetching in a sarong made out of a bed sheet?

4. In which book do characters think about going to Egypt to see the pyramids?

5. In which book does a character shop at Hugo's Building Supply, Rembrandt's Art Shop and a grocery store?

Molly's Pilgrim

Barbara Cohen. Illustrator: J. Deraney Michael. Lothrop, Lee & Shepard, 1983. ISBN: 0688021034.
URL: www.eduplace.com/tview/pages/m/Molly_s_Pilgrim_Barbara_Cohen.html (guide)
Subjects: tolerance; school stories; immigrants

Questions

1. In which book does the mother talk to her daughter in Yiddish?

2. In which book does a character make a clothespin doll for a school project?

3. In which book do you find out where the idea for the first Thanksgiving came from?

4. In which book does a character hate going to school because others tease and make fun of her?

5. In which book do you read about characters who came to America from Russia so they could worship God in their own way?

Moose Tales

Nancy Van Laan. Illustrator: Amy Rusch. Houghton Mifflin, 1999. ISBN: 0395908639.
Subject: animals

Questions

1. In which book does a character think a blue-sky, sunshiny day is a fine day for a walk?

2. In which book does a character get tired walking up and down, up and down many hills?

3. In which book does a beaver tail get stuck under a tree?

4. In which book do animals create a very unusual looking snow creature?

5. In which book does a character make a sign that reads "Do not nap here!"?

"More More More," Said the Baby

Vera B. Williams. Greenwillow Books, 1990. ISBN: 0688091733.
URL: www.kidsreads.com/authors/au-williams-vera.asp (author)
Award: Caldecott Honor Book
Subjects: family life; humorous fiction

Questions

1. In which book are the main characters Little Guy, Little Pumpkin and Little Bird?

2. In which book does a character have a perfect belly button?

3. In which book does the grandma taste her grandbaby's toes?

4. In which book does mama kiss her daughter on each of her little eyes?

5. In which book do a daddy, a grandma and a mamma have to move fast to catch their little ones?

Mouse Tales

Arnold Lobel. Harper, 1972. ISBN: 0060239417.
URL: www.eduplace.com/kids/hmr/mtai/lobel.html (author)
Subjects: animals; mice

Questions

1. In which book does Papa tell seven tales, one for each of his children?

2. In which book does a character throw a pillow and a penny into a well?

3. In which book is a character afraid of a cloud that looks like a cat?

4. In which book is a character blown around by north, south, east and west winds?

5. In which book does a character get a new pair of feet?

Mr. Gumpy's Motor Car

John Burningham. HarperCollins, 1973. ISBN: 0690007981.
URL: www.randomhouse.co.uk/catalog/authorcb.htm?authorid=309 (author)
Subject: travel

Questions

1. In which book are children and animals taken for a ride in an automobile?

2. In which book does a road keep getting muddier and muddier?

3. In which book do characters get into trouble when they take an old dirt road across a field?

4. In which book do tires finally grip the road?

5. In which book do you see a picture of a license plate that reads TYM 580?

Mrs. Wishy-Washy's Farm

Joy Cowley. Illustrator: Elizabeth Fuller. Philomel, 2003. ISBN: 0399238727.
URLs: www.eduplace.com/tview/pages/m/Mrs__Wishy-Washy_s_Farm_Joy_Cowley.html (guide)
  www.joycowley.com/ (author)
Subjects: animals; farm life

Questions

1. In which book do animals flee a bath and go to the city?

2. In which book does a character say, "You'll be a roast or toast if you don't get out"?

3. In which book are characters taken to jail in a van?

4. In which book do characters visit a hardware store and get covered in paint?

5. In which book do the characters go to the old tin tub for a scrub?

Mufaro's Beautiful Daughters: An African Tale

John Steptoe. Lothrop, Lee & Shepard Books, 1987. ISBN: 0688040462.
URLs: www.eduplace.com/tview/pages/m/Mufaro_s_Beautiful_Daughters_John_Steptoe.html (guide)
   www.sdcoe.k12.ca.us/score/mufaro/mufarotg.html (guide)
   www.harperchildrens.com/teacher/catalog/author_xml.asp?authorid=12770 (author)
Award: Caldecott Honor Book
Subject: folklore—Africa; Africa

Questions

1. In which book does a character grow millet, sunflowers, yams and vegetables?

2. In which book does a grove of trees laugh at a character?

3. In which book is a garden snake really a king?

4. In which book does a character like to sing while working in the garden?

5. In which book is one sister known for being unhappy while the other sister is known for being kind?

Mushroom in the Rain

Mirra Ginsburg. Illustrators: Jose Aruego and Ariane Dewey. Simon & Schuster, 1974. ISBN: 0027362418.
URLs: www.ri.net/schools/Central_Falls/ch/heazak/mushroom/mushroom.html (activities)
   www.eduplace.com/kids/hmr/mtai/aruego_dewey.html (illustrators)
Subject: animals

Questions

1. In which book does a character say, "Better crowded than wet"?

2. In which book does the story end with the words "It grows!"?

3. In which book does a character have tired, wet wings?

4. In which book does a frog say "Qua-ha-ha" and laugh at the other characters?

5. In which book does a plant act like an umbrella?

My Friend Rabbit

Eric Rohmann. Roaring Book Press, 2002. ISBN: 0761315357.
URLs: www.nancypolette.com/LitGuidesText/myfriendrabbit.htm (activities)
   www.randomhouse.com/kids/author/results_spotlight.pperl?authorid=26010 (author)
Award: Caldecott Medal
Subjects: friendship; humorous fiction

Questions

1. In which book are animals stacked one on top of another so they can rescue a toy airplane?

2. In which book do two characters try to move an elephant?

3. In which book is a plane caught in the branches of a tree?

4. In which book is a character rescued from angry animals by someone in an airplane?

5. In which book do the words "not to worry—I've got an idea" mean trouble?

The Napping House

Audrey Wood. Illustrator: Don Wood. Harcourt Brace, 1984. ISBN: 0152567089.
URLs: www.eduplace.com/tview/pages/n/The_Napping_House_Audrey_Wood.html (guide)
  www.audreywood.com/mac_site/auds_jumpstation/aud_jumpstation.htm (author)
  www.audreywood.com/mac_site/don_stuff/don_page/don_page.htm (illustrator)
  www.audreywood.com/mac_site/activity_pages/activities_page.html (activities)
Subjects: night; repetitive story

Questions

1. In which book do the pages get lighter and lighter as everyone wakes up?

2. In which book is the story about a place where people and animals sleep?

3. In which book do a snoozing cat and a dozing dog share a bed with a snoring granny?

4. In which book are there a slumbering mouse and a wakeful flea?

5. In which book does a flea biting a mouse cause everyone to wake up?

Nate the Great and the Missing Key

Marjorie Sharmat. Illustrator: Marc Simont. Bantam Doubleday Dell, 1981. ISBN: 044046191X.
URLs: www.kidsreads.com/series/series-nate-author.asp (author)
  www.eduplace.com/tview/pages/n/Nate_the_Great_and_the_Missing_Key_Marjorie_Weinman_Sharmat.html (guide)
Subject: mystery fiction

Questions

1. In which book does a character think something is hidden in a garbage can?

2. In which book is something hard to find because it mixes in with other shiny things?

3. In which book does a character collect cans and safety pins?

4. In which book does a dog get a lot of birthday presents?

5. In which book does a character lose something while getting ready for a party?

No, David!

David Shannon. Blue Sky Press, 1998. ISBN: 0590930028.
URLs: www.scholastic.com/titles/nodavid/davidshannon.htm (author)
  atozteacherstuff.com/lessons/writing_nodavid.shtml (activity)
Award: Caldecott Honor Book
Subjects: human behavior; humorous fiction

Questions

1. In which book do you see a picture of a character wearing a pirate hat in the bathtub?

2. In which book is something funny made from a potato, a chicken drumstick and green beans?

3. In which book is a character unhappy because he's not allowed to watch television?

4. In which book does a mother yell at her son for doing all sorts of things he isn't supposed to do?

5. In which book does a character get into trouble for playing baseball inside the house?

O'Diddy

Jocelyn Stevenson. Random House, 1988. ISBN: 0394896092.
Subject: imagination

Questions

1. In which book does a plot to trap someone in the bathroom backfire?

2. In which book do you learn how to play a game called "Hide and Spook"?

3. In which book is a character nicknamed Phinny?

4. In which book does the author suggest you read to Chapter Four before you decide if you want to read the whole book or give it away?

5. In which book do chairs at a workshop have painted snakes and clamps for hands and feet?

Officer Buckle and Gloria

Peggy Rathmann. Putnam, 1995. ISBN: 0399226168.
URLs: www.eduplace.com/tview/pages/o/Officer_Buckle_and_Gloria_Peggy_Rathmann.html (guide)
   www.peggyrathmann.com/peggyrathmann.html (author)
Award: Caldecott Medal
Subjects: school stories; dogs; safety education; animals

Questions

1. In which book does a character know a lot of safety tips?

2. In which book do a man and a dog give speeches in schools?

3. In which book do characters get thank-you notes from the students at Napville School?

4. In which book does an accident begin with a puddle of banana pudding?

5. In which book does a helmet save a character from getting hit on the head with a hammer?

Oh, Were They Ever Happy

Peter Spier. Doubleday, 1978. ISBN: 0385131755.
Subject: humorous fiction

Questions

1. In which book does the trouble begin when the babysitter doesn't show up?
2. In which book do the Noonan children decide to paint their house?
3. In which book is a clumsy person called Butterfingers?
4. In which book are windows and shutters hard to paint?
5. In which book are empty paint cans left for the garbage man?

One Fine Day

Nonny Hogrogian. Simon & Schuster, 1971. ISBN: 0027440001.
URL: www.harperchildrens.com/teacher/catalog/author_xml.asp?authorid=16974 (author)
Award: Caldecott Medal
Subject: folklore

Questions

1. In which book does a thirsty animal drink milk from an old woman's pail?
2. In which book is a character's tail chopped off with a knife?
3. In which book does a character go looking for a jug and a blue bead?
4. In which book does a peddler want to be paid with an egg?
5. In which book does a character get grain from a miller?

The One in the Middle Is a Green Kangaroo

Judy Blume. Illustrator: Irene Trivas. Bradbury Press, 1991. ISBN: 0027110559.
URLs: www.eduplace.com/tview/pages/o/The_One_in_the_Middle_is_the_Green_Kangaroo_Judy_Blume.html (guide)
  www.judyblume.com/jb-bio.html (author)
Subjects: family life; school stories

Questions

1. In which book does a character want to be in a school play?
2. In which book is a character told to "break a leg"?
3. In which book does the audience clap loudly after an actor takes a big, low bow?
4. In which book does a second grader get to do something special with the fifth and sixth graders?
5. In which book does a character feel like "the peanut butter part of a sandwich" squeezed between an older brother and a younger sister?

Owl Moon

Jane Yolen. Illustrator: John Schoenherr. Philomel Books, 1987. ISBN: 0399214577.
URLs: www.eduplace.com/tview/pages/o/Owl_Moon_Jane_Yolen.html (guide)
  www.janeyolen.com/janebio.html (author)
  www.embracingthechild.org/aschoenherr.html (illustrator)
Award: Caldecott Medal
Subjects: animals; night; family life

Questions

1. In which book do trains and dogs sing at night?

2. In which book do the characters have to be quiet, brave and make their own heat while they are outside looking for something?

3. In which book do trees and people make black shadows in the woods?

4. In which book does Pa call with a "whoo-whoo-who-who-who-whooo" sound?

5. In which book is a big flashlight used to see a bird sitting on a branch?

Ox-Cart Man

Donald Hall. Illustrator: Barbara Cooney. Viking, 1979. ISBN: 0670533289.
URLs: www.nashville.k12.tn.us/CyberGuides/Brookmeade/nanni.html (guide)
  www.eduplace.com/tview/pages/o/Ox-Cart_Man_Donald_Hall.html (guide)
  www.hbook.com/cooney.shtml (illustrator)
Award: Caldecott Medal
Subject: historical fiction

Questions

1. In which book is the wool from sheep used to make yarn for weaving and knitting?

2. In which book does a family make candles, shingles and brooms?

3. In which book is sap boiled and boiled to make maple syrup?

4. In which book are things sold and bought at the Portsmouth market?

5. In which book do characters eat wintergreen peppermint candy?

The Paperboy

Dav Pilkey. Scholastic, 1996. ISBN: 0590106414.
URLs: www.eduplace.com/tview/pages/p/The_Paper_Boy_Dav_Pilkey.html (guide)
  www.pilkey.com/bookview.php?id=11 (activities)
  www.pilkey.com/meet-dav.php (author)
Award: Caldecott Honor Book
Subjects: morning; work; realistic fiction

Questions

1. In which book does the story start with a delivery in the morning when it is still dark outside?

2. In which book do a boy and his dog finish their job before the sun comes up?

3. In which book does a character know what to do by heart so he can think of other things while doing it?

4. In which book do you learn it's hard to ride a bike when you're carrying something heavy?

5. In which book do characters snuggle back into bed when their morning work is done?

Paul Bunyan, A Tall Tale

Illustrator: Steven Kellogg. William Morrow and Company, 1984. ISBN: 0688038492.
URL: www.eduplace.com/tview/pages/p/Paul_Bunyan_Steven_Kellogg.html (guide)
  www.friend.ly.net/users/jorban/biographies/kelloggsteven/ (author)
Subjects: folklore—United States

Questions

1. In which book is the story about the largest, smartest and strongest baby ever born in the state of Maine?

2. In which book is a character interested in the logging business?

3. In which book does a character race with deer and wrestle with grizzlies?

4. In which book does a character become friends with a big blue ox?

5. In which book is there a gang of underground ogres called Gumberoos?

The Pig in the Pond

Martin Waddell. Illustrator: Jill Barton. Candlewick Press, 1992. ISBN: 1564020509.
URLs: www.eduplace.com/tview/pages/p/The_Pig_in_the_Pond_Martin_Waddell.html (guide)
  www.channel4.com/learning/microsites/B/bookbox/authors/waddell/ (author)
Subject: animals

Questions

1. In which book does the story begin at a place that belongs to Neligan?

2. In which book is there a lot of quack-quacking and honk-honking?

3. In which book does word of an event spread about, above and beyond?

4. In which book does a character undress before jumping into the water?

5. In which book do you find out that the main character doesn't swim?

Pinky and Rex and the Spelling Bee

James Howe. Illustrator: Melissa Sweet. Atheneum Publishers, 1991. ISBN: 0689316186.
URLs: www.melissasweet.net/index2.html (illustrator)
  www2.scholastic.com/teachers/authorsandbooks/authorstudies/authorhome.jhtml?authorID=1832&collateralID=10322&displayName=Biography (author)
Subjects: school stories; humorous fiction

Questions

1. In which book does a character know a lot about dinosaurs?

2. In which book does a character want to move to the moon right after school?

3. In which book do characters say special words while holding friendship stones?

4. In which book does a character drink too much milk and juice for lunch?

5. In which book does a character have to go to the bathroom very badly?

The Pioneer Cat

William H. Hooks. Illustrator: Charles Robinson. Random House, 1988. ISBN: 0394920384.
URL: www.randomhouse.com/kids/author/results_spotlight.pperl?authorid=13459 (author)
Subjects: historical fiction—frontier and pioneer life

Questions

1. In which book do children sleep on pallets on the kitchen floor?
2. In which book is a character asked to carve the number 49 in some wood?
3. In which book does a character have the job of putting axle grease on wheels?
4. In which book are buffalo chips used to keep the fires going?
5. In which book must every family give up one pound of sugar and a blanket?

Planting a Rainbow

Lois Ehlert. Harcourt, 1988. ISBN: 0152626093.
URL: www.eduplace.com/tview/pages/p/Planting_a_Rainbow_Lois_Ehlert.html (guide)
www.friend.ly.net/users/jorban/biographies/ehlertlois/ (author)
Subjects: plants; color

Questions

1. In which book do characters buy bulbs and put them in the ground?
2. In which book do characters order phlox, zinnia, aster and marigold seeds?
3. In which book do characters wait for spring to warm the soil?
4. In which book do characters grow all kinds of flowers?
5. In which book do characters go to the garden center to buy seedlings?

Polar Bears Past Bedtime

Mary Pope Osborne. Illustrator: Sal Murdocca. Harcourt, 1998. ISBN: 067988341X.
URLs: www.marypopeosborne.com/bio.htm (author)
www.randomhouse.com/kids/magictreehouse/ (activities)
Subjects: magic; Arctic region

Questions

1. In which book do you find out what causes the northern lights?
2. In which book do characters use a book called *Adventure In the Arctic*?
3. In which book do characters spend time with a seal hunter?
4. In which book do the main characters each get a magic library card?
5. In which book do characters wear fur clothes over their pajamas?

Poppleton

Cynthia Rylant. Illustrator: Mark Teague. Blue Sky Press, 1997. ISBN: 0590847821.
URLs: www.kidsreads.com/authors/au-rylant-cynthia.asp (author)
www.rif.org/art/illustrators/teague.mspx (illustrator)
Subject: friendship

Questions

1. In which book does a character tire of eating oatmeal, toasted cheese and spaghetti?
2. In which book does a character go to the library every Monday?
3. In which book does a character like to read adventure stories?
4. In which book is a pill hidden in a piece of Cherry Sue's Heavenly Cake?
5. In which book does a character soak a neighbor, then himself, with a hose?

Possum Magic

Mem Fox. Illustrator: Julie Vivas. Harcourt, 1983. ISBN: 0152005722.
URLs: www.eduplace.com/tview/pages/p/Possum_Magic_Mem_Fox.html (guide)
  www.memfox.net/ (author)
Subjects: animals; Australia

Questions

1. In which book does the story take place deep in the Australian bush?
2. In which book does a character want to be visible again?
3. In which book do characters eat a Vegemite sandwich, a piece of pavlova and half a lamington?
4. In which book does a character look through magic books to solve a problem?
5. In which book do characters spend time in Tasmania?

Princess Furball

Charlotte Huck. Illustrator: Anita Lobel. Mulberry Books, 1989. ISBN: 0688131077.
URLs: www.anitalobel.com/biographical.htm (illustrator)
  www.harperchildrens.com/teacher/catalog/author_xml.asp?authorid=17027 (author)
Subject: folklore

Questions

1. In which book is a character supposed to marry an ogre?
2. In which book does a character ask for three special dresses?
3. In which book does a character carry things in walnut shells?
4. In which book does a character fall asleep curled up inside the hollow of a tree?
5. In which book does a character make a delicious soup that pleases the king?

The Runaway Bunny

Margaret Wise Brown. Illustrator: Clement Hurd. HarperCollins, 1942. ISBN: 0060207663.
Subject: family life

Questions

1. In which book does a character decide to stay home instead of leaving his mother?

2. In which book do many of the sentences begin with the question "If you become…"?

3. In which book does the mother dress up like a mountain climber?

4. In which book does the mother consider being a gardener so she can find her son?

5. In which book does a character think about joining a circus and flying away on a trapeze?

Sheep in a Jeep

Nancy Shaw. Illustrator: Margot Apple. Houghton Mifflin, 1986. ISBN: 039541105X.
URLs: www.eduplace.com/tview/pages/s/Sheep_in_a_Jeep_Nancy_Shaw.html (guide)
  www.houghtonmifflinbooks.com/catalog/authordetail.cfm?authorID=978 (author)
Subjects: stories in rhyme; animals

Questions

1. In which book does something go beep beep on a hill that's steep?

2. In which book does the driver forget to steer?

3. In which book do characters weep when something ends up in a heap?

4. In which book is something for sale cheap?

5. In which book do two pigs help push something out of the mud?

The Sick Day

Patricia MacLachlan. Random House, 2001. ISBN: 0385321503.
URL: www.eduplace.com/kids/hmr/mtai/maclachlan.html (author)
Subject: family life

Questions

1. In which book does a character have a stomachache in her head and a headache in her throat?

2. In which book is a character's hair put into three ponytails?

3. In which book is a plastic giraffe added to a character's soup?

4. In which book does a character sing a song about a mouse to an ill parent?

5. In which book does a character use the words "swallowing up" instead of barfing?

Sleeping Ugly

Jane Yolen. Illustrator: Diane Stanley. Coward McCann, 1981. ISBN: 0698307216.
URLs: www.janeyolen.com/janebio.html (author)
  www.eduplace.com/tview/pages/s/Sleeping_Ugly_Jane_Yolen.html (guide)
Subject: fractured fairy tales

Questions

1. In which book is a fairy disguised as a little old lady asleep under a tree?

2. In which book do three characters take a famous hundred-year nap?

3. In which book does Plain Jane marry a prince and have three children?

4. In which book do wishes turn a character's foot into stone, then back to a foot again?

5. In which book is the story about a beautiful but mean, wicked and worthless princess?

Smoky Night

Eve Bunting. Illustrator: David Diaz. Harcourt Brace, 1994. ISBN: 0152699546.
URLs: www.friend.ly.net/users/jorban/biographies/buntingeve/ (author)
   www.eduplace.com/kids/hmr/mtai/diaz.html (illustrator)
Award: Caldecott Medal
Subjects: riots; friendship; city and town life; race relations

Questions

1. In which book does Mama explain about rioting?

2. In which book is a television stolen from an appliance store?

3. In which book do characters spend time in a church hall shelter?

4. In which book are two cats rescued from a burning building?

5. In which book is a character worried about a yellow cat named Jasmine?

Snowflake Bentley

Jacqueline Briggs Martin. Illustrator: Mary Azarian. Houghton Mifflin, 1998. ISBN: 0395861624.
URLs: www.eduplace.com/tview/pages/s/Snowflake_Bentley_Jacqueline_Briggs_Martin.html (guide)
   www.nancypolette.com/litguidestext/snowflake.htm (guide)
Award: Caldecott Medal
Subjects: snow; biography; photography

Questions

1. In which book does a character like to look at things through a microscope?

2. In which book does a character study ice crystals?

3. In which book does a character keep a record of weather and do experiments with rain drops?

4. In which book does a character call a two-day storm a gift from King Winter?

5. In which book does a Vermont farmer develop a way to photograph very tiny things?

The Snowy Day

Ezra Jack Keats. Viking, 1962. ISBN: 0670654000.
URLs: www.eduplace.com/tview/pages/s/The_Snowy_Day_Ezra_Jack_Keats.html (guide)
   www.ezra-jack-keats.org/aboutezra/biography.htm (author)
Award: Caldecott Medal
Subject: snow

Questions

1. In which book do a character's feet go crunch, crunch, crunch as they sink into the snow?

2. In which book does a character make angels in the snow?

3. In which book does a character put a snowball in a pocket?

4. In which book does a character use a stick to smack snow out of a tree?

5. In which book is a character too young to be in a snowball fight?

Song and Dance Man

Karen Ackerman. Illustrator: Stephen Gammell. Knopf, 1988. ISBN: 0679819959.
URLs: www.teachers.net/lessons/posts/1532.html (activities)
  community-2.webtv.net/KAbooks/KarenAckermanBooks/ (author)
  www.bookpage.com/0006bp/stephen_gammell.html (illustrator)
Award: Caldecott Medal
Subjects: family life; grandparents

Questions

1. In which book is there a character who once danced on the vaudeville stage?

2. In which book does a character tell about the good old days before people watched television?

3. In which book does a character have tap shoes, bowler hats and bow ties?

4. In which book is a silver dollar pulled out from somebody's hair?

5. In which book do characters laugh so hard they get the hiccups?

So You Want to Be President?

Judith St. George. Illustrator: David Small. Philomel Books. 2000. ISBN: 0399234071.
URLs: www.randomhouse.com/kids/author/results_spotlight.pperl?authorid=28746 (illustrator)
  www.eduplace.com/tview/pages/s/So_You_Want_to_Be_President_Judith_St__George.html (guide)
Award: Caldecott Medal
Subject: presidents

Questions

1. In which book do the characters live in the White House?

2. In which book do you read about McKinley, Taft, Harrison and Roosevelt?

3. In which book does a pony ride in an elevator to cheer up a sick boy?

4. In which book do you learn about a man who designed his own house, started a university, wrote the Declaration of Independence and was an expert on agriculture, music and botany?

5. In which book do characters take an oath to preserve, protect and defend the Constitution of the United States?

The Statue of Liberty

Lucille Recht Penner. Illustrator: Jada Rowland. Random House, 1995. ISBN: 067986928X.
URLs: www.surfnetkids.com/statueofliberty.htm (activities)
  members.aol.com/jadarowland/ (illustrator)
Subject: historical fiction—United States

Questions

1. Which book is the story about a lady who stands in New York harbor?

2. In which book do people send nickels and dimes so a huge pedestal can be built?

3. In which book is something so big it's made in smaller pieces, then put together outside?

4. In which book do you read about a right hand holding a torch?

5. In which book is something carried from France to New York in 214 crates?

Stellaluna

Janell Cannon. Harcourt, 1993. ISBN: 0152802177.
URLs: www.eduplace.com/tview/pages/s/Stellaluna_Janell_Cannon.html (guide)
  www.sdcoe.k12.ca.us/score/stella/stellatg.html (guide)
  projects.edtech.sandi.net/chavez/batquest/batquest.html (activities)
Subjects: animals; friendship; bats

Questions

1. In which book do characters search for ripe fruit to eat?

2. In which book does a character eat bugs even though they taste awful?

3. In which book is a character told to obey all the rules of a house, which is a nest?

4. In which book is a character separated from her mother after an owl attack?

5. In which book does a character's name mean "large hand-wing"?

The Stonecutter: A Japanese Folk Tale

Gerald McDermott. Viking Press, 1975. ISBN: 067067074X.
URLs: www.eduplace.com/tview/pages/s/The_Stonecutter_Gerald_McDermott.html (guide)
  www.geraldmcdermott.com/biography.htm (author)
Subject: folklore—Japan

Questions

1. In which book does a character use a hammer and a chisel to chip away at a mountain?

2. In which book does a character want to be as rich as a prince?

3. In which book does a character ask the spirit of the mountain for help?

4. In which book does a character become the sun?

5. In which book does a character learn a lesson about power?

The Stories Julian Tells

Ann Cameron. Illustrator: Ann Strugnell. Pantheon Books, 1981. ISBN: 0394843010.
URLs: www.kyrene.org/schools/brisas/sunda/litpack/julian_sample.htm (guide)
www.eduplace.com/kids/hmr/mtai/cameron.html (author)
Subject: family life

Questions

1. In which book do a whipping and a beating turn into a delicious lemon pudding?

2. In which book do characters find out what a catalog is?

3. In which book do characters plant corn of the ancients and a house of flowers?

4. In which book does a character get a fig tree for a birthday present?

5. In which book does a character learn about different ways to remove a loose tooth from the mouth?

Strega Nona

Tomie de Paola. Simon & Schuster, 1975. ISBN: 067166283X.
URLs: www.eduplace.com/tview/pages/s/Strega_Nona_Tomie_de Paola.html (guide)
www.tomie.com/about_tomie/index.html (author)
Award: Caldecott Honor Book
Subject: folklore—Italy

Questions

1. In which book does the story take place in Calabria?

2. In which book does a character cure headaches and get rid of warts?

3. In which book does a pasta pot bubble?

4. In which book is it important to blow three kisses?

5. In which book does a character say, "The punishment must fit the crime"?

Sunken Treasure

Gail Gibbons. HarperCollins, 1988. ISBN: 0690047347.
URLs: www.eduplace.com/tview/pages/s/Sunken_Treasure_Gail_Gibbons.html (guide)
www.gailgibbons.com/ (author)
Subject: buried treasure

Questions

1. In which book is a Spanish galleon found and salvaged?

2. In which book do divers use underwater metal detectors?

3. In which book do you read about an invention called a mailbox?

4. In which book does a marine archaeologist insist that the mother lode not be disturbed?

5. In which book are artifacts sketched, photographed and cataloged?

Tar Beach

Faith Ringgold. Crown, 1991. ISBN: 0517580306.
URLs: www.princetonol.com/groups/iad/lessons/elem/TarBeach.html (activity)
 www.faithringgold.com/ringgold/bio.htm (author)
Award: Caldecott Honor Book
Subjects: New York City; family life

Questions

1. In which book does a character tell about hoisting cables on the George Washington Bridge?
2. In which book does a character dream about flying above a city?
3. In which book does a family picnic on the roof of an apartment building?
4. In which book does Mama dream about sleeping late like Mrs. Honey?
5. In which book are the pictures in the story taken from a "story quilt"?

Teammates

Peter Golenbock. Illustrator: Paul Bacon. Harcourt, 1990. ISBN: 0152006036.
Subjects: baseball; race relations

Questions

1. In which book is the story about Jack Roosevelt Robinson and Harold Reese?
2. In which book do the Dodgers play the Reds in an important ball game?
3. In which book do characters wear blue and gray uniforms on the field?
4. In which book does a character value skill over skin color?
5. In which book do you see pictures of Joe DiMaggio, Ty Cobb, Lou Gehrig, Ted Williams and Babe Ruth?

There's a Monster Under My Bed

James Howe. Illustrator: David Rose. Atheneum, 1986. ISBN: 0689311788.
Subjects: night; counting; monsters

Questions

1. In which book does a character feel the mattress on a bed jump?
2. In which book does a character tell his mom he's too old for a night light?
3. In which book is a character afraid of being munched for a midnight snack?
4. In which book is a character sorry for putting a dead fish in Mrs. Grover's drawer?
5. In which book do two brothers decide to sleep together to feel safe?

There Was an Old Lady Who Swallowed a Fly

Simms Taback. Viking 1997. ISBN: 0670869392.
Award: Caldecott Honor Book
Subjects: humorous fiction; songs; repetitive story

Questions

1. In which book do you see a picture of unusual food in a character's stomach?

2. In which book do you see a picture of animals on the page before it is eaten?

3. In which book does a character make headlines in several newspapers and magazines?

4. In which book is the story based on a poem by an unknown poet?

5. In which book is the moral of the story to never eat a horse?

Three By the Sea

Edward Marshall. Illustrator: James Marshall. Dial, 1981. ISBN: 0803786875.
Subject: friendship

Questions

1. In which book does a character tell a story about a dog, a cat and a rat?

2. In which book does a character buy a cat for ten cents in a pet shop?

3. In which book do two friends sit on a beach and eat cheese?

4. In which book does a character with sharp green teeth and long black claws like to eat kids on toast?

5. In which book do two characters jump ten feet in the air after hearing a scary story?

Three Days on a River in a Red Canoe

Vera B. Williams. Greenwillow Books, 1981. ISBN: 0688803075.
Subjects: family life; camping

Questions

1. In which book do characters look at maps to plan a boating trip?

2. In which book do characters learn how to make knots?

3. In which book are there pictures and instructions for putting up a tent?

4. In which book does a character promise to catch a fish for his cat?

5. In which book do characters see the Big Dipper and the Milky Way?

The Three Little Wolves and the Big Bad Pig

Eugene Trivizas. Illustrator: Helen Oxenbury. Margaret K. McElderry, 1993. ISBN: 0689505698.
Subject: humorous fiction

Questions

1. In which book does a kangaroo push a wheelbarrow full of bricks?

2. In which book do characters play croquet, battledore, shuttlecock and hopscotch?

3. In which book are houses built of straw, sticks and bricks?

4. In which book does a character use a sledgehammer, a pneumatic drill and dynamite?

5. In which book does a character sing and dance the tarantella?

The Three Pigs

David Wiesner. Clarion Books, 2001. ISBN: 0618007016.
Award: Caldecott Medal
Subject: folklore

Questions

1. In which book is an about-to-be slain dragon rescued at the last minute?

2. In which book are the story pages folded into a paper airplane?

3. In which book do the characters meet the cow who jumped over the moon?

4. In which book does a character get blown right out of the story?

5. In which book is a prince sent after a golden rose?

Throw Your Tooth on the Roof: Tooth Traditions from Around the World

Selby B. Beeler. Illustrator: G. Brian Karas. Houghton Mifflin, 1998. ISBN: 0395891086.
Subjects: teeth; culture

Questions

1. In which book is something hidden under a pillow for fairies, rats and mice to find?

2. In which book do parents bury something in the garden of a hospital if they want their child to be a doctor?

3. In which book is a mouse called La Petite Souris, Ratoncito Perez, El Ratoncito or El Raton Miguelito?

4. In which book is something put in a mouse hole in the ground?

5. In which book do you find out the meaning of the words crown, dentin, pulp and gum?

The Titanic Lost ... and Found

Judy Donnelly. Illustrator: Keith Kohler. Random House, 1987. ISBN: 0394986695.
Subjects: historical fiction; shipwrecks

Questions

1. In which book does a wonder ship travel across the Atlantic Ocean?

2. In which book is something given the nickname "The Rich Man's Special"?

3. In which book is a robot used to find a missing ship?

4. In which book does a giant iceberg cause a lot of trouble?

5. In which book are lifeboats used to save some of the passengers?

Today Was a Terrible Day

Patricia Reilly Giff. Illustrator: Susanna Natti. Penguin, 1980. ISBN: 0670718300.
Subject: school stories

Questions

1. In which book is the main character called Snakey?
2. In which book does a character get into trouble for spraying water on Joy Farley's dress?
3. In which book is a character in the Rocket reading group?
4. In which book does the plant monitor forget to water the plants?
5. In which book does a character read a note from the teacher all by himself?

Too Many Tamales

Gary Soto. Illustrator: Ed Martinez. Putnam, 1992. ISBN: 0399221468.
Subjects: family life; Christmas; Mexican Americans

Questions

1. In which book does a character knead masa?
2. In which book does a missing ring create a problem for the main character?
3. In which book do characters try to find something hard inside the Christmas dinner?
4. In which book are cornhusks used to make the dinner?
5. In which book does a character think the second batch always tastes better than the first batch?

Tops and Bottoms

Janet Stevens. Harcourt, 1994. ISBN: 0152928510.
Award: Caldecott Honor Book
Subjects: animals, humorous fiction; trickster tales

Questions

1. In which book does a very lazy character have a lot of money and a lot of land?
2. In which book do two characters agree to split the profit right down the middle?
3. In which book does a character sleep through three seasons of planting and harvesting?
4. In which book does a clever rabbit want to be a business partner with a lazy bear?
5. In which book do characters plant carrots, radishes, beets, lettuce, broccoli and celery?

The Treasure

Uri Shulevitz. Farrar, Straus and Giroux, 1978. ISBN: 0374377405.
Award: Caldecott Honor Book
Subjects: folklore—England; folklore—Jewish

Questions

1. In which book does a character finally pay attention to a dream?
2. In which book does a character look for something under a bridge in the capital city?
3. In which book is an inscription put in the corner of a house of prayer?
4. In which book is the captain of the guards sent a priceless ruby?
5. In which book do you learn "sometimes one must travel far to discover what is near"?

The Ugly Duckling

Hans Christian Anderson. Illustrator: Jerry Pinkney. William Morrow and Company, 1999. ISBN: 068815932X.
Award: Caldecott Honor Book
Subjects: character; birds; animals

Questions

1. In which book is one egg in a nest a different shape from all the others?
2. In which book is an animal so ugly that a hunting dog ignores him?
3. In which book are a character's legs and body frozen in the river ice?
4. In which book does the biggest egg take the longest to hatch?
5. In which book is a character scared by some children wanting to play?

The Very Busy Spider

Eric Carle. Philomel Books, 1984. ISBN: 0399211667.
Subject: animals

Questions

1. In which book does a character spend a lot of time making a web?
2. In which book does a thin, silky thread trail from a character's body?
3. In which book is something made on a fencepost near a farmyard?
4. In which book does a character keep spinning instead of doing things with the other farm animals?
5. In which book does a character **not** answer when others ask questions?

The Very Worst Monster

Pat Hutchins. Greenwillow Books, 1985. ISBN: 0688040101.
Subject: family life

Questions

1. In which book does a character feel ignored when the baby brother gets all the attention?
2. In which book does a character try to eat the judge?

3. In which book does a character scare the postman?

4. In which book does a character try to eat a prize?

5. In which book do all the characters have long nails and pointed ears?

The Village of Round and Square Houses

Ann Grifalconi. Little, Brown and Company, 1986. ISBN: 0316328626.
Award: Caldecott Honor Book
Subject: folklore—Africa; Africa

Questions

1. In which book does a character grow up on her grandmother's farm in the village of Tos?

2. In which book does a character pound and soften the white cassava root to make fou-fou?

3. In which book are people covered with ashes?

4. In which book are children told to pick small gray stones out of the fields?

5. In which book does Gran'ma tell a story about an active volcano?

The Wall

Eve Bunting. Illustrator: Ronald Himler. Clarion Books, 1990. ISBN: 0395515882.
Subjects: historical fiction; grandfathers

Questions

1. In which book do characters visit the Vietnam Veterans Memorial?

2. In which book does a character look for his grandfather's name on a list?

3. In which book does a character meet a wounded soldier?

4. In which book does a character regret he never got to know his grandfather?

5. In which book does a character make a rubbing of his father's written name?

Weird Stories from the Lonesome Café

Judy Cox. Illustrator: Diane Kidd. Scholastic, 2000. ISBN: 0439219426.
Award: Nevada Young Reader Award
Subject: West (U.S.)

Questions

1. In which book does the Channel 4 newsroom team miss the big stories?

2. In which book does Bigfoot get a job flipping hamburgers?

3. In which book does Santa Claus drive a red station wagon while hauling a white trailer?

4. In which book does a character use a pink Cadillac to deliver supplies?

5. In which book does a character move to Nevada in order to write in peace and quiet?

When Bluebell Sang

Lisa Campbell Ernst. Simon & Schuster, 1992. ISBN: 0027335615.
Subject: farm life

Questions

1. In which book do you find out why cows often gather in the shade of large trees?

2. In which book does a character sing in concert halls, theaters and auditoriums?

3. In which book does a talent agent get greedier and greedier?

4. In which book do characters travel by train to Chicago, Philadelphia, New York and Boston?

5. In which book does a famous singer get homesick for life on the farm?

Where Does the Sun Go at Night?

Mirra Ginsburg. Illustrators: Jose Aruego and Ariane Dewey. ISBN: 0688802451.
Subject: songs

Questions

1. In which book is grandpa the wind?

2. In which book is grandma the deep blue sky?

3. In which book do characters sleep in the clouds?

4. In which book does a character dream about the moon and the stars?

5. In which book does a rooster in the village wake up all the other animals?

Wild, Wild Wolves

Joyce Milton. Illustrator: Larry Schwinger. Random House, 1992. ISBN: 0679910522.
Subject: wolves

Questions

1. In which book do you find out why certain animals howl?

2. In which book does an animal's powerful jaw crack the leg bone of a moose?

3. In which book are you warned to watch out if an animal wags just the tip of its tail?

4. In which book do the pups have to learn how to be good hunters?

5. In which book do you see a picture of a paw that is as large as a grownup's hand?

Will and Orv

Walter A. Schulz. Illustrator: Janet Schulz. Carolrhoda Books, 1991. ISBN: 0876146698.
Subjects: biography; flight

Questions

1. In which book does the story take place on the sand dunes of Kitty Hawk, North Carolina?

2. In which book do two brothers fly big gliders down a hill?

3. In which book do characters spend time in a machine called the Flyer?

4. In which book does a character bring fish to men at the life-saving station?

5. In which book does a young boy watch a historical event that happened on December 17, 1903?

Will's Mammoth

Rafe Martin. Illustrator: Stephen Gammell. Putnam, 1989. ISBN: 0399216278.
Subjects: imagination; prehistoric animals

Questions

1. In which book does a character find out that certain animals disappeared ten thousand years ago?

2. In which book does a character pretend to ride on the back of something very large and woolly?

3. In which book is a character's room filled with creatures from prehistoric times?

4. In which book does a character climb up a hill and up onto a giant boulder covered in snow?

5. In which book does a character's make-believe adventure end when it is time for supper?

Winter Days in the Big Woods

Laura Ingalls Wilder. Illustrator: Renée Graef. HarperCollins, 1994. ISBN: 0060230142.
Subject: historical fiction—frontier and pioneer life

Questions

1. In which book does a character live in Wisconsin in a house made of logs?

2. In which book does Pa say, "Where's my little half-pint of sweet cider half drunk up?"

3. In which book do characters play with rag dolls and cut out paper dolls?

4. In which book do characters use a thimble to make patterns on frosted windows?

5. In which book does each day of the week have certain work that needs to be done?

The Wolf's Chicken Stew

Keiko Kasza. Putnam, 1987. ISBN: 0399214003.
Subject: animals

Questions

1. In which book does a character try to fatten up his prey?

2. In which book is everything a character makes described as being scrumptious?

3. In which book does a cake weigh one hundred pounds?

4. In which book does a character receive one hundred kisses?

5. In which book is the main character called the best cook in the world at the end of the story?

Yoko

Rosemary Wells. Hyperion, 1998. ISBN: 0786803959.
Subjects: school stories; culture

Questions

1. In which book is a character called My Little Cherry Blossom?

2. In which book does a character bring lunch to school in a willow-covered cooler?

3. In which book does a character eat rice rolls filled with secret treasures?

4. In which book do characters celebrate International Food Day?

5. In which book does the class sing "Good Morning, School Bus" and Clean Hands, Snack Time and Friendly songs?

Intermediate Books

Ace: The Very Important Pig

Dick King-Smith. Illustrator: Lynette Hemmant. Bullseye Books, 1992. ISBN: 0679819312.
URL: falcon.jmu.edu/~ramseyil/kingsmith.htm
Subjects: animals; farm life; humorous fiction

Questions

1. In which book does a cat explain that it is rude to speak with a full mouth?

2. In which book does a character teach that in life it doesn't matter who you are, it's what you are that counts?

3. In which book does a character teach that MYOB means Mind Your Own Business?

4. In which book does a character's name come from a mark on his skin?

5. In which book do you learn how to address the Queen and her family?

Across Five Aprils

Irene Hunt. Viking, 1964. ISBN 0813672023.
URLs: www.sunsite.utk.edu/civil-war/
www.civilwar.com
Award: Newbery Medal
Subjects: historical fiction—United States, Civil War

Questions

1. In which book are the loyalties of a border state family divided between the North and the South during the Civil War?

2. In which book does an angry Union mob burn a barn and put coal oil in a well?

3. In which book does an Illinois farm boy get in trouble because his brother has joined the Rebel army?

4. In which book do the "cracker barrel heroes" pick on a character for defending a southern soldier?

5. In which book does the enemy of a family protect their youngest son from an attack?

All About Sam

Lois Lowry. Bantam, 1988. ISBN: 0440402212.
URLs: scils.rutgers.edu/special/kay/lowry
  www.carolhurst.com/authors/llowry
Subjects: Scotland; family life

Questions

1. In which book does a character expect goldfish to rain out of the sky?

2. In which book is the living room rug lumpy because there is broccoli underneath it?

3. In which book do moving men drive toy trucks down a hallway?

4. In which book does a character take a pack of Dentyne gum from a supermarket?

5. In which book does a character learn to send Morse code with a flashlight?

Amber Brown Sees Red

Paula Danziger. Illustrator: Tony Ross. Putnam, 1998. ISBN: 0399229019.
URL: www.scholastic.com/titles/paula/
Subjects: divorce; school stories

Questions

1. In which book does a fourth grader's wish that a math test be cancelled come true?

2. In which book does a character feel part of a team, even if the team doesn't always do what she wants?

3. In which book does a girl get really mad at the way her parents act toward each other?

4. In which book does a character work on her announcing skills by starting conversations with: Bulletin, Bulletin, Bulletin?

5. In which book does a character agree to coach a bowling team?

Among the Hidden

Margaret Haddix. Aladdin, 2000. ISBN: 0689824750.
URL: falcon.jmu.edu/~ramseyil/haddix.htm
Award: ALA Best Book for Young Adults
Subject: science fiction

Questions

1. In which book is a character unable to play outside or look out of the windows of a house?

2. In which book are people worried about the Population Police?

3. In which book does a character taste potato chips for the very first time?

4. In which book do characters use a chat room to plan a secret meeting?

5. In which book does the government tell farmers which crops they can plant and which animals they are allowed to raise?

Babysitting Is a Dangerous Job

Willo Davis Roberts. Aladdin, 1996. ISBN: 0689806574.
URL: cbcbooks.org/autindex/falcon.jmu.edu/~ramseyil
Subjects: mystery fiction; contemporary issues

Questions

1. In which book are two friends followed by a strange black car?

2. In which book do intruders use a garage door opener to gain entry to a house?

3. In which book does a little girl make friends with two large dogs?

4. In which book does a character hide in a tree house after running away from home?

5. In which book does a housekeeper have many dental appointments?

Battle for the Castle

Elizabeth Winthrop. Bantam, 1993. ISBN: 044040942X.
URL: www.elizabethwinthrop.com/castleindex.html
Subject: fantasy; time travel

Questions

1. In which book are characters expected to "jump the trains" when they are 12 years old?

2. In which book does a character on a bicycle joust with a knight on horseback?

3. In which book do characters set fire to a ship filled with bones?

4. In which book is a party besieged by an army of rats?

5. In which book does a character learn that it is better to rely on himself than on a magic token to solve problems?

Because of Winn-Dixie

Kate DiCamillo. Candlewick Press, 2000. ISBN: 0763607762.
URL: www.teenreads.com/authors/au-dicamillo-kate.asp
Award: Newbery Honor Book
Subjects: dogs; friendship

Questions

1. In which book does the heroine rescue a mischievous dog?

2. In which book does a character get a library for her birthday?

3. In which book does a character who cares for animals let them out of their cages because he knows what it is like to be in jail?

4. In which book do you learn that the secret ingredient of a candy is "sorrow" because of the Civil War?

5. In which book does a character say she sees with her heart instead of her eyes?

The Best School Year Ever

Barbara Robinson. HarperCollins, 1994. ISBN: 0064404927.
URL: Usawrites4kids.Drury.Edu/Authors/Robinson/
Award: Nene Award (Hawaii)
Subjects: humorous fiction; school stories

Questions

1. In which book does a character release a group of adults locked in the teachers' lounge?

2. In which book does a character smash walnuts on his forehead in a talent show?

3. In which book does a character give up an old baby blanket to an upset little boy who has lost his own blanket?

4. In which book do children put their brother on a leash because they don't have a dog?

5. In which book does a character tie a snake to a light cord in the teacher's supply closet?

The BFG

Roald Dahl. Illustrator: Quentin Blake. Farrar, Straus and Giroux, 1982. ISBN: 0374304696.
URL: falcon.jmu.edu/~ramseyil/dahl.htm
Subject: fantasy

Questions

1. In which book do we hear of the witching hour?

2. In which book does a giant catch dreams and blow good dreams into little children's minds?

3. In which book are grandmothers thought to be tougher to eat than children?

4. In which book does an orphan take a trip in a pocket?

5. In which book do characters believe Jack from "Jack and the Beanstalk" has returned?

Blister

Susan Shreve. Scholastic, 2001. ISBN: 0439193141.
Award: ALA Notable Book
Subject: family life

Questions

1. In which book does a family move from a farmhouse with cats, chickens and a goat to a small city apartment?

2. In which book does a grandmother dance and sing to swing music on the radio?

3. In which book does a character find a suitcase full of clothing underneath a bed?

4. In which book does a character lie about being invited to cheerleading practice?

5. In which book does a character unwillingly return a ring she has taken?

The Boggart and the Monster

Susan Cooper. Aladdin, 1998. ISBN: 0689822863.
URL: scholastic.com/authorsandbooks
Subjects: fantasy; Scotland

Questions

1. In which book do two characters from Canada visit Scotland?

2. In which book are two long-lost cousins reunited?

3. In which book does a character meet a well-known scientist on an airplane?

4. In which book does the crash of a car with an ice cream truck effect more than those who are involved in the collision?

5. In which book are two seals especially friendly to several characters?

Bound for Oregon

Jean Van Leeuwen. Penguin, 1996. ISBN: 0140383190.
URL: eduplace.com/kids/hmr/mtai
Subject: historical fiction—frontier and pioneer life

Questions

1. In which book is a grandmother admired for shooting a panther out of a tree?

2. In which book is a pet animal washed away in a flooded river?

3. In which book do characters become ill in a cholera epidemic?

4. In which book is a baby born during a family's long journey?

5. In which book do two sisters work many days digging sacks of potatoes?

Can't You Make them Behave, King George?

Jean Fritz. Illustrator: Tomie De Paola. Puffin, 1996. ISBN: 0698114027.
URL: falcon.jmu.edu/~ramseyil/fritz.htm
Subjects: George III; history—United States, Revolutionary War

Questions

1. In which book does the main character follow these rules: stay thin, don't swear and keep your promises?

2. In which book is a stamp tax created to help pay for a war?

3. In which book does a king feel he has to be firm with the Massachusetts "children"?

4. In which book do you learn about France joining America in a war against England?

5. In which book do you learn about a character who had 15 children?

Case of the Muttering Mummy

E. W. Hildick. Illustrator: Blanche Sims. Macmillan, 1986. ISBN: 0027439607.
URL: falcon.jmu.edu/~ramseyil/levine.htm
Subject: mystery fiction

Questions

1. In which book is the notice "don't jump the gun" memorized?

2. In which book does a man try to scare kids with an ancient Egyptian curse?

3. In which book do you learn about an alley that looks like gold?

4. In which book is a man a suspected thief because of ordering food in Greek?

5. In which book is a birthday present really a stolen museum piece?

Catwings

Ursula Le Guin. Scholastic, 1990. ISBN: 0590428330.
URLs: ursulakleguin.com
   teenreads.com/authors/au_leguin_ursula.asp
Subject: fantasy

Questions

1. In which book does a mother want her children to move away from their rundown neighborhood?

2. In which book do three city dwellers find a very different home in the country?

3. In which book does a character catch a fish for dinner for the first time in his life?

4. In which book does an owl attack unusual new neighbors?

5. In which book are three homeless animals adopted by a brother and sister?

The Chalk Box Kid

Clyde Bulla. Illustrator: Thomas Allen. Random House, 1987. ISBN: 0394891023.
URL: mowrites4kids.drury.edu/authors/bulla/
Subjects: imagination; friendship; family life

Questions

1. In which book does a character have to share a bedroom with an uncle?

2. In which book does a third grade class visit a picture garden?

3. In which book does a photograph help a character make new friends?

4. In which book does an old burned-out building become a place of inner beauty?

5. In which book does a shy girl help a shy boy make friends?

Changes for Felicity

Valerie Tripp. Illustrator: Dan Andreasen. Pleasant Co., 1992. ISBN: 156247037X.
URL: www.childrenslit.com/f_valerietripp.html
Subjects: historical fiction—United States, Revolutionary War; friendship

Questions

1. In which book is the question "Is death the end of everything?" answered by "No change, not even death, can end love"?

2. In which book are the families of two best friends on the opposite sides of a war?

3. In which book does Grandfather leave money for a man in jail so he can pay his debts and go home?

4. In which book does an act of kindness in the shape of a blanket and medicine bring out the goodness in a mean character?

5. In which book do you learn that not all changes are bad; that growing up and learning new skills are good changes?

The Chicken Doesn't Skate

Gordon Korman. Scholastic, 1998. ISBN: 0590853015.
URLs: www2.scholastic.com/teachers/authorsandbooks/authorstudies/authorhome.jhtml?authorID=138&collateralID=5206&displayName=Biography
  gordonkorman.com
Subjects: school stories; contemporary issues; humorous fiction

Questions

1. In which book does a seventh grader have to take sixth grade science?

2. In which book does a character work on a project about the food chain?

3. In which book is the fire department called at the end of a party?

4. In which book is a character's father a Nobel Prize winner?

5. In which book is a character accused of cattle rustling?

The Devil's Arithmetic

Jane Yolen. Penguin, 1990. ISBN: 0140345353.
URLs: ipl.org/youth/askauthor/yolen
  www.janeyolen.com.
Award: National Jewish Book Award
Subjects: historical fiction—twentieth century—Holocaust, 1933–1945

Questions

1. In which book does a family hold a special feast for remembering history?

2. In which book does a character receive crocks of butter and two cages of chickens among other wedding presents?

3. In which book does a character find herself in another time and place after opening an apartment door?

4. In which book are people who are returning to their village carried away by soldiers and then imprisoned?

5. In which book does a character save someone's life by putting on a blue scarf?

Dovey Coe

Frances O. Dowell. Aladdin, 2001. ISBN: 0689846673.
Subjects: family life; historical fiction—twentieth century

Questions

1. In which book does a pretty girl's flattery win her younger sibling a much-wanted knife?

2. In which book are two dogs named for Tom Sawyer and Huckleberry Finn?

3. In which book does a character interrupt a barn dance to make a marriage proposal?

4. In which book is a character who is deaf threatened by an older bully?

5. In which book does a young lawyer struggle as he tries his first case?

Earthquake Terror

Peg Kehret. Penguin, 1996. ISBN: 0140383433.
URL: eduplace.com/kids/hmr/mtai/kehret.html
Subjects: adventure; survival

Questions

1. In which book does a family go camping on a small island?

2. In which book does a golden retriever save a character from drowning?

3. In which book do two characters sing the itsy-bitsy spider song?

4. In which book do characters eat squished sandwiches and broken cookie crumbs?

5. In which book does a town burn during a flood because the firefighters cannot get water?

Ella Enchanted

Gail Carson Levine. HarperCollins, 1997. ISBN: 0064407055.
URL: falcon.jmu.edu/~ramseyil/levine.htm
Award: Newbery Honor Book
Subject: fantasy

Questions

1. In which book does a gift for learning languages help a character on a dangerous journey?

2. In which book do you learn that gifts are not always appreciated or wanted by those who receive them?

3. In which book does eating mushrooms lead to love?

4. In which book does a character write letters which are never sent?

5. In which book does a character have to follow every command given?

An Enemy at Green Knowe

L. M. Boston. Harcourt, 1964. ISBN: 0152259732.
URL: www.literatureforkids.com/kids/boston.html
Subject: fantasy

Questions

1. In which book do two characters bring home unusual pebbles from their trip to the sea?

2. In which book is a special ball hung in the attic of an old house?

3. In which book does a character dislike a teacher's strong forefinger and strange roving eye?

4. In which book does an unpleasant guest ask many rude questions?

5. In which book do two characters get excited when their fathers return home from a journey?

Escape to Witch Mountain

Alexander Key. Illustrator: Leon B. Wisdom. Westminster Press, 1980. ISBN: 0671560441.
Subjects: science fiction; adventure

Questions

1. In which book does a character remember seeing an old letter with a double star at the top?

2. In which book are two children sure that the man who tries to claim them is not really their uncle?

3. In which book are two half-starved bears let out of their cage?

4. In which book do characters remember a long-ago journey in a boat?

5. In which book do two characters communicate without speaking?

Esperanza Rising

Pam Muñoz Ryan. Scholastic, 2000. ISBN: 043912042X.
URL: www.pammunozryan.com/
Awards: Jane Addams Children's Book Award; Willa Cather Award
Subjects: historical fiction—California; migrant labor

Questions

1. In which book does a family escape from their home by hiding under a load of guavas?
2. In which book does a traveler receive a present of two live chickens?
3. In which book does a character learn to sweep with a broom?
4. In which book does a character pray to be chosen Queen of the May?
5. In which book does a character lie down on the ground to feel the heartbeat of the world?

Everything on a Waffle

Polly Horvath. Farrar, Straus and Giroux, 2001. ISBN: 0374322368.
URL: falcon.jmu.edu/~ramseyil/horvath.htm
Subject: realistic fiction

Questions

1. In which book are a character's parents believed to be drowned in a storm at sea?
2. In which book does a character's uncle hope to develop a small town as a tourist attraction?
3. In which book does a character enter a boiled potatoes contest?
4. In which book does a character cut a guinea pig's hair after the animal catches fire?
5. In which book does a character lose a baby toe and the tip of a little finger?

Fair Weather

Richard Peck. Dial, 2001. ISBN: 0803725167.
URL: www.carolhurst.com/authors/rpeck.html
Subject: fairs; historical fiction—Chicago 1893; humorous fiction

Questions

1. In which book does Granddad turn out to be an old friend of Buffalo Bill?
2. In which book do characters go to Chicago to visit the Columbian Exposition?
3. In which book does a character meet the real actress Lillian Russell?
4. In which book are children upset because the cook keeps a dirty kitchen?
5. In which book does a family dog jump into a stagecoach as it races around the show ring?

The Family Under the Bridge

Natalie Savage Carlson. Illustrator: Garth Williams. HarperCollins, 1989. ISBN: 0064402509.
Award: Newbery Honor Book
Subjects: homeless persons; friendship; gypsies

Questions

1. In which book does a church provide dinner for the homeless on Christmas Eve?
2. In which book does a character lose his wallet and leave town before he gets it back?
3. In which book do kids ask for a house for Christmas and get one?
4. In which book does a character teach the alphabet to kids who have never gone to school?
5. In which book does a mother have to leave her children alone so that she can go to work?

Finding Buck McHenry

Alfred Slote. HarperCollins, 1993. ISBN: 0064404692.
Subjects: sports; prejudices

Questions

1. In which book does a character own 30,000 baseball cards?
2. In which book does a grandfather tell a lie to help his grandchild?
3. In which book does a school custodian become a celebrity?
4. In which book do two characters hiding under a porch hear some shocking news?
5. In which book does a character move to a new town when both parents are killed?

Flaming Arrows

William O. Steele. Harcourt, 1990. ISBN: 0152284273.
Subject: historical fiction—West (U.S.)

Questions

1. In which book does a character have to card wool for his mother?
2. In which book are characters sent to a spring to carry water for their families?
3. In which book does a boy lose friends when his father helps an unpopular family?
4. In which book does a group of people become very thirsty?
5. In which book are a character's hands burned trying to put out a fire?

Flight of the Dragon Kyn

Susan Fletcher. Atheneum, 1993. ISBN: 0689318804.
Subjects: fantasy; dragons

Questions

1. In which book does a character get in trouble for calling birds?

2. In which book is Skava the name of a white falcon?

3. In which book does a character disobey the king?

4. In which book does a character cause the death of an animal who saved her as a baby?

5. In which book does a character learn the art of falconry?

The Friendship

Mildred D. Taylor. Illustrator: Max Ginsburg. Puffin, 1987. ISBN: 0140389644.
URLs: falcon.jmu.edu/ramseyil/taylor.htm
   indiana.edu/~reading/ieo/bibs
Subjects: prejudices; historical fiction—Mississippi 1933

Questions

1. In which book does an old man like to buy sardines and peppermint?

2. In which book does a store clerk threaten a six-year-old when he puts his hands on a glass case?

3. In which book does a young man promise his rescuer he can always call him by name?

4. In which book does a group of men urge a character to mistreat an elder?

5. In which book does a character defy a group of bullies even after he is injured?

Frindle

Andrew Clements. Aladdin, 1998. ISBN: 0689818769.
URLs: www.frindle.com/
   www.eduplace.com/kids/hmr/mtai/clements.html
Subjects: humorous fiction; school stories

Questions

1. In which book is the idea expressed that in every good story there is a bad guy?

2. In which book do you learn that an idea shared is no longer controlled by the person who thought of it?

3. In which book does a school receive one million dollars in a trust fund?

4. In which book is the dictionary introduced as the finest tool ever made?

5. In which book does the question "where did all those words come from" lead to an extra homework assignment?

The Frog Princess of Pelham

Ellen Conford. Little, Brown and Company, 1997. ISBN: 0316152463.
Subjects: orphans; fantasy; humorous fiction

Questions

1. In which book do the CIA and the National Institute of Science search a house in the name of national security?

2. In which book does a character have to go to Survival Camp in Idaho?

3. In which book does an old aquarium with a bowl of water in it make a safe home?

4. In which book are a character's favorite foods chili and tiny shrimp?

5. In which book does an animal trash a room by trying to get a little exercise?

The Gate in the Wall

Ellen Howard. Atheneum, 1999. ISBN: 0689822952.
URL: falcon.jmu.edu/~ramseyil/howard.htm
Subject: historical fiction—West (U.S.)

Questions

1. In which book is a character told she'll have to take horses along a towpath in order to pay for eating a potato?

2. In which book does a character work as a huffler for a narrowboat?

3. In which book does a character have a talent for painting tinware?

4. In which book is a character torn between helping her sister or helping Granny Minshull?

5. In which book does a character learn to crew a boat through the locks?

Ghost in the Family

Betty Ren Wright. Scholastic, 1998. ISBN: 059002955X.
Subjects: ghost stories; mystery fiction

Questions

1. In which book are characters trapped in a room where fog streams in the window, a toothbrush is flying in the air and humongous beetles crawl over the bed?

2. In which book does the message "Go Home" appear on a mirror then suddenly disappear?

3. In which book do characters try to discover who stole a diamond bracelet?

4. In which book can a character see into the window of a neighbor from his room?

5. In which book does a character stay in a room with the spirit of a dead dentist?

The Ghosts of Austwick Manor

Reby MacDonald. Aladdin, 1991. ISBN: 0689715331.
Subjects: fantasy; time travel

Questions

1. In which book does a character inherit a dollhouse because he will one day become head of the family?

2. In which book is a present-day character threatened by a sixteenth-century curse?

3. In which book does a character ask for a stargazey pie and a hedgehog as a birthday meal?

4. In which book do a teenager's parents disapprove of a friend who drives a sporty red car?

5. In which book does a mother think her children may be mentally disturbed?

Gib and the Gray Ghost

Zilpha Keatley Snyder. Bantam, 2000. ISBN: 0440415187.
URL: www.zksnyder.com/Autobiography.html
Subjects: orphans; horses; animals

Questions

1. In which book is a character adopted by the same family for a second time?

2. In which book do two characters drive a team of horses when they go to school?

3. In which book does a rancher lose stock over the winter because the foreman is weak and lazy?

4. In which book does a frightened animal find shelter from a snowstorm in an unfamiliar barn?

5. In which book does a character earn the nickname "Cowboy"?

Ginger Pye

Eleanor Estes. Harcourt, 1951. ISBN: 0152025057.
Award: Newbery Medal
Subjects: dogs; family life; animals

Questions

1. In which book do characters earn a dollar by dusting the pews of a church?

2. In which book are characters followed by a stranger in a yellow hat?

3. In which book does a pet climb through a classroom window?

4. In which book does a character observe a classmate on the platform of a train going to New York?

5. In which book do school-age children have a three-year-old uncle?

Guests

Michael Dorris. Hyperion. 1999. ISBN: 0786811080.
URL: www2.scholastic.com/teachers/authorsandbooks/authorstudies/authorhome.jhtml;jsessionid=SNUXVEYU132BWCQVALDSFFAKCUBJWIWA?authorID=30&collateralID=5150&displayName=Biography&_requestid=506342
Subject: historical fiction—United States, colonial period

Questions

1. In which book is a boy angry that company has been invited to a special meal?

2. In which book does a boy break a very old object that belongs to his grandfather?

3. In which book does a character slip away instead of helping his family prepare for a celebration?

4. In which book does a mother tell a story even though she is very shy?

5. In which book does a character have a friend whose name is Trouble?

Hatchet

Gary Paulsen. Aladdin, 1996. ISBN: 0689808828.
URL: www.trelease-on-reading.com/paulsen
Award: Newbery Honor Book
Subjects: survival; divorce

Questions

1. In which book does a last-minute gift help save a character's life?

2. In which book does a pilot die of a heart attack while flying an airplane?

3. In which book does a skunk steal turtle eggs?

4. In which book is a character's shelter destroyed by a tornado?

5. In which book is a character surprised when company arrives just as his dinner is ready?

The Hobbit

J. R. R. Tolkien. Houghton Mifflin, 1997. ISBN: 0618002219.
Subject: fantasy

Questions

1. In which book is there a dragon named Smaug?

2. In which book does a character live in a nice round hole in a hill?

3. In which book does a great bee-keeper change his skin and become a huge black bear?

4. In which book do characters ask riddles?

5. In which book do spiders web-wrap dwarves for dinner?

Home From Far

Jean Little. Little Brown, 1965. ISBN: 0316528021.
Subject: family life

Questions

1. In which book does a family take in two characters after their own son is killed in an accident?

2. In which book does a dog perform as a lion in a backyard circus?

3. In which book does a fire start when a character carries a candle to explore a secret hideaway?

4. In which book does a character overcome a fear of caterpillars?

5. In which book does a character love both Pop and Dad?

House on Hackman's Hill

Joan Lowery Nixon. Scholastic, 1985. ISBN: 0590423703.
URLs: teacher.scholastic.com/authorsandbooks/
  randomhouse.com/teachers/authors
Subjects: haunted houses; mystery fiction

Questions

1. In which book is a character employed by a college professor to help set up a museum?

2. In which book do characters hear an exciting story from their grandparents' neighbor?

3. In which book do characters hope to claim a large reward?

4. In which book does a collector of artifacts come under the curse of an ancient god?

5. In which book does a mysterious fire blaze up just at the end of a snowstorm?

The House with a Clock in its Walls

John Bellairs. Illustrator: Edward Gorey. Puffin, 1993. ISBN: 014036336X.
URL: www.bellairsia.com
Award: New York Times Outstanding Book of the Year
Subjects: witchcraft; haunted houses; occult fiction

Questions

1. In which book does a character move to a town called New Zebedee?

2. In which book do two characters have a frightening Halloween experience in the town cemetery?

3. In which book do characters avoid their pursuers by driving across an old iron bridge?

4. In which book is a character interested in the Spanish Armada and the Napoleonic Wars?

5. In which book is an old parlor organ set to play chopsticks on "infinite replay"?

Humbug Mountain

Sid Fleischman. Bantam, 1997. ISBN: 0440414032.
URLs: www2.scholastic.com/teachers/authorsandbooks/authorstudies/authorhome.jhtml?authorID=34&collateralID=5158&displayName=Biography
  www.carr.org/authco/fleis-inf.htm
Subjects: historical fiction—West (U.S.); humorous fiction

Questions

1. In which book is a goose stolen to be the target in a "goose pull"?

2. In which book does a father start newspapers in several small towns?

3. In which book does a family travel on a steamboat called *The Prairie Buzzard?*

4. In which book do travelers find they have made a long journey to a ghost town?

5. In which book do saloons go out of business when a river changes course?

The Hundred Penny Box

Sharon Bell Mathis. Illustrators: Leo and Diane Dillon. Puffin Books, 1986. ISBN: 0670387878.
URL: falcon.jmu.edu/~ramseyil/mathis.htm
Award: Newbery Honor Book
Subjects: grandparents; family life

Questions

1. In which book do we understand that a thing might be old and broken but is still loved because it holds memories?

2. In which book do we hear that forgetting is the only bad thing about getting old?

3. In which book does Ruth feel unhappy in her own house because of an old lady?

4. In which book does a boy love to hear the stories of when his father was young?

5. In which book is there a favorite dusty, chipped, recording of the hymn "Precious Lord, Take My Hand"?

In the Year of the Boar and Jackie Robinson

Bette Bao Lord. Illustrator: Marc Simont. HarperCollins, 1984. ISBN: 0064401758.
URL: falcon.jmu.edu/~ramseyil/lord.htm
Subjects: immigrants; sports

Questions

1. In which book does a character choose a new name at the new year's festivities?

2. In which book does a parrot help a character play the piano?

3. In which book does a character have good luck after getting two black eyes?

4. In which book does a character borrow coins from a piggy bank?

5. In which book do two characters swear in blood to keep a secret?

An Island Far From Home

John Donahue. Carolrhoda, 1995. ISBN: 0876148593.
Subjects: historical fiction—United States, Civil War; friendship; family life

Questions

1. In which book does a character end up in jail as a spy?

2. In which book does a mother teach her son that slavery takes away a person's dignity and dreams?

3. In which book does war look different if you know someone on the other side?

4. In which book does a brass button with the letter "A" lead to a story more than 100 years old?

5. In which book do a Confederate prisoner of war and the nephew of a Union major become pen pals and friends?

Jason's Gold

Will Hobbs. Harper Trophy, 1999. ISBN: 0688150934.
URL: falcon.jmu.edu/~ramseyil/hobbs.htm
Subjects: survival; Alaska

Questions

1. In which book does a character meet Jack London?

2. In which book does a character struggle up the Dead Horse Trail?

3. In which book does a character try to follow others to the Klondike?

4. In which book is a character rescued by Jamie Dunavant?

5. In which book is a character trampled by a moose?

Joey Pigza Loses Control

Jack Gantos. HarperCollins, 2000. ISBN: 0064410226.
URLs: cbcbooks.org
   www2.scholastic.com/teachers/authorsandbooks/authorstudies/authorhome.jhtml;
jsessionid=SNUXVEYU132BWCQVALDSFFAKCUBJWIWA?authorID=5570&collateralID=11023&
displayName=Biography&_requestid=506627
Subjects: learning disabilities—ADHD; humorous fiction

Questions

1. In which book does a character shoot a dog's ear with an arrow?

2. In which book does a grandmother carry an oxygen tank and ride in a grocery cart?

3. In which book does a character spend a day alone seeing the sights of Pittsburgh?

4. In which book does a character pretend to be a department store mannequin?

5. In which book does a baseball team lose its championship game because of its pitcher?

Journey to America

Sonia Levitin. Aladdin, 1970. ISBN: 0689711301.
URL: falcon.jmu.edu/~ramseyil/levitin.htm
Subjects: historical fiction—twentieth century—Holocaust, 1933–1945; immigrants

Questions

1. In which book does a character give her little sister a special bride doll so she will not tell a secret?

2. In which book does a character hide money in a violin case?

3. In which book do characters steal potatoes for a cookout?

4. In which book does a mother become ill while traveling?

5. In which book are Christians forbidden to work for Jews?

Just So Stories

Rudyard Kipling. Viking Press, 1993. ISBN: 0670851965.
URL: www.online-literature.com/kipling/
Subjects: animals; humorous fiction

Questions

1. In which book does the author call the reader "O Best beloved"?

2. In which book is a kangaroo chased by a dingo until five o'clock in the afternoon?

3. In which book does a Bi-Colored Python Rock Snake save a small elephant from a crocodile?

4. In which book does a shipwrecked sailor wear blue canvas breeches and a pair of suspenders?

5. In which book does a Parsee rub cake crumbs into an animal's skin?

Kävik the Wolf Dog

Walt Morey. Illustrator: Peter Parnall. Puffin, 1997. ISBN: 0140384235.
Subjects: Alaska; survival; animals

Questions

1. In which book does an over-confident pilot crash his plane in a sudden storm?

2. In which book does a character want a puppy to grow up tough and mean?

3. In which book does a doctor wait until after dark to treat a patient's broken leg?

4. In which book does a fussy housewife insist that her husband lock up a new pet?

5. In which book does a character find courage to take out a fishing boat again?

The Kid in the Red Jacket

Barbara Park. Random House, 1987. ISBN: 0394805712.
URL: randomhouse.com/teachers/authors
Subjects: family life; moving

Questions

1. In which book is a pet given sleeping pills when the family travels across the country?

2. In which book is a character embarrassed by the street name in the family's new address?

3. In which book does a character's baby brother seem to be the only one who listens to him?

4. In which book do two older children play keep-away with a little girl's doll?

5. In which book does a child color pictures using only lavender and lime green?

The Kid Who Ran for President

Dan Gutman, Scholastic, 1996. ISBN: 0590939882.
URL: www.dangutman.com/
Subjects: elections; school stories; humorous fiction

Questions

1. In which book does a character promise to abolish all homework if his classmates convince their parents to vote for him?

2. In which book do you hear the promise "give the customer what he wants" even if it isn't a good choice?

3. In which book does a character ask his former babysitter to be a running mate in a campaign?

4. In which book is the question, "Who caused all the problems the country faces today?" answered with "the grown-ups!"

5. In which book does the author tell you not to read the end of the story first as there are no shortcuts in life?

A Killing in Plymouth Colony

Carol Otis Hurst and Rebecca Otis. Houghton Mifflin, 2003. ISBN: 0618275975.
URL: www.carolhurst.com/bios/carolbio.html
Subject: historical fiction—United States, colonial period

Questions

1. In which book does a character try to teach a crow to speak?

2. In which book do characters save a man who fell overboard?

3. In which book does a character become very ill after seeing a murder?

4. In which book does a character feel his father is always disappointed in him, no matter what he does?

5. In which book does a character resent being left behind in Holland?

The Kite Fighters

Linda Sue Park. Illustrator: Eung Won Park. Clarion Books, 2000. ISBN: 0395940419.
URL: www.lindasuepark.com/
Subject: historical fiction—Korea

Questions

1. In which book is a character expected to be studious just because he's the elder?

2. In which book does a character decide to coat a toy's string with powdered pottery?

3. In which book does the king honor those who crafted an item as well as those who used them well?

4. In which book does a boy king leave his palace to play games with some brothers?

5. In which book does an important competition take place during a New Year's festival?

The Land I Lost

Huynh Quang Nhuong. HarperCollins, 1986. ISBN: 0064401839.
URL: seaox.com/thich.html
Award: ALA Notable Book
Subject: historical fiction—Vietnam War

Questions

1. In which book is a buffalo trained to fight tigers?

2. In which book do characters mistake a python for a dead tree trunk and sit down on it?

3. In which book does a character cut off a large piece of a crocodile's tail?

4. In which book does a grandmother take a character to see a long opera about The Faithful One and the Flatterer?

5. In which book does an elderly character know just when she will die?

The Last Battle

C. S. Lewis. Harper, 1956. ISBN: 0064409414.
URLs: narnia.com
   cslewis.drzeus.net
Subject: fantasy

Questions

1. In which book is a donkey disguised as a lion?

2. In which book does a false leader tell followers that freedom means doing what he tells them to do?

3. In which book do strange things happen behind the door of an old shed?

4. In which book do people and animals swim up a waterfall?

5. In which book are children happy to hear that they will not have to return home?

Lily's Crossing

Patricia Reilly Giff. Dell Yearling, 1997. ISBN: 0440414539.
URL: falcon.jmu.edu/~ramseyil/giff.htm
Award: Newbery Honor Book
Subjects: historical fiction—World War, 1939–1945; friendship

Questions

1. In which book does a character send a secret message by writing a series of book titles?

2. In which book is a character worried about her sister Ruth, last seen in France?

3. In which book is a character caught breaking into her own house by crawling in the second floor window?

4. In which book does a friendship start with the rescue of a cat from drowning?

5. In which book is a birthday present the key to an empty house?

Love, Ruby Lavender

Deborah Wiles. Harcourt, 2002. ISBN: 0152045686.
URLs: www.deborahwiles.com/ruby.htm
   www.aea10.k12.ia.us/communityofreaders/2002/wiles.html
Awards: ALA Notable Book; NCTE Notable Children's Trade Book
Subjects: grandparents; death

Questions

1. In which book does a grandmother drive the getaway car when her grandchild carries off some chickens?

2. In which book is a character invited to a root beer party by a teacher new to town?

3. In which book do characters use a hole under a maple tree to exchange letters in pink envelopes?

4. In which book is a character's head shaved after a bucket of blue paint spills on it?

5. In which book do characters who consider themselves enemies meet at a special spot on a bridge?

Love that Dog

Sharon Creech. HarperCollins, 2003. ISBN: 0064409597.
URL: falcon.jmu.edu/~ramseyil/creech.htm
Subjects: school stories; poetry

Questions

1. In which book does a character believe that poetry is written only by girls?

2. In which book does a blue car play an important part in the story?

3. In which book do a father and son choose a pet at an animal shelter?

4. In which book does a character write a letter to a famous author?

5. In which book does a teacher sometimes bake brownies for the class?

Mandy

Julie Edwards. HarperCollins, 1971. ISBN: 0064402967.
URL: julieandrewscollection.com
Subjects: orphans

Questions

1. In which book is a character often sad in spite of a pleasant life in an orphanage?

2. In which book does a character keep a secret from a best friend?

3. In which book does a character replace small items that have been taken from cupboards and drawers without permission?

4. In which book does a character pretend to be ill in order to avoid a day trip to the seashore?

5. In which book is a character rescued during a storm by a rider on a tall dark horse?

Max and Me and the Time Machine

Gery Greer. HarperCollins, 1983. ISBN: 0064402223.
URL: www.eduplace.com/tview/pages/m/Max_and_Me_and_the_Time_Machine_Gery_Greer.html
Subjects: fantasy; time travel

Questions

1. In which book does a character get more than his money's worth from a garage sale purchase?

2. In which book does a horse play jokes on its rider?

3. In which book is a character invited to join the Crusades?

4. In which book is a character reminded that it is bad manners to wipe one's nose on the tablecloth or butter bread with one's thumb?

5. In which book does a bully accuse a character of stealing his ancestor's ear?

The Midnight Fox

Betsy Byars. Puffin, 1996. ISBN: 0140314504 .
URLs: betsybyars.com
  randomhouse.com/teachers/authors
Subjects: family life; animals

Questions

1. In which book is a character angry about spending vacation time in the country?

2. In which book do characters exchange many letters during vacation?

3. In which book does a character spend many hours watching for a special animal?

4. In which book does a mother bring food to her baby who has been stolen from their home?

5. In which book does a girl's boyfriend say he will not marry her unless she loses twenty pounds?

The Monsters of Morley Manor

Bruce Coville. Harcourt, 2001. ISBN: 0152047050.
URLs: brucecoville.com
  teacher.scholastic.com/authorsandbooks
Subject: science fiction

Questions

1. In which book does a character get a monkey for her fortieth birthday?

2. In which book do two characters buy a box containing five small figurines?

3. In which book does a character fall through a hole in the world?

4. In which book do several characters escape pursuit by opening a black door decorated with a circle of stars?

5. In which book are a character's elderly grandparents briefly reunited?

Morning Girl

Michael Dorris. Hyperion, 1992. ISBN: 1562822845.
URLs: teacher.scholastic.com/authorsandbooks
  dir.yahoo.com/arts/humanities/literature/authors/literary_fiction/dorris__michael__1945_1997_/?o=a
Subjects: historical fiction; family life

Questions

1. In which book do a brother and sister have different feelings about night and day?

2. In which book is a family disappointed when they do not get a new sister?

3. In which book does a character pretend to be a rock when he believes his parents are disappointed in him?

4. In which book do characters celebrate after a hurricane?

5. In which book do characters meet strangers from a ship they have never seen before?

Mossflower

Brian Jacques. Ace, 1998. ISBN: 0442005489.
URLs: redwall.org/dave/jacques
  teacher.scholastic.com/authorsandbooks/
Subjects: fantasy; animals

Questions

1. In which book does an evil character usurp the throne from a brother who is the rightful heir?

2. In which book do Gloomer and Stormfin engage in a deadly battle?

3. In which book do characters follow clues deciphered from a hidden manuscript as they search for a missing leader?

4. In which book does a young warrior carry a broken sword?

5. In which book is a sailing ship sunk to make a dam across a river?

Mr. Tucket

Gary Paulsen. Bantam, 1994. ISBN: 0441005764.
URL: www.trelease-on-reading.com/paulsen
Subject: historical fiction—West (U.S.)

Questions

1. In which book does a character receive a new rifle as a birthday present?

2. In which book do two characters compete in a wrestling match?

3. In which book do two travelers learn that an Indian uprising is being planned?

4. In which book is the object of a game to touch your opponent's thumb to the table?

5. In which book does a fur trapper take care to avoid trapping too many animals?

The Music of Dolphins

Karen Hesse. Scholastic, 1996. ISBN: 0590897977.
URL: falcon.jmu.edu/~ramseyil/hesse.htm
Subjects: dolphins; fantasy; survival

Questions

1. In which book is a character considered to be a scientific study owned by the government?

2. In which book does a character call an old man "abuelo"?

3. In which book is a character brought up by sea mammals?

4. In which book does a character love learning new things to do with her hands?

5. In which book is there a place where the sounds of traffic seem like sounds of the sea?

My Side of the Mountain

Jean Craighead George. Puffin, 2001. ISBN: 0141312424.
URL: falcon.jmu.edu/~ramseyil/george.htm
Award: Newbery Honor Book
Subject: survival

Questions

1. In which book is a character's hair cut by a librarian?

2. In which book do you find a recipe for frog soup served in a turtle shell?

3. In which book does a character train a falcon to hunt?

4. In which book does a character run away to find his great-grandfather's land?

5. In which book does a kind man teach a character how to make a fire?

Nekomah Creek

Linda Crew. Illustrator: Charles Robinson. Dell, 1993. ISBN: 0440407885.
URL: www.teenreads.com/authors/au-crew-linda.asp
Subjects: family life; school stories

Questions

1. In which book is a character teased because his father stays home and keeps house?

2. In which book is a character worried that the school counselor will think his family isn't normal?

3. In which book does a character get in trouble for reading books on the school playground?

4. In which book does a father auction off an elegant dinner that the school counselor wins?

5. In which book does a character make a neat diorama that the teacher wants to give as a retirement present?

Number the Stars

Lois Lowry. Dell, 1989. ISBN: 0440403278.
URL: falcon.jmu.edu/~ramseyil/lowry.htm
Award: Newbery Medal
Subjects: historical fiction—World War, 1939–1945; friendship

Questions

1. In which book is a handkerchief used to keep dogs from finding hidden people?

2. In which book do neighbors leave their daughter with her friend's family and disappear during the night?

3. In which book does a character pull a necklace from her friend's neck when they are awakened by strangers in the night?

4. In which book does a family hold a funeral for a great aunt, who never lived?

5. In which book does a character wear shoes made from fish skin because leather shoes are not available?

Once on this Island

Gloria Whelan. HarperCollins, 1995. ISBN: 0064406199.
URL: gloriawhelan.com
Subjects: Native Americans; historical fiction

Questions

1. In which book is an Indian child rescued and adopted by a white family?

2. In which book does a father leave his children behind with the enemy when he goes to enlist in the American army?

3. In which book do a storyteller's listeners hear that their land is resting on a turtle's back?

4. In which book does an adopted child rescue his foster parents from captivity?

5. In which book is a cow hidden in a house to keep from being stolen?

On My Honor

Marion Bauer. Clarion, 1986. ISBN: 0899194397.
URL: www.childrensliteraturenetwork.org/authors/bauer.html
Award: Newbery Honor Book
Subjects: accidents; friendship; character

Questions

1. In which book does a character's best friend drown?

2. In which book do best friends want to be on the high school swim team?

3. In which book does the title refer to promises a boy makes to his father?

4. In which book does a character feel guilty because of his friend's accident?

5. In which book does a character usually do what a friend wants to do instead of what he wants to do?

Out of the Deep

Gloria Skurzynski. National Geographic Society, 2002. ISBN: 0792282310.
Subjects: mystery fiction; Acadia National Park (ME); whales; foster home care

Questions

1. In which book do you read about the problem of dying whales?

2. In which book does an animal's damaged ears signal a possible cause of death?

3. In which book does a character overhear a telephone conversation that puts her life in danger?

4. In which book is a clue to the mystery found in a silver suitcase?

5. In which book does the fate of two kidnapped kids lie in the hands of a character who tells lies?

Parsifal's Page

Gerald Morris. Houghton Mifflin, 2001. ISBN: 0618055096.
Subjects: knighthood; fantasy

Questions

1. In which book does the son of a blacksmith yearn to travel with a knight?

2. In which book is a woodcutter really Sir Lancelot?

3. In which book does a character meet the daughter of the Lady of the Lake?

4. In which book does a character save his uncle when he finally asks "what ails you?"

5. In which book does an enchanted garland turn into a river?

Perloo the Bold

Avi. Scholastic, 1998. ISBN: 0590110039.
URLs: www.avi-writer.com
   teacher.scholastic.com/authorsandbooks/
Subjects: animals; fantasy

Questions

1. In which book is an important document torn in half?

2. In which book do characters stumble into an enemy stronghold during a winter storm?

3. In which book do two plotters become enemies as they try to seize power?

4. In which book is a character bothered by a serious itching at important moments?

5. In which book does a character win an important battle by throwing a snowball?

Pippi Longstocking

Astrid Lindgren. Illustrator: Louis S. Glanzman. Viking, 1950. ISBN: 0670557455.
URL: falcon.jmu.edu/~ramseyil/lindgren.htm
Subjects: fantasy; orphans; friendship; humorous fiction

Questions

1. In which book do policemen chase a girl onto the roof of a house?

2. In which book does a character go to school to get a Christmas vacation?

3. In which book are someone's shoes twice as big as needed so the owner has something to grow into?

4. In which book does a nine-year-old live all alone?

5. In which book does a character excuse her bad manners by saying she can't behave?

Poppy and Rye

Avi. Illustrator: Brian Floca. HarperCollins, 1998. ISBN: 0380797178.
URL: teacher.scholastic.com/authorsandbooks/
   www.avi-writer.com
Subjects: animals; fantasy; environment

Questions

1. In which book is a family's home flooded when a dam is built nearby?

2. In which book do two characters meet and dance together without learning each other's names?

3. In which book is a character upset by believing he can never be as good as his older brother?

4. In which book does a rescuer climb down a vine to reach a prisoner?

5. In which book is a condo development destroyed by a large boulder?

Ramona's World

Beverly Cleary. Morrow, 1999. ISBN: 0688168167.
URLs: www.beverlycleary.com
  falcon.jmu.edu/~ramseyil/cleary.htm
Subjects: family life; humorous fiction

Questions

1. In which book do two nine-year-olds write to a business because their ad contains misspelled words?

2. In which book does a character find a new best friend named Daisy?

3. In which book does a character fall through the ceiling while pretending to be a princess?

4. In which book does a character figure out how to get a baby's head out of a cat condo?

5. In which book does a cat enjoy being vacuumed?

Rats!

Jane Cutler. Illustrator: Tracey Pearson. Farrar, Strauss and Giroux, 1998. ISBN: 0-374-46203-8.
URL: www.janecutler.com/linkspages/janelinks.html
Subjects: humorous fiction; family life

Questions

1. In which book do you learn people will go into haunted houses because they like to be scared?

2. In which book does an accident with a bicycle lead to a funny Christmas photograph?

3. In which book is a boy unable to hit a baseball because he closes his eyes when the ball comes toward him?

4. In which book does a boy wear a yellow curly wig while wandering around a department store?

5. In which book does a boy believe ghosts are real because a girl who never lies has seen one?

Rescue of Josh McGuire

Ben Mikaelsen. Hyperion, 1991. ISBN: 1562820990.
URL: www.benmikaelsen.com/
Subjects: bears; animals; pets

Questions

1. In which book does a character save a bear cub?

2. In which book does a character carry an animal in a milk crate on a motorcycle?

3. In which book does a bear save a character's life?

4. In which book does a character learn he can't own a wild animal?

5. In which book does a character team up with a man who runs an animal rehabilitation center?

The Riddle of Penncroft Farm

Dorothea Jensen. Harcourt, 1989. ISBN: 0152669086.
Subjects: historical fiction—United States, Revolutionary War; ghost stories

Questions

1. In which book does a great-aunt hide a will in a special secret place?

2. In which book do characters frequently say, "Where there's a will there's a way"?

3. In which book does a father disown his son when he joins the colonial army?

4. In which book does a character boast constantly about distinguished ancestors?

5. In which book does a character suddenly become interested in American history?

Riding Freedom

Pam Muñoz Ryan. Scholastic, 1998. ISBN: 0439087961.
URL: teacher.scholastic.com/authorsand books/
Subjects: historical fiction—California; friendship

Questions

1. In which book does a character grow up in an orphanage for boys?

2. In which book does a character wear a leather bracelet?

3. In which book does a character learn to drive a team of horses?

4. In which book does a character lose sight in one eye?

5. In which book does a sign say "Private Property"?

Rip-Roaring Russell

Johanna Hurwitz. Illustrator: Lillian Hoban. Penguin, 1983. ISBN: 0140329390.
URLs: teacher.scholastic.com/authorsandbooks
  falcon.jmu.edu/~ramseyil/hurwitz.htm
Subjects: family life; humorous fiction

Questions

1. In which book is a character angry because it is raining on Columbus Day?

2. In which book does a character eat in a Chinese restaurant for the first time?

3. In which book does a character learn that it isn't fun for a five-year-old to be a baby?

4. In which book does an old lady in a wheelchair join a children's parade?

5. In which book does a character fall asleep after begging to watch a late TV show?

Rising Water

P. J. Petersen. Simon & Schuster, 2002. ISBN: 0689841485.
URL: usawrites4kids.drury.edu/authors/petersen/
Subjects: floods; animals; self esteem

Questions

1. In which book does a character pay for a crime by cleaning rat cages?
2. In which book does a character get caught in a house that is being burgled?
3. In which book does a character knock a shotgun out of a man's reach?
4. In which book is a "borrowed" knife used to flatten truck tires?
5. In which book does a character earn self respect for thinking of others first?

Rodzina

Karen Cushman. Clarion, 2003. ISBN: 0618133518.
URL: falcon.jmu.edu/~ramseyil/cushman.htm
Subjects: orphans

Questions

1. In which book does a character tell everyone she is slow?
2. In which book is a lady doctor in charge of a group of orphans traveling west?
3. In which book does a character discover Mr. Clench wants her for a wife, not a daughter?
4. In which book does a character tell stories from her Polish mama to keep other children quiet?
5. In which book does a character insist his brother is not really his brother?

Rosa Parks: Fight for Freedom

Keith Brandt. Illustrator: Gershom Griffith. Troll, 1993. ISBN: 0816728321.
URL: teacher.scholastic.com/rosa/
Subjects: civil rights; biography; family life

Questions

1. In which book does the Supreme Court change the segregation laws in Alabama?
2. In which book does a character leave school to take care of her grandmother and then her mother?
3. In which book do we learn about a terrorist group known as the Ku Klux Klan?
4. In which book do you learn that a boycott is the first step in trying to change a law?
5. In which book do you read about the "mother of the civil rights movement"?

Royal Diaries: Cleopatra VII, Daughter of the Nile

Kristiana Gregory. Scholastic, 1999. ISBN: 0590819755.
URL: falcon.jmu.edu/~ramseyil/gregory.htm
Subject: historical fiction—Egypt

Questions

1. In which book do the characters have a leopard and a baboon for pets?

2. In which book is a character the only family member who can speak the native language of their people?

3. In which book does a character hear songs in the streets that cause fear for the safety of the family?

4. In which book does a fire burn night and day to maintain the lighthouse in a great harbor?

5. In which book does a character love her father but fear his intentions toward her?

Run Away Home

Patricia McKissack. Scholastic, 1997. ISBN: 0590467514.
URL: falcon.jmu.edu/~ramseyil/pmckissack.htm
Subjects: friendship; African Americans; Native Americans

Questions

1. In which book does a boy think animals are divided into two groups (clean and unclean), which means he will not eat pork but will eat rat?

2. In which book do you learn that president Andrew Jackson freed all the black men who fought in the war with him?

3. In which book does a character call spring "the time of little leaves"?

4. In which book is Booker T. Washington's Tuskeegee School introduced?

5. In which book do Apache Indians work alongside former slaves and share food and recipes?

Runt

Marion Bauer. Clarion Books, 2002. ISBN: 0618212612.
URL: www.childrensliteraturenetwork.org/authors/bauer.html
Subjects: wolves; animals

Questions

1. In which book does a raven warn another animal about poisoned meat?

2. In which book do humans remove porcupine quills from a wild animal?

3. In which book does another animal feel sorry for a dog?

4. In which book is a character constantly washed to get rid of a human smell?

5. In which book does a pup earn a new name?

Sable

Karen Hesse. Illustrator: Marcia Sewall. Henry Holt & Company, 1994. ISBN: 0805057722.
URL: falcon.jmu.edu/~ramseyil/hesse.htm
Subjects: dogs; fathers and daughters; family life; animals

Questions

1. In which book is a mother afraid of dogs because she was bitten as a child?
2. In which book does a doctor solve a mother's problem but cause her daughter to feel awful?
3. In which book do a box of sawdust and a quilt make a good bed?
4. In which book does a character prove capable of working with a hammer and nails?
5. In which book is the same animal rescued twice?

Sadako

Eleanor Coerr. Illustrator: Ed Young. Putnam, 1993. ISBN: 0399217711.
URLs: www.sadako.org/sadakostory.htm
 falcon.jmu.edu/~ramseyil/young.htm
Subjects: friendship; death; historical fiction—World War, 1939–1945

Questions

1. In which book are dizzy spells after running the first signs of sickness?
2. In which book do classmates finish an origami project started by a student?
3. In which book is a spider considered a sign of good luck by many people?
4. In which book do characters buy a kokeshi doll for a fellow student?
5. In which book do you learn about the celebration of "Peace Day" on August 6 in Japan?

The School Story

Andrew Clements. Aladdin, 2001. ISBN: 0689825943.
URL: www.eduplace.com/kids/hmr/mtai/clements.html
Subjects: authorship; school stories

Questions

1. In which book is one friend the writer and one friend the talker?
2. In which book does a teacher decide she's not a coward and will help her students?
3. In which book does a sixth grader set up a business?
4. In which book is a mother totally surprised by her daughter's writing talent?
5. In which book is a character known for being totally persuasive since birth?

Search for the Shadowman

Joan Lowery Nixon. Bantam, 1996. ISBN: 0440411289.
URL: falcon.jmu.edu/~ramseyil/nixon.htm
Subjects: family life; mystery fiction; friendship

Questions

1. In which book does a character receive a college scholarship named after a long dead relative?

2. In which book does a school assignment help a character understand the feud between a great-aunt and a friend's grandmother?

3. In which book does a character contact a college professor through the Internet to get help with a school project?

4. In which book does a character wonder about a family photograph which is folded to hide a member of the family?

5. In which book does a snake head on a tombstone stand for the quotation, "How much sharper than a serpent's tooth it is to have a thankless child"?

Secret In St. Something

Barbara Brooks Wallace. Aladdin, 2003. ISBN: 0689856016.
Subjects: historical fiction; cities and towns

Questions

1. In which book do a character and a baby brother steal out into the night and run away?

2. In which book does a character meet new friends after opening an unlocked door?

3. In which book does a character meet a wealthy man with frightening eyes?

4. In which book does a pawnbroker lie about the value of a watch?

5. In which book does a character confess to a crime after being fatally stabbed in a brawl?

Shadows In the Glasshouse

Megan McDonald. Pleasant Co., 2000. ISBN: 1584850922.
URL: www.meganmcdonald.net
Subjects: historical fiction—United States, colonial period; mystery fiction

Questions

1. In which book are a set of dishes made as a present for the main character's sister?

2. In which book does a character tell a lie to keep a friend out of prison?

3. In which book is the villain the wife of the boss?

4. In which book does the story take place in Jamestown colony?

5. In which book does a character have a secret formula for making crystal?

A Single Shard

Linda Sue Park. Clarion Books, 2001. ISBN: 0395978270.
URL: www.lindasuepark.com
Award: Newbery Medal
Subjects: historical fiction—Korea; travelers—Korea

Questions

1. In which book does a character live under a bridge with a crippled man?
2. In which book does a character spy on a master potter?
3. In which book does a character learn to dig and drain clay?
4. In which book is a character trusted to take a prized vase to Songdo?
5. In which book does a character agree to work nine days to pay for a broken box?

Stepping on the Cracks

Mary Downing Hahn. Avon, 1991. ISBN: 0380719002.
URLs: www.carr.org/authco/hahn.htm
   www.childrensbookguild.org/hahn.htm
Subjects: historical fiction—World War, 1939–1945; conscientious objectors

Questions

1. In which book do characters try to injure Hitler by playing a children's game?
2. In which book do families have stars in their windows to show they have sons at war?
3. In which book does a character living in the woods become ill with pneumonia?
4. In which book do characters disobey their parents by crossing the train tracks?
5. In which book do characters rebuild a tree house they have ruined?

Sun and Spoon

Kevin Henkes. Puffin, 1998. ISBN: 0141300957.
URLs: falcon.jmu.edu/~ramseyil/henkes.htm
   www.carolhurst.com/authors/khenkes.html
Subjects: death; grandmothers

Questions

1. In which book does "M" always stand for Martha?
2. In which book did Pa think finding something that belonged to Grams was a sign from her in Heaven?
3. In which book does Frederick's nickname come from something his mother found in the front yard?
4. In which book is a Grandmother's collection focus part of the title?
5. In which book does a boy take something from Grandpa's house to keep a memory alive?

The Tale of Despereaux

Kate DiCamillo. Candlewick Press, 2003. ISBN: 0763617229.
Subjects: mice; princesses

Questions

1. In which book does Miggery Sow want to become a princess?
2. In which book does the author often interrupt the story to talk to the reader?
3. In which book does a mouse fall in love with the Princess Pea?
4. In which book is a mouse sent to a dungeon inhabited by rats?
5. In which book does a king ban the making and eating of soup?

Tales of a Fourth Grade Nothing

Judy Blume. Illustrator: Roy Doty. Bantam, 1972. ISBN: 044048474X.
URL: judyblume.com
Subjects: family life; humorous fiction

Questions

1. In which book does a father dump a bowl of cereal over a child's head?
2. In which book does a character lose two front teeth by trying to fly from a jungle gym?
3. In which book does a committee of three students do a project on transportation?
4. In which book does a character appear in a TV commercial?
5. In which book does a character swallow a pet turtle?

Tallahassee Higgins

Mary Downing Hahn. Avon, 1987. ISBN: 0380705001.
URLs: www.childrensbookguild.org/hahn.htm
www.carr.org/authco/hahn.htm
Subjects: family life; single parents

Questions

1. In which book does a character worry about being abandoned by an irresponsible mother?
2. In which book are pictures of a character's parents found in an old high school album?
3. In which book does a character get in to trouble for pushing an old dog in a doll carriage?
4. In which book does a character find a grandmother?
5. In which book does a character hold conversations with an ugly doll?

Thirteen Ways to Sink a Sub

Jamie Gilson. Illustrator: Linda Edwards. Pocket Books, 1982. ISBN: 0671625675.
URL: jamiegilson.com/
Subjects: school stories; humorous fiction

Questions

1. In which book is going into the "spit pit" to retrieve balls the result of a lost bet?
2. In which book does the substitute teacher, used to kindergartners, have to work with the fourth grade?
3. In which book does a character pretend to speak only Japanese in order to make origami airplanes all day?
4. In which book do characters stick up for a teacher when the principal questions the classroom activities?
5. In which book do characters take notes during oral reports so they can pass a test at the end of the report?

Three Against the Tide

D. Anne Love. Bantam, 1998. ISBN: 0440416345.
URL: www.dannelove.com/
Subject: historical fiction—United States, Civil War

Questions

1. In which book does a doctor travel to visit military hospitals in wartime?
2. In which book do old family servants behave in an unexpected way?
3. In which book does fire destroy a family's home in the city?
4. In which book does a character hope to become a doctor?
5. In which book do characters hurrying to catch a ferry stop to care for an injured person?

Three Days

Donna Jo Napoli. Puffin, 2001. ISBN: 0142500259.
URL: falcon.jmu.edu/~ramseyil/napoli.htm
Subject: kidnapping

Questions

1. In which book does a character travel with her father on a business trip to Italy?
2. In which book does a character have a heart attack while driving a car on the highway?
3. In which book is a character held captive in a house in a foreign country?
4. In which book does a newspaper show a picture of a character's father on the front page?
5. In which book is a character kidnapped to take the place of someone who has died?

The Tiger Rising

Kate DiCamillo. Candlewick Press, 2002. ISBN: 0763618985.
Award: National Book Award Finalist
Subject: friendship

Questions

1. In which book does a character work as a motel handyman?
2. In which book is a character kept out of school because of a severe skin rash?
3. In which book does a character refuse to cry for any reason?
4. In which book does a character who wears very bright clothes love to fight?
5. In which book is an animal killed after characters unlock its cage and set it free?

Toughboy and Sister

Kirkpatrick Hill. Puffin, 1992. ISBN: 0140348662.
URL: yahooligans.yahoo.com/school_bell/language_arts/authors
Subjects: Alaska; survival
Note: Some Alaskan native groups have objected to this book because of the alcohol issue.

Questions

1. In which book do two characters fear they will be separated after their mother's death?
2. In which book does a family spend every summer camping?
3. In which book do two children do their own washing?
4. In which book does a bear break a cabin window?
5. In which book does a character figure out how to change radio batteries?

Trapped in Death Cave

Bill Wallace. Aladdin, 2002. ISBN: 0689853416.
URL: falcon.jmu.edu/~ramseyil/bwallace.htm
Subject: mystery fiction

Questions

1. In which book do rattlesnakes live in honeycombs in cave walls?
2. In which book does a wooden box keep three people from drowning?
3. In which book are two boys "grounded" for falling into an open sewer?
4. In which book does a rice paper map overlay lead to treasures and the discovery of a murderer?
5. In which book is the sheriff the bad guy?

The Trolls

Polly Horvath. Sunburst, 2001. ISBN: 0374479917.
URL: falcon.jmu.edu/~ramseyil/horvath.htm
Award: Boston Globe Horn Book Award
Subject: family life

Questions

1. In which book does a Canadian relative stay with three children when their parents travel to Paris?

2. In which book do characters who hate vegetables learn to like green beans?

3. In which book does someone come to visit for two weeks and stays six years?

4. In which book is a sister jealous when her younger brother wins an art contest?

5. In which book does a grown-up build a tree house for a character?

Tucket's Gold

Gary Paulsen. Dell, 1999. ISBN: 0440413761.
URLs: scils.rutgers.edu/special/kay/paulsen
www.trelease-on-reading.com/paulsen
Subject: historical fiction—West (U.S.)

Questions

1. In which book does a thunderstorm help three travelers escape a band of outlaws called Comancheros?

2. In which book do characters discover an old gravesite and bars of gold and silver?

3. In which book is a character badly bitten by a poisonous snake?

4. In which book are characters sheltered in a village high above a desert?

5. In which book does a character kill two outlaws with a bow and arrow?

Tut, Tut

Jon Scieszka. Illustrator: Lane Smith. Puffin, 1996. ISBN: 0140363602.
URL: falcon.jmu.edu/~ramseyil/scieszka.htm
Subjects: Ancient Egypt; time travel; fantasy; humorous fiction

Questions

1. In which book does a cat save the lives of four kids?

2. In which book does a king wear magic sandals called "sneakers"?

3. In which book is a contest of strength between a little girl and a grown man won by the little girl?

4. In which book is a coffin lid used like a surfboard?

5. In which book do people use amulets like a blue hippo, a green crocodile and a paper clip to ward off danger?

The Voyage of Patience Goodspeed

Heather Vogel Frederick. Simon & Schuster, 2002. ISBN: 068984851X.
Subjects: whaling; historical fiction

Questions

1. In which book does a character put laudanum in muffins?

2. In which book does a character use the knowledge of astronomical navigation to find the island where her father has been left?

3. In which book is a character unhappy because she won't be able to study mathematics with Maria Mitchell?

4. In which book do two sailors who bullied some characters in town turn up on the same sailing ship?

5. In which book is netting stretched across a window on a ship's stern so a character won't fall overboard?

Walk Two Moons

Sharon Creech. HarperCollins, 1994. ISBN: 006440516.
URL: falcon.jmu.edu/~ramseyil/creech.htm
Award: Newbery Medal
Subjects: friendship; family life; death

Questions

1. In which book does a character go to the police because she believes her mother has been kidnapped or murdered?

2. In which book does a character take a trip west with her grandparents?

3. In which book does a character search for her mother by retracing the route she had taken on her journey?

4. In which book does a character tell a story of a mother who disappeared?

5. In which book is a woman bitten by a snake?

Wanted ... Mud Blossom

Betsy Byars. Dell, 1991. ISBN: 0440407613.
URL: falcon.jmu.edu/~ramseyil/byars.htm
Subjects: dogs; humorous fiction; family life; animals

Questions

1. In which book is a bag with a dead possum in it a sign of trouble?

2. In which book is a dog accused of murder?

3. In which book does an old woman wake up frightened because she doesn't know where she is?

4. In which book do you find out that in America everyone is innocent until proven guilty?

5. In which book is a hamster given a tunnel to play in?

The Warm Place

Nancy Farmer. Orchard Books, 1995. ISBN: 0531068889.
Subjects: animals; zoos; fantasy

Questions

1. In which book does a tiny mouse peek out in every picture?
2. In which book does a boy boil pokeweed berries to make red dye?
3. In which book does a sheep watch his fleece being spun?
4. In which book do you see a sheep covered in soap bubbles?
5. In which book does a mouse take things to his home in a hollow stump?

The War with Grandpa

Robert Kimmel Smith. Bantam, 1984. ISBN: 0440492769.
URL: randomhouse.com/teachers/authors
Subjects: family life; grandparents

Questions

1. In which book is a class assigned to write about something that has really happened?
2. In which book is an alarm clock set to go off at three o'clock in the morning?
3. In which book is a character frightened by a sound in the hallway and a light flickering on the ceiling?
4. In which book does a character find Monopoly game pieces missing?
5. In which book does a character's toothbrush disappear?

The Water Horse

Dick King-Smith. Illustrator: David Parkins. Crown, 1998. ISBN: 0517800268.
URL: falcon.jmu.edu/~ramseyil/kingsmith.htm
Subjects: monsters; Scotland

Questions

1. In which book does a family go beachcombing after a storm?
2. In which book is a character called Grumble because of his constant complaining?
3. In which book does a character come home from sea just in time to help with an important project?
4. In which book does a pet learn to come only when it is called?
5. In which book is a cattle truck used to haul an unusual load?

Where Do You Think You're Going, Christopher Columbus?

Jean Fritz. Illustrator: Margot Tomes. Puffin, 1997. ISBN: 0698115805.
URL: falcon.jmu.edu/~ramseyil/fritz.htm
Subjects: explorers; biography

Questions

1. In which book is the sight of three mountains in a row a sign to name an island Trinidad?

2. In which book does a character have to wait for a war with the Moors to be over before there is money for a trip?

3. In which book does a character dress like a monk and wear an itchy shirt so he'll look humble?

4. In which book does a cook put chains on the arms and legs of his boss?

5. In which book does the main character read a travel book written by Marco Polo?

Which Witch?

Eva Ibbotson. Penguin, 1979. ISBN: 0141304278.
URL: penguinputnam.com/static/rguides/us/eva_ibbotson
Subjects: fantasy

Questions

1. In which book is a character disliked for being kind and lovable?

2. In which book does a group of contestants camp out in a meadow?

3. In which book does a character have a pet worm?

4. In which book are two characters unable to tell their pets apart?

5. In which book does an orphanage character get revenge on a mean and cruel matron?

The White Mountains

John Christopher. Aladdin, 1967. ISBN: 0020427115.
URL: www.gnelson.demon.co.uk/tripage/jc.html
Subject: science fiction

Questions

1. In which book do all citizens wear special caps after a certain age?

2. In which book does a character have to travel with a disliked cousin?

3. In which book do three characters discover ruins of a long-ago city?

4. In which book does a character learn to speak French and ride a horse?

5. In which book do characters destroy an enemy with stolen hand grenades?

The Wild Whale Watch

Eva Moore. Illustrator: John Speirs. Scholastic, 2000. ISBN: 0439109906.
Subject: whales

Questions

1. In which book does Captain Gil create handbooks for the kids?

2. In which book do you learn that blowholes can identify animals?

3. In which book are animals grouped into "baleen" and "toothed"?

4. In which book do students feel like goldfish in a bowl as they are stared at?

5. In which book does a class collect money to sponsor an animal?

The Winter of Red Snow: The Revolutionary War Diary of Abigail Jane Stewart

Kristiana Gregory. Scholastic, 1996. ISBN: 0590226533.
URL: teacher.scholastic.com/authorsandbooks/
Subject: historical fiction—United States, Revolutionary War

Questions

1. In which book do bystanders give away their cloaks as soldiers march in the cold of winter?

2. In which book do girls embroider their names in garments they sew for soldiers?

3. In which book does a wife use 40 eggs in a cake for her husband's birthday?

4. In which book is a special gift given to a soldier but worn by a dog?

5. In which book do a girl's parents shave her head after she has a haircut?

The Year of Miss Agnes

Kirkpatrick Hill. Aladdin, 2000. ISBN: 0689851243.
URL: yahooligans.yahoo.com/school_bell/language_arts/authors
Subjects: Alaska; school stories

Questions

1. In which book is a village moved to keep it from flooding?

2. In which book does a character think it is a waste of time for children to go to school?

3. In which book does a deaf character learn to use sign language?

4. In which book do characters see pictures of themselves for the first time?

5. In which book do the characters act in the play "A Christmas Carol"?

Yolonda's Genius

Carol Fenner. Aladdin, 1997. ISBN: 0689813279.
URL: web.syr.edu/~avanbode/yolanda/authorinfo.htm
Award: Newbery Honor Book
Subjects: African Americans; family life; musicians

Questions

1. In which book does a family move to a smaller community after a classroom shooting in Chicago?

2. In which book does a character lie about being able to turn jump ropes for double Dutch?

3. In which book is a treasured harmonica destroyed?

4. In which book does a very large lady require three seats in an airplane?

5. In which book does a character decide to be a police officer when she grows up?

Bibliography

Appendix 1

About Battle of the Books

Cook, Sybilla, and Cheryl A. Page. *Books, Battles & Bees*. ALA, 1994. ISBN: 0-8389-0626-5.

Cook, Sybilla, Frances Corcoran and Beverley Fonnesbeck. *Battle of the Books and More: Reading Activities for Middle School Students*. Alleyside Press, 2001. ISBN: 1-57950-047-1.

Greeson, Janet. *Name That Book!* 2nd ed. Scarecrow, 1998. ISBN: 0-8108-3151-1.

Kelly, Joanne. *The Battle of Books, K-8*. Teacher Ideas Press, 1990. ISBN: 0-87287-779-5.

Toor, Ruth, and Hilda K. Weisburk. *Raising Readers: Appealing Approaches & Successful Strategies*. Library Learning Resources, l997. ISBN: 0931315093. A compilation of reading activities previously published between 1980 and 1997 in *The School Librarian's Workshop*. Part I focuses on "Battle of the Books" including history, formats, thinking skills, writing questions and sample forms.

About Literature and Reading

Bartch, Marian R. *Literature Activities Across the Curriculum: Ready-To-Use Ideas, Projects & Worksheets for Grades 4–8*. The Center for Applied Research in Education, 1992. ISBN: 0-87628-544-2. Uses 73 award-winning books as vehicles for teaching in various content areas. Includes a short synopsis, discussion facts or questions, projects and research activities, interest center ideas and reproducible activity sheets for books.

Canavan, Diane D., and LaVonne H. Sanborn. *Using Children's Books in Reading/Language Arts Programs*. Neal-Schuman, 1992. ISBN: 1555701019. A practical guide for locating and using children's books that illustrate reading, language and literacy instructional concepts in grade K-8. Included are examples of books and activities that develop decoding skills, sight vocabulary, comprehension, language concepts and literary awareness.

Gillespie, John T., and Corinne J. Naden. *The Newbery Companion: Booktalk and Related Materials for Newbery Medal and Honor Books*, 2nd ed. Libraries Unlimited, 2001. ISBN: 1563088134. A wealth of information about Newbery award winners and honor books (1922-2001). Plot summaries, booktalks, suggestions for read-alikes and ideas for introducing the books to young readers.

Girard, Sherry. *20 Irresistible Reading-Response Projects Based on Favorite Picture Books: Adorable Reproducible Patterns with Engaging Writing Prompts*. Scholastic Professional Books, 2002. ISBN: 0439205727. Children enjoy a well-loved story together, then create their own meaningful responses through hands-on art and writing projects.

Hall, Susan. *Using Picture Storybooks to Teach Literary Devices: Recommended Books for Children and Young Adults*. Volume 3. Oryx Press, 2001. ISBN: 1573563501. All-ages picture storybooks, which can be enjoyed by adults as well as children, are included in this perfect tool to teach literary devices to students in grades K–12. For each device, a definition is given as well as descriptions of appropriate storybooks, with information on how to use them, the art style used in the book and a curriculum tie-in. Among the literary devices included are alliteration, analogy, flashback, irony, metaphor, paradox, tone and 34 more. Indexes by author, title, art style and curriculum tie-in add to this outstanding book's great value.

Huffman, Ru Story. *Caldecott on the Net: Reading and Internet Activities*, vol. 2. Highsmith Press, 2002. ISBN: 1579500765. Various activities direct students to specific Internet Web sites that are used to answer questions about Caldecott Medal books.

Kurstedt, Rosanne and Maria Koutras. *Teaching Writing with Picture Books as Models*. Scholastic, 2000. ISBN: 0439135168. Using picture books to teach mood, voice, character traits, theme and other devices. Includes lessons from all stages of the writing process for both fiction and memoir writing plus lists of recommended books.

Licciardo-Musso, Lori. *25 Terrific Literature Activities: For Readers of All Learning Styles*. Scholastic Professional Books, 1996. ISBN: 0590599321. Easy, motivating activities such as Film Strips and "candy-bar wrapper" letters take students "into," "through" and "beyond" literature. Activities are designed for wide-ranging appeal. Includes rubrics for assessing written student responses.

Littlejohn, Carol. *Talk that Book: Booktalks to Promote Reading*. Linworth Publishing, l999. ISBN: 0-938865-757. Includes tips and strategies for using booktalks, including the purpose, ways to use booktalks, how to write and present booktalks and a bibliography of resources. Chapter two includes booktalks for 100 titles for grades 4-6.

Livo, Norma J. *Bringing Out Their Best: Values Education and Character Development Through Traditional Tales*. Libraries Unlimited, 2003. ISBN: 1563089343. More than

60 tales that support the character education being mandated in state after state throughout the country. Grouped into 12 sections based on specific values, such as love, perseverance, fairness and cooperation (with a separate chapter on dealing with bullies), these tales have come from many world cultures and traditions. Livo offers activity ideas and suggestions for discussions pertinent to specific stories and values. In addition, there is an appendix of general activity ideas that can be used in character education.

McElmeel, Sharron, and Deborah L. McElmeel. *An Author a Month (for Pennies); An Author a Month (for Nickels); An Author a Month (for Dimes).* Teacher Ideas Press. Includes interesting biographical information, a black-and-white photo and an idea cupboard with extension activities for reading skills.

Miller, Pat. *Reaching Every Reader: Promotional Strategies For the Elementary School Library Media Specialist.* Linworth Publishing, 2001. ISBN: 1586830015. Includes lessons based on picture books and easy nonfiction titles that can be completed in one library session. The book extensions include storytelling, puppetry, games, songs and creative dramatics.

Moen, Christine Boardman. *25 Fun and Fabulous Literature Response Activities and Rubrics: Quick, Engaging Activities and Reproducible Rubrics That Help Kids Understand Literary Elements and Use Reading Strategies for Better Comprehension.* Scholastic Professional Books, 2002. ISBN: 0439282357. Projects and rubrics to help students explore such literary elements as plot, character, setting and theme.

Nespeca, Sue McCleaf, and Joan B. Reeve. *Picture Books Plus: 100 Extension Activities in Art, Drama, Music, Math and Science.* American Library Association, 2003. ISBN: 0-8389-0840-3. Includes detailed background information and procedures to implement extension activities in the areas of math, science, music, drama and art for 100 carefully selected picture books. Additional sections include information on sharing picture books with children and art and color techniques in illustrations.

Newman, Marilyn Dover. *Cyberlit: Online Connections to Children's Literature for the Primary Grades.* Scarecrow Press, 2004. ISBN: 0810849038. Includes Web sites for authors, illustrators and storybook characters and lesson plans and book-related activities for classroom projects and units.

Novelli, Joan. *Using Caldecotts Across the Curriculum.* Scholastic Professional Books, l998. ISBN: 0590110330. Caldecott winners are used as springboards to provide lively, literature-based learning experiences across the curriculum.

O'Brien-Palmer, Michelle. *Beyond Book Report: 50 Totally Terrific Literature Response Activities that Develop Great Readers And Writers.* Scholastic Professional Books, l997. ISBN: 059076991X. Creative "read and respond" activities to cultivate students' critical-thinking skills and broaden their story comprehension. Students can predict outcomes, retell their favorite stories and share their personal responses to a story through paper genre pizzas, character report cards, 3-D setting maps and more. Simple step-by-step directions, student samples and ready-to-go, reproducible graphic organizers accompany each activity.

O'Brien-Palmer Michelle. *Great Graphic Organizers to Use With Any Book! 50 Fun Reproducibles & Activities to Explore Literature & Develop Kids' Writing.* Scholastic Professional Books, l997. ISBN: 0590769901. Students learn about plot, character and setting while becoming motivated readers and writers. Includes 50 versatile projects and activities to use with any book, along with student samples, step-by-step directions and ready-to-go graphic organizers.

Pinnel, Gay Sue, and Irene C. Fountas. *Guided Reading: Good First Teaching for All Children.* Heinemann, 1996. ISBN: 0435088637. Most comprehensive guided reading resource available today and the first systematic offering of instructional support for guided reading adherents. Organizational strategies, templates and a list of books to use for guided reading with their reading ranges.

Raines, Shirley C., and Robert J. Canady. *Story S-T-R-E-T-C-H-E-R-S for the Primary Grades: Activities to Expand Children's Favorite Books.* Gryphon House, 1992. ISBN: 0-87659-157-8. Includes learning center, art, drama, music, movement, science, nature, writing and special project and event activities for 90 children's classic and favorite books. Books are grouped into 20 thematic units. For each title there is a synopsis of the story, read-aloud suggestions and 5 story stretcher activities. Additional references and resources conclude each unit.

Robb, Anina. *40 Graphic Organizers that Build Comprehension During Independent Reading: Engaging Reproducibles that Help Students Use Reading Strategies, Learn About Literary Elements, and Explore Genre.* Scholastic Professional Books, 2003. ISBN: 0439387825. Forty interactive graphic organizers help students use key reading strategies, including making predictions, summarizing, inferring information, identifying main ideas and so much more. Includes organizers for fiction and nonfiction genres.

Tarlow, Ellen. *Teaching Story Elements with Favorite Books: Creative and Engaging Activities to Explore Character, Plot, Setting, and Theme That Work with ANY Book!* Scholastic Professional Books, l998. ISBN: 059076988X. Activities to help students learn to identify and explore the story elements essential to every good book. Includes reading discussion ideas, reproducible graphic organizers and hands-on activities geared towards diverse learning styles.

Walker, Christine, and Sarah Shaw. *Teaching Reading Strategies in the School Library.* Libraries Unlimited, 2004. ISBN: 1591581206. Suggestions for ways school librarians can support reading instruction. Links 10 reading strategies to new picture book titles. Each title is accompanied by a graphic organizer, model lesson and extensive bibliography of additional books for each strategy.

Webliography

Appendix 2

Battle of the Books—Some National and Statewide Programs

Alaska Association of School Librarians Battle of the Books
www.akla.org/akasl/bb/bbhome.html
Includes booklists and general information. Rules and questions are available upon registration.

America's Battle of the Books
www.battleofthebooks.org
Offers resources to students, parents, schools (public or private), librarians, home schools and international schools.

Daily-Tangents Battle of the Books
www.daily-tangents.com/BOB/national
Includes a list of links to the United States and a few worldwide schools and libraries that have already set up a Battle of the Books program.

New Mexico Battle of the Books
www.nmbattleofthebooks.org
Includes booklists, rules and practice questions.

North Carolina School Library Media Association Battle of the Books
www.ncslma.org
Includes booklists and a program timeline.

Wisconsin Educational Media Association: Battle of the Books: A Statewide Contest
www.wemaonline.org/ev.bb.overview.cfm
Includes booklists, suggestions for forming teams, rules and frequently asked questions.

Battle of the Books Program Strategies— Organization, Rules and Questions

Birchwood Elementary School Battle of the Books
www.nisk.k12.ny.us/birchwood/readingincentiveprograms/goforgoldbattleofthebooks.html
Includes rules and sample questions using an alternative to the "In which book…?" format.

Cooper Elementary School
internal.vusd.solanocoe.k12.ca.us/Cooper/Intranet/read/battleQ.htm
Includes rules and sample questions for a fourth through sixth grade battle program.

Do You Want to Rumble?.... A Battle of the Books Webquest
www.ga.unc.edu/NCTA/NCTA/WebQuests2001/BunnMiddle1/BattleoftheBooks
Describes the use of the Battle of the Books program to meet a variety of educational standards and student activities for reading and sharing books on the list.

Teachers Net Lesson #834
www.teachers.net/lessons/posts/834.html
Describes how to set up a Battle of the Books as a classroom literature appreciation program.

Literature Connections—Book Selection

Barrie Public Library Battle of the Books
www.library.barrie.on.ca/kids/Bob/battle.htm
Includes booklists by category and an art project idea.

Best Of & Other Lists
www.readingrockets.org/books/bestof.php
Includes links to award winning, notable and highly recommended books.

Carol Hurst's Children's Literature Site
www.carolhurst.com
Includes comprehensive book reviews and theme lists.

Cooperative Children's Book Center: Publications on the Web
www.soemadison.wisc.edu/ccbc/books/bibBio.asp
Includes links to theme or age level specific booklists.

Database of Award Winning Children's Literature
www.dawcl.com
Enables viewer to create a tailored reading list of quality children's literature or to find out if a book has won one of the indexed awards. The list can be searched by a large variety of criteria, including age, setting, format and genre.

The Horn Book Inc. Children's Classics A Booklist for Parents
www.hbook.com/childclass1.shtml
Includes annotated booklists for the very young, picture books, beginning readers, classics, myths, legends, folklore and nonfiction.

The Innovative Teaching Newsletter
surfaquarium.com/NEWSLETTER/books.htm
Walter McKenzie's site offers a tremendous array of information and activities about books.

Kim's Korner for Teacher Talk
www.kimskorner4teachertalk.com/
This site by a middle school language arts teacher has a wide variety of activities, presented in a clear and simple format.

Literature and Reading Activities and Lesson Plans
www.richmond.k12.va.us/readamillion/literatureactivities.htm

Nancy Keane's Children's Literature Webpage
www.nancykeane.com
Includes links to ready-to-use booktalks, lists of

165

recommended reading, book reviews by children and other information about children's literature.

Reading Rockets-Monthly Recommended Kids Books
www.readingrockets.org/books/booksbytheme.php
Includes lists of recommended books for children ages 0-9 based on reading interests.

Literature Connections—Author and Illustrator Information

Children's and Young Adults' Authors & Illustrators
falcon.jmu.edu/~ramseyil/biochildhome.htm#AUT
Includes links to author and illustrator biographies, birthdays, appearances, online interviews and name pronunciations.

Children's Book Council: About Authors & Illustrators
www.cbcbooks.org/contacts/
Links to author and illustrator biographical and contact information.

Houghton Mifflin Authors and Illustrators
www.eduplace.com/kids/hmr/mtai/index.html
Includes information about authors and illustrators who appear in the Houghton Mifflin Reading series.

Kay E. Vandergrift Learning About the Author and Illustrator Pages
www.scils.rutgers.edu/~kvander/AuthorSite/index.html
Includes more than 600 links to author/illustrator sites.

Reading Rockets: Children's Books and Authors: Interviews
www.readingrockets.org/books/authorinterviews.php
Includes exclusive interviews with children's book authors and illustrators

Scholastic: Authors and Books
www2.scholastic.com/teachers/authorsandbooks/authorstudies/authorstudies.jhtml
Includes biographical information, booklists and classroom activities.

Teachers At Random: Authors & Illustrators
www.randomhouse.com/teachers/authors/
Includes information about authors and illustrators whose works are published by Random House.

Yahooligans: Authors
yahooligans.yahoo.com/School_Bell/Language_Arts/Authors/
Links author sites, audio clips and pictures.

Literature Connections—Literature Guides

Doucette Index: K-12 Literature-Based Teaching Ideas: An Index to Books and Web sites
www.educ.ucalgary.ca/litindex/
Provides access to books and Web sites containing useful teaching suggestions related to books for children and young adults, and the creators of those books.

Metro Nashville Public School Cyberguides
www.nashville.k12.tn.us/CyberGuides/cyberguide.html
Includes interdisciplinary, multimedia, web-based resources to develop units of instruction based on works of literature for grades K-6.

Nancy Polette's Children's Literature Site
www.nancypolette.com/litguides.asp
Includes sample guides for many well-known children's books. A new title is added each month.

Random House Teacher Guides
www.randomhouse.com/teachers/guides/title
Includes guides for literature appropriate for upper elementary readers.

S.C.O.R.E. Cyberguides: Teacher Guides and Student Activities
www.sdcoe.k12.ca.us/SCORE/cyberguide.html
Includes supplementary, standards-based, web-delivered units of instruction centered on core works of literature.

Scholastic: Lesson Plans-Discussion Guides
www2.scholastic.com/teachers/authorsandbooks/authorstudies/authorstudies.jhtml
Includes a variety of pre- and post-reading discussion questions with links to other information about the book.

Literature Connections—Lessons and Activities

The Bestkidsbooksite.com
www.thebestkidsbooksite.com
Includes lists of topic related books, crafts, fingerplays, songs and Web sites.

Book Adventure
www.bookadventure.org
Encourages students to create their own booklists from over 6,000 recommended titles, take multiple choice quizzes on the books they've read offline and earn points and prizes for their literary successes.

Freeology: Free Graphic Organizers
www.freeology.com/graphicorgs/
Includes printable templates for a Venn diagram, Pro/Con chart, Story Web, Short Story Plot, Character Study Chart and Timeline which can be used to help students analyze literature.

Golden Duck Awards for Excellence in Children's Science Fiction Literature
www.goldenduck.org
Includes award-winning science fiction books listed by grade level, lesson plans for the selected books and teacher resources.

Houghton Mifflin Teacher Views
www.eduplace.com/tview/index.html
Includes reviews and classroom activities for favorite K-8 books.

Read.Write.Think
www.readwritethink.org/lessons/
Includes lesson plans and activities tying together language, reading and writing skills, research skills and literature studies.

Web English Teacher: Children's Literature Authors
www.webenglishteacher.com/childlit1.html
Includes lesson plans and activity links organized by author.

Other Resources

Appendix 3

Study Guides

Many publishers issue study guides. We've listed some that can be found easily. Check their Web sites for information.

Learning Links, 1300 Marcus Avenue, New Hyde Park, NY 11042.
www.learninglinks.com/

Mari, Inc., 1025 25th Street, Santa Monica, CA 90403.
www.mariinc.com/paperlit.html

Perfection Learning, 1000 N. Second Ave, Logan, IA 51546-1061.
www.perfectionlearning.com/elementary/

Scholastic, 555 Broadway, New York, NY 10012-3999.
teacher.scholastic.com/

Sundance Publishing, P.O. Box 1326, Littleton, MA 01460.
www.sundancepub.com/c/@qdx7uD_Zfcr6A/Pages/prek6lit.html

Teacher Created Materials, 6421 Industry Way, Westminster, CA 92683.
www.teachercreated.com/

Story Puppet Sources

Folkmanis, Inc., 1219 Park Avenue, Emeryville, CA 94608.
www.folkmanis.com

Lakeshore Learning (Multicultural family puppet sets.)
www.lakeshorelearning.com

Buzzer Systems and Materials for Academic Competitions

These academic competition systems can make the battles easier for the director and more fun for the participants. Bob Kuest, a retired media specialist,(bkuest@aol.com) has prepared a list of various systems available in March 2004. The price indicated is for a basic six to eight player system and is given for comparison. Check the Web sites for more details.

Buzzer Systems	www.groupics.com	$250
BZR-200	www.jemdesigns.com	$280
CAB-16 Buzzer System	www.quizbowlonline.com	$499
Challenger I, II, III	www.zeecraft.com	$424
Eggspert Learning Game	www.edin.com	$50
GS76 Game Show	www.rolls.com/new/gs76.html	$240

The Judge	612-781-9588	$350
Questronic Learning System	bkuest@aol.com	$300
Quick Pro	www.specialtydesigncorp.com	$289
Quizbot Show	www.quizbot.com	$500
Quiz Machine	www.quizco.com	$315
Quiz Pro 2000	www.cp4e.com	$499
Quizsystem	www.quizsystems.com	$230
Quizzer!	www.quizzerltd.com	$560
Sho-me Smart Lights	www.tripleqquestions.com	$240
TieBreaker	www.tiebreaker.com	$300
Tournament Master	www.buzzersystems.com	$389

Other Sources

Game Show Presenter (software)	www.groupics.com
List of links, etc.	www.cwru.edu/orgs/triv
Quiz competition question books, etc.	www.patrickspress.com
Questions, etc.	www.academicbowlonline.com
Quiz Bowl for Windows (software)	www.advancedsp.com

Author, Subject and Award Index

Authors

A

Aardema, Verna
Bringing the Rain to Kapiti Plain: A Nandi Tale, 67

Ackerman, Karen
Song and Dance Man, 108

Ahlberg, Janet and Allan
Each Peach Pear Plum, 73

Allard, Harry
Miss Nelson Is Missing!, 94

Anderson, Hans Christian
The Ugly Duckling, 115

Anno, Masaichiro and Mitsumasa
Anno's Mysterious Multiplying Jar, 64

Archambault, John, and Bill Martin Jr.
Knots On a Counting Rope, 87

Arnosky, Jim
Crinkleroot's Guide to Walking in Wild Places, 70–71

Avi
Perloo the Bold, 146
Poppy and Rye, 146

B

Barrett, Judi
Cloudy with a Chance of Meatballs, 69–70

Bauer, Marion
On My Honor, 145
Runt, 150

Beeler, Selby B.
Throw Your Tooth on the Roof: Tooth Traditions from Around the World, 113

Bellairs, John
The House with a Clock in its Walls, 134

Berger, Barbara
Grandfather Twilight, 79

Birdseye, Tom
Airmail to the Moon, 62

Blume, Judy
The One in the Middle Is a Green Kangaroo, 101
Tales of a Fourth Grade Nothing, 154

Boston, L. M.
An Enemy at Green Knowe, 127

Bourgeois, Paulette
Franklin in the Dark, 76

Brandt, Keith
Rosa Parks: Fight for Freedom, 149

Brenner, Martha
Abe Lincoln's Hat, 61

Brett, Jan
The Mitten: A Ukrainian Folktale, 95

Brighton, Catherine
The Fossil Girl: Mary Anning's Dinosaur Discovery, 76

Brown, Jeff
Flat Stanley, 75

Brown, Marc
Arthur's Birthday, 64

Brown, Margaret Wise
The Runaway Bunny, 105–106

Bulla, Clyde
The Chalk Box Kid, 125

Bunting, Eve
Smoky Night, 107
The Wall, 116

Burleigh, Robert
Flight: The Journey of Charles Lindbergh, 75

Burningham, John
Mr. Gumpy's Motor Car, 97

Byars, Betsy
The Golly Sisters Ride Again, 79
The Midnight Fox, 141
Wanted ... Mud Blossom, 158

C

Calmenson, Stephanie
Dinner at the Panda Palace, 71

Cameron, Ann
The Stories Julian Tells, 110

Cannon, Janell
Stellaluna, 109

Carle, Eric
The Very Busy Spider, 115

Carlson, Natalie Savage
The Family Under the Bridge, 129

Carlstrom, Nancy White
Jesse Bear, What Will You Wear?, 84–85

Cazet, Denys
A Fish in His Pocket, 74
Minnie and Moo Save the Earth, 93

Christopher, John
The White Mountains, 160

Cleary, Beverly
Ramona's World, 147

Clement, Rod
Just Another Ordinary Day, 86

Clements, Andrew
Frindle, 130
The School Story, 151

Coerr, Eleanor
The Big Balloon Race, 65–66
Buffalo Bill and the Pony Express, 67
The Josefina Story Quilt, 85
Sadako, 151

Cohen, Barbara
Molly's Pilgrim, 96

Cohen, Miriam
First Grade Takes a Test, 74

Cole, Joanna
The Magic School Bus Lost in the Solar System, 90

Conford, Ellen
The Frog Princess of Pelham, 130–131

Cooney, Barbara
Miss Rumphius, 95

Cooper, Susan
The Boggart and the Monster, 123

Coville, Bruce
The Monsters of Morley Manor, 142

Cowley, Joy
Mrs. Wishy-Washy's Farm, 97

Cox, Judy
Butterfly Buddies, 67
Weird Stories from the Lonesome Café, 116

Creech, Sharon
Love that Dog, 140
Walk Two Moons, 158

Crew, Linda
Nekomah Creek, 144

Crews, Donald
Bigmama's, 66
Cronin, Doreen
Click, Clack, Moo Cows that Type, 69
Cushman, Karen
Rodzina, 149
Cutler, Jane
Rats!, 147

D

Dahl, Roald
The BFG, 122–123
Dalgliesh, Alice
The Courage of Sarah Noble, 70
Danziger, Paula
Amber Brown Sees Red, 120
de Paola, Tomie
The Legend of the Bluebonnet, 87
Strega Nona, 110
Deedy, Carmen Agra
The Library Dragon, 88
DiCamillo, Kate
Because of Winn-Dixie, 121–122
The Tale of Despereaux, 154
The Tiger Rising, 156
Donahue, John
An Island Far From Home, 135–136
Donnelly, Judy
The Titanic Lost ... and Found, 113
Dorris, Michael
Guests, 132–133
Morning Girl, 142
Dowell, Frances O.
Dovey Coe, 126

E

Edwards, Julie
Mandy, 140–141
Ehlert, Lois
Planting a Rainbow, 104
Emberley, Barbara
Drummer Hoff, 72–73
Ernst, Lisa Campbell
When Bluebell Sang, 117
Estes, Eleanor
Ginger Pye, 132

F

Farmer, Nancy
The Warm Place, 159
Fenner, Carol
Yolonda's Genius, 161–162
Fleischman, Sid
Humbug Mountain, 134–135
Fleming, Candace
Boxes for Katje, 66
Fletcher, Susan
Flight of the Dragon Kyn, 129–130

Fox, Mem
Possum Magic, 105
Frasier, Debra
Miss Alaineus, 94
Frederick, Heather Vogel
The Voyage of Patience Goodspeed, 158
Friedman, Ina R.
How My Parents Learned to Eat, 82
Fritz, Jean
Can't You Make them Behave, King George?, 124
George Washington's Mother, 78
Where Do You Think You're Going, Christopher Columbus?, 160

G

Galdone, Paul
The Little Red Hen, 89
Gantos, Jack
Joey Pigza Loses Control, 136
George, Jean Craighead
My Side of the Mountain, 143
Gerstein, Mordicai
The Man Who Walked Between the Towers, 91
Gibbons, Gail
Sunken Treasure, 110
Giff, Patricia Reilly
In the Dinosaur's Paw, 84
Lily's Crossing, 139–140
Today Was a Terrible Day, 114
Gilson, Jamie
Thirteen Ways to Sink a Sub, 155
Ginsburg, Mirra
The Chick and the Duckling, 68–69
Mushroom in the Rain, 98
Where Does the Sun Go at Night?, 117
Goble, Paul
The Girl Who Loved Wild Horses, 78
Golenbock, Peter
Teammates, 111
Greer, Gery
Max and Me and the Time Machine, 141
Gregory, Kristiana
Royal Diaries: Cleopatra VII, Daughter of the Nile, 149–150
The Winter of Red Snow: The Revolutionary War Diary of Abigail Jane Stewart, 161
Grifalconi, Ann
The Village of Round and Square Houses, 116
Guarino, Deborah
Is Your Mama a Llama?, 84
Gutman, Dan
The Kid Who Ran for President, 138

H

Haddix, Margaret
Among the Hidden, 120–121

Hahn, Mary Downing
Stepping on the Cracks, 153
Tallahassee Higgins, 154
Hall, Donald
Ox-Cart Man, 102
Henkes, Kevin
Lilly's Purple Plastic Purse, 88–89
Sun and Spoon, 153
Hesse, Karen
The Music of Dolphins, 143
Sable, 150–151
Hildick, E. W.
Case of the Muttering Mummy, 124
Hill, Kirkpatrick
Toughboy and Sister, 156
The Year of Miss Agnes, 161
Hippely, Hilary Horder
Adventure on Klickitat Island, 61–62
Hobbs, Will
Jason's Gold, 136
Hoberman, Mary Ann
A House Is a House for Me, 82
Hogrogian, Nonny
One Fine Day, 101
Hooks, William H.
The Pioneer Cat, 104
Horvath, Polly
Everything on a Waffle, 128
The Trolls, 157
Howard, Ellen
The Gate in the Wall, 131
Howe, James
Harold and Chester in Hot Fudge, 80–81
Pinky and Rex and the Spelling Bee, 103
There's a Monster Under My Bed, 111
Huck, Charlotte
Princess Furball, 105
Hunt, Irene
Across Five Aprils, 119–120
Hurd, Thacher
Mama Don't Allow, 91
Hurst, Carol Otis, and Rebecca Otis
A Killing in Plymouth Colony, 138
Hurwitz, Johanna
Rip-Roaring Russell, 148
Hutchins, Pat
The Doorbell Rang, 72
The Very Worst Monster, 115–116

I

Ibbotson, Eva
Which Witch?, 160

J

Jacques, Brian
Mossflower, 142–143
Jensen, Dorothea
The Riddle of Penncroft Farm, 148

K

Kasza, Keiko
The Wolf's Chicken Stew, 118–119
Kay, Verla
Gold Fever, 79
Keats, Ezra Jack
The Snowy Day, 107–108
Kehret, Peg
Earthquake Terror, 126
Kellogg, Steven (illustrator)
Paul Bunyan, A Tall Tale, 103
Key, Alexander
Escape to Witch Mountain, 127
Kimmel, Eric A.
Anansi and the Moss-Covered Rock, 63
The Erie Canal Pirates, 74
King-Smith, Dick
Ace: The Very Important Pig, 119
The Water Horse, 159
Kipling, Rudyard
The Elephant's Child, 73–74
Just So Stories, 137
Korman, Gordon
The Chicken Doesn't Skate, 125
Kraus, Robert
Milton the Early Riser, 93
Kulling, Monica
Edgar Badger's Fishing Day, 73

L

Le Guin, Ursula
Catwings, 124
Leedy, Loreen
The Furry News: How to Make a Newspaper, 77
Lester, Julius
John Henry, 85
Levine, Gail Carson
Ella Enchanted, 127
Levinson, Nancy Smiler
Clara and the Bookwagon, 69
Levitin, Sonia
Journey to America, 136–137
Lewis, C. S.
The Last Battle, 139
Lindgren, Astrid
Pippi Longstocking, 146
Little, Jean
Home From Far, 133–134
Lobel, Arnold
Frog and Toad Are Friends, 76–77
Ming Lo Moves the Mountain, 93
Mouse Tales, 97
London, Jonathan
Froggy Gets Dressed, 77
Long, Melinda
How I Became a Pirate, 82

Lord, Bette Bao
In the Year of the Boar and Jackie Robinson, 135
Love, D. Anne
Three Against the Tide, 155
Low, Joseph
Mice Twice, 92
Lowry, Lois
All About Sam, 120
Number the Stars, 144

M

MacDonald, Reby
The Ghosts of Austwick Manor, 131–132
MacLachlan, Patricia
The Sick Day, 106
Mahy, Margaret
17 Kings and 42 Elephants, 61
Marshall, Edward
Three By the Sea, 112
Marshall, James
James Marshall's Mother Goose, 84
Martin, Bill
Chicka Chicka Boom Boom, 68–69
Martin, Bill, Jr., and John Archambault
Knots On a Counting Rope, 87
Martin, Jacqueline Briggs
Snowflake Bentley, 107
Martin, Rafe
Will's Mammoth, 118
Mathis, Sharon Bell
The Hundred Penny Box, 135
McCloskey, Robert
Make Way for Ducklings, 90–91
McDermott, Gerald
Anansi the Spider: A Tale from Ashanti, 63
The Stonecutter: A Japanese Folk Tale, 109
McDonald, Megan
Shadows In the Glasshouse, 152
McKissack, Patricia C.
Flossie and the Fox, 75–76
Run Away Home, 150
McPhail, David
The Bear's Toothache, 65
Mikaelsen, Ben
Rescue of Josh McGuire, 147–148
Miles, Miska
Annie and the Old One, 63–64
Milton, Joyce
Wild, Wild Wolves, 117
Moore, Eva
The Wild Whale Watch, 161
Morey, Walt
Kävik the Wolf Dog, 137
Morris, Gerald
Parsifal's Page, 145
Murphy, Frank
Ben Franklin and the Magic Squares, 65

N

Napoli, Donna Jo
Three Days, 155
Nhuong, Huynh Quang
The Land I Lost, 139
Nixon, Joan Lowery
House on Hackman's Hill, 134
Search for the Shadowman, 151–152
Noble, Trinka Hakes
The Day Jimmy's Boa Ate the Wash, 71
Numeroff, Laura
If You Give a Pig a Pancake, 83

O

Osborne, Mary Pope
Polar Bears Past Bedtime, 104

P

Park, Barbara
The Kid in the Red Jacket, 137–138
Park, Linda Sue
The Kite Fighters, 138–139
A Single Shard, 153
Patterson, Katherine
The King's Equal, 86–87
Paulsen, Gary
Hatchet, 133
Mr. Tucket, 143
Tucket's Gold, 157
Peck, Richard
Fair Weather, 128
Peet, Bill
Hubert's Hair-Raising Adventure, 83
Penner, Lucille Recht
The Statue of Liberty, 109
Petersen, P. J.
Rising Water, 149
Peterson, John
The Littles, 89
Pilkey, Dav
The Paperboy, 102
Polacco, Patricia
Babushka's Doll, 64–65

R

Rappaport, Doreen
Martin's Big Words: The Life of Dr. Martin Luther King Jr., 92
Rathmann, Peggy
Officer Buckle and Gloria, 100
Redmond, Shirley-Raye
Lewis and Clark: A Prairie Dog for the President, 87–88
Ringgold, Faith
Tar Beach, 111
Roberts, Willo Davis
Babysitting Is a Dangerous Job, 121

Robinson, Barbara
The Best School Year Ever, 122

Rohmann, Eric
My Friend Rabbit, 98–99

Roop, Peter and Connie
Ahyoka and the Talking Leaves, 62
Keep the Lights Burning, Abbie, 86

Ryan, Pam Muñoz
Esperanza Rising, 128
Riding Freedom, 148

Ryder, Joanne
Catching the Wind, 68

Rylant, Cynthia
The Case of the Climbing Cat, 68
Henry and Mudge in the Sparkle Days, 81
Poppleton, 104–105

S

Schulz, Walter A.
Will and Orv, 117–118

Scieszka, Jon
Tut, Tut, 157

Seuss, Dr.
Green Eggs and Ham, 80

Shannon, David
No, David!, 99–100

Shannon, George
Lizard's Song, 89–90

Sharmat, Mitchell
Gregory the Terrible Eater, 80
Nate the Great and the Missing Key, 99

Shaw, Nancy
Sheep in a Jeep, 106

Shreve, Susan
Blister, 123

Shulevitz, Uri
The Treasure, 114–115

Skurzynski, Gloria
Out of the Deep, 145

Slate, Joseph
Miss Bindergarten Gets Ready for Kindergarten, 94

Slote, Alfred
Finding Buck McHenry, 129

Small, David
Imogene's Antlers, 83

Smith, Robert Kimmel
The War with Grandpa, 159

Snyder, Zilpha Keatley
Gib and the Gray Ghost, 132

Soto, Gary
Too Many Tamales, 114

Spier, Peter
Oh, Were They Ever Happy, 100–101

St. George, Judith
So You Want to Be President?, 108

Stanley, Diane
Moe the Dog in Tropical Paradise, 95–96

Steele, William O.
Flaming Arrows, 129

Steig, William
Amos and Boris, 62–63
Doctor De Soto, 71–72

Steptoe, John
Mufaro's Beautiful Daughters: An African Tale, 98

Stevens, Janet
Tops and Bottoms, 114

Stevenson, Jocelyn
O'Diddy, 100

Stewart, Sarah
The Gardener, 78
The Library, 88

T

Taback, Simms
Joseph Had a Little Overcoat, 85–86
There Was an Old Lady Who Swallowed a Fly, 111–112

Taylor, Mildred D.
The Friendship, 130

Thurber, James
Many Moons, 91–92

Tolkien, J. R. R.
The Hobbit, 133

Tripp, Valerie
Changes for Felicity, 125

Trivizas, Eugene
The Three Little Wolves and the Big Bad Pig, 112–113

Turkle, Brinton
Do Not Open, 72

V

Van Laan, Nancy
Moose Tales, 96

Van Leeuwen, Jean
Bound for Oregon, 123

W

Waddell, Martin
The Pig in the Pond, 103

Wallace, Barbara Brooks
Secret In St. Something, 152

Wallace, Bill
Trapped in Death Cave, 156

Ward, Lynd
The Biggest Bear, 66

Wells, Rosemary
Yoko, 119

Whelan, Gloria
Once on this Island, 144–145

Wiesner, David
The Three Pigs, 113

Wilder, Laura Ingalls
Winter Days in the Big Woods, 118

Wiles, Deborah
Love, Ruby Lavender, 140

Williams, Karen Lynn
Galimoto, 77

Williams, Vera B.
"More More More," Said the Baby, 96–97
Three Days on a River in a Red Canoe, 112

Winthrop, Elizabeth
Battle for the Castle, 121

Wood, Audrey
Heckedy Peg, 81
The Napping House, 99

Wright, Betty Ren
Ghost in the Family, 131

Y

Yolen, Jane
Commander Toad and the Planet of the Grapes, 70
The Devil's Arithmetic, 126
Owl Moon, 101–102
Sleeping Ugly, 106–107

Yorinks, Arthur
Hey, Al, 81

Young, Ed
Lon Po Po: A Red-Riding Hood Story from China, 90

Subjects

A

Acadia National Park (ME)
Out of the Deep, 145

accidents
On My Honor, 145

adventure
Earthquake Terror, 126
Escape to Witch Mountain, 127

Africa
Anansi and the Moss-Covered Rock, 63
Anansi the Spider: A Tale from Ashanti, 63
Bringing the Rain to Kapiti Plain: A Nandi Tale, 67
Galimoto, 77
Mufaro's Beautiful Daughters: An African Tale, 98
The Village of Round and Square Houses, 116

African Americans
Run Away Home, 150
Yolonda's Genius, 161–162

Alaska
Jason's Gold, 136
Kävik the Wolf Dog, 137
Toughboy and Sister, 156
The Year of Miss Agnes, 161

alphabet
Chicka Chicka Boom Boom, 68–69
Miss Bindergarten Gets Ready for Kindergarten, 94

Ancient Egypt
Tut, Tut, 157

animals
17 Kings and 42 Elephants, 61
Amos and Boris, 62–63
The Biggest Bear, 66
Catching the Wind, 68
The Chick and the Duckling, 68–69
Click, Clack, Moo Cows that Type, 69
Dinner at the Panda Palace, 71
Do Not Open, 72
Doctor De Soto, 71–72
The Elephant's Child, 73–74
Flossie and the Fox, 75–76
Franklin in the Dark, 76
Gib and the Gray Ghost, 132
Ginger Pye, 132
The Girl Who Loved Wild Horses, 78
Just So Stories, 137
Kävik the Wolf Dog, 137
Make Way for Ducklings, 90–91
Mice Twice, 92
The Midnight Fox, 141
Milton the Early Riser, 93
Moose Tales, 96
Mossflower, 142–143
Mouse Tales, 97
Mrs. Wishy-Washy's Farm, 97
Mushroom in the Rain, 98
Officer Buckle and Gloria, 100
Owl Moon, 101–102
Perloo the Bold, 146
The Pig in the Pond, 103
Poppy and Rye, 146
Possum Magic, 105
Rescue of Josh McGuire, 147–148
Rising Water, 149
Runt, 150
Sable, 150–151
Sheep in a Jeep, 106
Stellaluna, 109
Tops and Bottoms, 114
The Ugly Duckling, 115
The Very Busy Spider, 115
The Very Important Pig, 119
Wanted ... Mud Blossom, 158
The Warm Place, 159
The Wolf's Chicken Stew, 118–119

Arctic region
Polar Bears Past Bedtime, 104

Australia
Possum Magic, 105

authorship
The School Story, 151

B

baseball
Teammates, 111

bats
Stellaluna, 109

bears
The Biggest Bear, 66
Rescue of Josh McGuire, 147–148

biography
Abe Lincoln's Hat, 61
Ahyoka and the Talking Leaves, 62
Ben Franklin and the Magic Squares, 65
Buffalo Bill and the Pony Express, 67
Flight: The Journey of Charles Lindbergh, 75
The Fossil Girl: Mary Anning's Dinosaur Discovery, 76
George Washington's Mother, 78
Keep the Lights Burning, Abbie, 86
Lewis and Clark: A Prairie Dog for the President, 87–88
Martin's Big Words: The Life of Dr. Martin Luther King Jr., 92
Rosa Parks: Fight for Freedom, 149
Snowflake Bentley, 107
Where Do You Think You're Going, Christopher Columbus?, 160
Will and Orv, 117–118

birds
Catching the Wind, 68
The Chick and the Duckling, 68–69
Make Way for Ducklings, 90–91
The Ugly Duckling, 115

birthdays
Arthur's Birthday, 64

books and reading
Clara and the Bookwagon, 69
The Library, 88

Boston
Make Way for Ducklings, 90–91

buried treasure
Sunken Treasure, 110

C

camping
Three Days on a River in a Red Canoe, 112

cats
Do Not Open, 72

character
The Courage of Sarah Noble, 70
Miss Rumphius, 95
On My Honor, 145
The Ugly Duckling, 115

Christmas
Too Many Tamales, 114

cities and towns
Secret in St. Something, 152

city and town life
Smoky Night, 107

civil rights
Martin's Big Words: The Life of Dr. Martin Luther King Jr., 92
Rosa Parks: Fight for Freedom, 149

Clark, William
Lewis and Clark: A Prairie Dog for the President, 87–88

clothing
Joseph Had a Little Overcoat, 85–86

color
Planting a Rainbow, 104

conscientious objectors
Stepping on the Cracks, 153

contemporary issues
Babysitting Is a Dangerous Job, 121
The Chicken Doesn't Skate, 125

counting
Dinner at the Panda Palace, 71
The Doorbell Rang, 72
There's a Monster Under My Bed, 111

country life
Bigmama's, 66

culture
How My Parents Learned to Eat, 82
Throw Your Tooth on the Roof: Tooth Traditions from Around the World, 113
Yoko, 119

D

death
Annie and the Old One, 63–64
Love, Ruby Lavender, 140
Sadako, 151
Sun and Spoon, 153
Walk Two Moons, 158

dentists
Doctor De Soto, 71–72

detective stories
The Case of the Climbing Cat, 68

dinosaurs
The Fossil Girl: Mary Anning's Dinosaur Discovery, 76

divorce
Amber Brown Sees Red, 120
Hatchet, 133

dogs
Because of Winn-Dixie, 121–122
Ginger Pye, 132
Officer Buckle and Gloria, 100
Sable, 150–151
Wanted ... Mud Blossom, 158

dolphins
The Music of Dolphins, 143

dragons
Flight of the Dragon Kyn, 129–130

E

eating customs
 How My Parents Learned to Eat, 82
elections
 The Kid Who Ran for President, 138
encyclopedias and dictionaries
 Miss Alaineus, 94
environment
 Poppy and Rye, 146
explorers
 Lewis and Clark: A Prairie Dog for the President, 87–88
 Where Do You Think You're Going, Christopher Columbus?, 160

F

fairs
 Fair Weather, 128
fairy tales
 Heckedy Peg, 81
 The King's Equal, 86–87
family life
 Airmail to the Moon, 62
 All About Sam, 120
 Bigmama's, 66
 Blister, 123
 The Chalk Box Kid, 135
 Dovey Coe, 126
 The Gardener, 78
 Ginger Pye, 132
 Home From Far, 133–134
 How My Parents Learned to Eat, 82
 The Hundred Penny Box, 135
 An Island Far From Home, 135–136
 The Kid in the Red Jacket, 137–138
 The Midnight Fox, 141
 "More More More," Said the Baby, 96–97
 Morning Girl, 142
 Nekomah Creek, 144
 The One in the Middle Is a Green Kangaroo, 101
 Owl Moon, 101–102
 Ramona's World, 147
 Rats!, 147
 Rip-Roaring Russell, 148
 Rosa Parks: Fight for Freedom, 149
 The Runaway Bunny, 105–106
 Sable, 150–151
 Search for the Shadowman, 151–152
 The Sick Day, 106
 Song and Dance Man, 108
 The Stories Julian Tells, 110
 Tales of a Fourth Grade Nothing, 154
 Tallahassee Higgins, 154
 Tar Beach, 111
 Three Days on a River in a Red Canoe, 112
 Too Many Tamales, 114
 The Trolls, 157
 The Very Worst Monster, 115–116
 Walk Two Moons, 158
 Wanted ... Mud Blossom, 158
 The War with Grandpa, 159
 Yolonda's Genius, 161–162
fantasy
 Battle for the Castle, 121
 The BFG, 122
 The Boggart and the Monster, 123
 Catwings, 124
 Ella Enchanted, 127
 An Enemy at Green Knowe, 127
 Flight of the Dragon Kyn, 129–130
 The Frog Princess of Pelham, 130–131
 The Ghosts of Austwick Manor, 131–132
 Hey, Al, 81
 The Hobbit, 133
 The Last Battle, 139
 The Littles, 89
 The Magic School Bus Lost in the Solar System, 90
 Max and Me and the Time Machine, 141
 Mossflower, 142–143
 The Music of Dolphins, 143
 Parsifal's Page, 145
 Perloo the Bold, 146
 Pippi Longstocking, 146
 Poppy and Rye, 146
 Tut, Tut, 157
 The Warm Place, 159
 Which Witch?, 160
farm life
 Mrs. Wishy-Washy's Farm, 97
 The Very Important Pig, 119
 When Bluebell Sang, 117
fathers and daughters
 Sable, 150–151
fear
 Franklin in the Dark, 76
fishing
 Edgar Badger's Fishing Day, 73
flight
 The Big Balloon Race, 65–66
 Flight: The Journey of Charles Lindbergh, 75
 Will and Orv, 117–118
floods
 Rising Water, 149
folklore
 The Little Red Hen, 89
 One Fine Day, 101
 Princess Furball, 105
 The Three Pigs, 113
folklore—Africa
 Anansi and the Moss-Covered Rock, 63
 Anansi the Spider: A Tale from Ashanti, 63
 Bringing the Rain to Kapiti Plain: A Nandi Tale, 67
 Mufaro's Beautiful Daughters: An African Tale, 98
 The Village of Round and Square Houses, 116
folklore—China
 Lon Po Po: A Red-Riding Hood Story from China, 90
folklore—England
 The Treasure, 114–115
folklore—Italy
 Strega Nona, 110
folklore—Japan
 The Stonecutter: A Japanese Folk Tale, 109
folklore—Jewish
 Joseph Had a Little Overcoat, 85–86
 The Treasure, 114–115
folklore—Native American
 The Girl Who Loved Wild Horses, 78
 The Legend of the Bluebonnet, 87
folklore—Ukraine
 The Mitten: A Ukrainian Folktale, 95
folklore—United States
 John Henry, 85
 Paul Bunyan, A Tall Tale, 103
foster home care
 Out of the Deep, 145
fractured fairy tales
 Sleeping Ugly, 106–107
friendship
 Amos and Boris, 62–63
 Because of Winn-Dixie, 121–122
 The Chalk Box Kid, 135
 Changes for Felicity, 125
 Edgar Badger's Fishing Day, 73
 The Family Under the Bridge, 129
 Frog and Toad Are Friends, 76–77
 An Island Far From Home, 135–136
 Lily's Crossing, 139–140
 Moe the Dog in Tropical Paradise, 95–96
 My Friend Rabbit, 98–99
 On My Honor, 145
 Pippi Longstocking, 146
 Poppleton, 104–105
 Number the Stars, 144
 Riding Freedom, 148
 Run Away Home, 150
 Sadako, 151
 Search for the Shadowman, 151–152
 Smoky Night, 107
 Stellaluna, 109
 Three By the Sea, 112
 The Tiger Rising, 156
 Walk Two Moons, 158

G

gardening
The Gardener, 78

George III
Can't You Make them Behave, King George?, 124

ghost stories
Ghost in the Family, 131
The Riddle of Penncroft Farm, 148

gold mines and mining
Gold Fever, 79

grandfathers
The Wall, 116

grandmothers
Sun and Spoon, 153

grandparents
The Hundred Penny Box, 135
Knots On a Counting Rope, 87
Love, Ruby Lavender, 140
Song and Dance Man, 108
The War with Grandpa, 159

Great Depression
The Gardener, 78

gypsies
The Family Under the Bridge, 129

H

haunted houses
House on Hackman's Hill, 134
The House with a Clock in its Walls, 134

historical fiction
Clara and the Bookwagon, 69
Drummer Hoff, 72–73
Gold Fever, 79
Morning Girl, 142
Once on this Island, 144–145
Ox-Cart Man, 102
Secret in St. Something, 152
The Titanic Lost ... and Found, 113
The Voyage of Patience Goodspeed, 158
The Wall, 116

historical fiction—California
Esperanza Rising, 128
Riding Freedom, 148

historical fiction—Chicago 1893
Fair Weather, 128

historical fiction—Egypt
Royal Diaries: Cleopatra VII, Daughter of the Nile, 149–150

historical fiction—frontier and pioneer life
Bound for Oregon, 123
The Courage of Sarah Noble, 70
The Golly Sisters Ride Again, 79
The Josefina Story Quilt, 85
The Pioneer Cat, 104
Winter Days in the Big Woods, 118

historical fiction—Korea
The Kite Fighters, 138–139
A Single Shard, 153

historical fiction—Mississippi 1933
The Friendship, 130

historical fiction—twentieth century
Dovey Coe, 126

historical fiction—twentieth century—Holocaust, 1933–1945
The Devil's Arithmetic, 126
Journey to America, 136–137

historical fiction—United States
The Statue of Liberty, 109

historical fiction—United States, Civil War
Across Five Aprils, 119–120
An Island Far From Home, 135–136
Three Against the Tide, 155

historical fiction—United States, colonial period
Guests, 132–133
A Killing in Plymouth Colony, 138
Shadows In the Glasshouse, 152

historical fiction—United States, Revolutionary War
Changes for Felicity, 125
The Riddle of Penncroft Farm, 148
The Winter of Red Snow: The Revolutionary War Diary of Abigail Jane Stewart, 161

historical fiction—Vietnam War
The Land I Lost, 139

historical fiction—West (U.S.)
Flaming Arrows, 129
The Gate in the Wall, 131
Humbug Mountain, 134–135
Mr. Tucket, 143
Tucket's Gold, 157

historical fiction—World War, 1939–1945
Boxes for Katje, 66
Lily's Crossing, 139–140
Number the Stars, 144
Sadako, 151
Stepping on the Cracks, 153

history—United States, Revolutionary War
Can't You Make them Behave, King George?, 124

homeless persons
The Family Under the Bridge, 129

horses
Gib and the Gray Ghost, 132

houses
Ming Lo Moves the Mountain, 93

human behavior
Babushka's Doll, 64–65
Gregory the Terrible Eater, 80
Miss Nelson Is Missing!, 94
No, David!, 99–100

humorous fiction
17 Kings and 42 Elephants, 61
Abe Lincoln's Hat, 61
The Bear's Toothache, 65
The Best School Year Ever, 122
Butterfly Buddies, 67
The Chicken Doesn't Skate, 125
Click, Clack, Moo Cows that Type, 69
Cloudy with a Chance of Meatballs, 69–70
The Day Jimmy's Boa Ate the Wash, 71
Do Not Open, 72
Doctor De Soto, 71–72
The Elephant's Child, 73–74
Fair Weather, 128
Flat Stanley, 75
Frindle, 130
The Frog Princess of Pelham, 130–131
The Golly Sisters Ride Again, 79
Green Eggs and Ham, 80
Gregory the Terrible Eater, 80
Harold and Chester in Hot Fudge, 80–81
Henry and Mudge in the Sparkle Days, 81
Hey, Al, 81
Hubert's Hair-Raising Adventure, 83
Humbug Mountain, 134–135
Is Your Mama a Llama?, 84
Joey Pigza Loses Control, 136
Just Another Ordinary Day, 86
Just So Stories, 137
The Kid Who Ran for President, 138
Milton the Early Riser, 93
My Friend Rabbit, 98–99
No, David!, 99–100
Oh, Were They Ever Happy, 100–101
Pinky and Rex and the Spelling Bee, 103
Pippi Longstocking, 146
Ramona's World, 147
Rats!, 147
Rip-Roaring Russell, 148
Tales of a Fourth Grade Nothing, 154
There Was an Old Lady Who Swallowed a Fly, 111–112
Thirteen Ways to Sink a Sub, 155
The Three Little Wolves and the Big Bad Pig, 112–113
Tops and Bottoms, 114
Tut, Tut, 157
The Very Important Pig, 119
Wanted ... Mud Blossom, 158

I

imagination
The Chalk Box Kid, 135
The Day Jimmy's Boa Ate the Wash, 71
How I Became a Pirate, 82
Imogene's Antlers, 83
Just Another Ordinary Day, 86

O'Diddy, 100

Will's Mammoth, 118

immigrants

Journey to America, 136–137

Molly's Pilgrim, 96

In the Year of the Boar and Jackie Robinson, 135

K

kidnapping

Three Days, 155

knighthood

Parsifal's Page, 145

L

learning disabilities—ADHD

Joey Pigza Loses Control, 136

Lewis, Meriwether

Lewis and Clark: A Prairie Dog for the President, 87–88

libraries

The Library Dragon, 88

M

magic

Polar Bears Past Bedtime, 104

mathematics

Anno's Mysterious Multiplying Jar, 64

Ben Franklin and the Magic Squares, 65

Mexican Americans

Too Many Tamales, 114

mice

Doctor De Soto, 71–72

Mouse Tales, 97

The Tale of Despereaux, 154

migrant labor

Esperanza Rising, 128

monsters

There's a Monster Under My Bed, 111

The Water Horse, 159

morning

The Paperboy, 102

moving

The Kid in the Red Jacket, 137–138

musicians

Yolonda's Genius, 161–162

mystery fiction

Babysitting is a Dangerous Job, 121

The Case of the Climbing Cat, 68

Case of the Muttering Mummy, 124

Ghost in the Family, 131

House on Hackman's Hill, 134

Nate the Great and the Missing Key, 99

Out of the Deep, 145

Search for the Shadowman, 151–152

Shadows In the Glasshouse, 152

Trapped in Death Cave, 156

N

Native Americans

Ahyoka and the Talking Leaves, 62

Annie and the Old One, 63–64

The Girl Who Loved Wild Horses, 78

Knots On a Counting Rope, 87

Once on this Island, 144–145

Run Away Home, 150

nature study

Crinkleroot's Guide to Walking in Wild Places, 70–71

New York City

The Gardener, 78

The Man Who Walked Between the Towers, 91

Tar Beach, 111

newspapers

The Furry News: How to Make a Newspaper, 77

night

Grandfather Twilight, 79

The Napping House, 99

Owl Moon, 101–102

There's a Monster Under My Bed, 111

nursery rhymes

James Marshall's Mother Goose, 84

O

occult fiction

The House with a Clock in its Walls, 134

orphans

The Frog Princess of Pelham, 130–131

Gib and the Gray Ghost, 132

Mandy, 140–141

Pippi Longstocking, 146

Rodzina, 149

P

peace

Drummer Hoff, 72–73

pets

Henry and Mudge in the Sparkle Days, 81

Rescue of Josh McGuire, 147–148

photography

Snowflake Bentley, 107

pirates

How I Became a Pirate, 82

plants

Miss Rumphius, 95

Planting a Rainbow, 104

poetry

Love that Dog, 140

prehistoric animals

Will's Mammoth, 118

prejudices

Finding Buck McHenry, 129

The Friendship, 130

presidents

So You Want to Be President?, 108

princesses

Many Moons, 91–92

The Tale of Despereaux, 154

R

race relations

Smoky Night, 107

Teammates, 111

railroads

John Henry, 85

realistic fiction

Everything on a Waffle, 128

The Paperboy, 102

repetitive story

If You Give a Pig a Pancake, 83

Lizard's Song, 89–90

The Napping House, 99

There Was an Old Lady Who Swallowed a Fly, 111–112

riots

Smoky Night, 107

S

safety education

Officer Buckle and Gloria, 100

school stories

Amber Brown Sees Red, 120

The Best School Year Ever, 122

Butterfly Buddies, 67

The Chicken Doesn't Skate, 125

In the Dinosaur's Paw, 84

First Grade Takes a Test, 74

A Fish in His Pocket, 74

Frindle, 130

Just Another Ordinary Day, 86

The Kid Who Ran for President, 138

The Library Dragon, 88

Lilly's Purple Plastic Purse, 88–89

Love that Dog, 140

The Magic School Bus Lost in the Solar System, 90

Miss Alaineus, 94

Miss Bindergarten Gets Ready for Kindergarten, 94

Miss Nelson Is Missing!, 94

Molly's Pilgrim, 96

Nekomah Creek, 144

Officer Buckle and Gloria, 100

The One in the Middle Is a Green Kangaroo, 101

Pinky and Rex and the Spelling Bee, 103

The School Story, 151

Thirteen Ways to Sink a Sub, 155

Today Was a Terrible Day, 114

The Year of Miss Agnes, 161
Yoko, 119
science fiction
Among the Hidden, 120–121
Commander Toad and the Planet of the Grapes, 70
Escape to Witch Mountain, 127
Minnie and Moo Save the Earth, 93
The Monsters of Morley Manor, 142
The White Mountains, 160
Scotland
All About Sam, 120
The Boggart and the Monster, 123
The Water Horse, 159
self esteem
Rising Water, 149
shipwrecks
The Titanic Lost ... and Found, 113
single parents
Tallahassee Higgins, 154
snow
Snowflake Bentley, 107
The Snowy Day, 107–108
solar system
The Magic School Bus Lost in the Solar System, 90
songs
The Erie Canal Pirates, 74
Lizard's Song, 89–90
Mama Don't Allow, 91
There Was an Old Lady Who Swallowed a Fly, 111–112
Where Does the Sun Go at Night?, 117
sports
Finding Buck McHenry, 129
In the Year of the Boar and Jackie Robinson, 135
stories in rhyme
17 Kings and 42 Elephants, 61
Adventure on Klickitat Island, 61–62
Bringing the Rain to Kapiti Plain: A Nandi Tale, 67
Chicka Chicka Boom Boom, 68–69
Dinner at the Panda Palace, 71
Drummer Hoff, 72–73
Each Peach Pear Plum, 73
Green Eggs and Ham, 80
A House Is a House for Me, 82
Hubert's Hair-Raising Adventure, 83
Is Your Mama a Llama?, 84
Jesse Bear, What Will You Wear?, 84–85
The Library, 88
Miss Bindergarten Gets Ready for Kindergarten, 94
Sheep in a Jeep, 106

storytelling
Joseph Had a Little Overcoat, 85–86
survival
Earthquake Terror, 126
Hatchet, 133
Jason's Gold, 136
Kävik the Wolf Dog, 137
The Music of Dolphins, 143
My Side of the Mountain, 143
Toughboy and Sister, 156

T

teeth
Airmail to the Moon, 62
The Bear's Toothache, 65
Doctor De Soto, 71–72
Throw Your Tooth on the Roof: Tooth Traditions from Around the World, 113
time travel
Battle for the Castle, 121
The Ghosts of Austwick Manor, 131–132
Max and Me and the Time Machine, 141
Tut, Tut, 157
tolerance
Molly's Pilgrim, 96
toys
Babushka's Doll, 64–65
Galimoto, 77
travel
Flat Stanley, 75
Flight: The Journey of Charles Lindbergh, 75
Mr. Gumpy's Motor Car, 97
travelers—Korea
A Single Shard, 153
trickster tales
Tops and Bottoms, 114

W

war
Drummer Hoff, 72–73
weather
Cloudy with a Chance of Meatballs, 69–70
West (U.S.)
Weird Stories from the Lonesome Café, 116
West (U.S.)—exploration
Lewis and Clark: A Prairie Dog for the President, 87–88
whales
Out of the Deep, 145
The Wild Whale Watch, 161
whaling
The Voyage of Patience Goodspeed, 158
winter
Froggy Gets Dressed, 77
Henry and Mudge in the Sparkle Days, 81
witchcraft
The House with a Clock in its Walls, 134

wolves
Runt, 150
Wild, Wild Wolves, 117
work
The Paperboy, 102

Z

zoos
The Warm Place, 159

Award Winning Books

A

ALA Best Books for Young Adults
Among the Hidden, 120–121
ALA Notable Books
Amos and Boris, 62–63
Blister, 123
The Land I Lost, 139
Love, Ruby Lavender, 140
American Book Award winners
Miss Rumphius, 95

B

Boston Globe Horn Book Award winners
The Trolls, 157

C

Caldecott Honor Books
Anansi the Spider: A Tale from Ashanti, 63
Click, Clack, Moo Cows that Type, 69
Frog and Toad Are Friends, 76–77
John Henry, 85
Martin's Big Words: The Life of Dr. Martin Luther King Jr., 92
Mice Twice, 92
"More More More," Said the Baby, 96–97
Mufaro's Beautiful Daughters: An African Tale, 98
No, David!, 99–100
The Paperboy, 102
Strega Nona, 110
Tar Beach, 111
There Was an Old Lady Who Swallowed a Fly, 111–112
Tops and Bottoms, 114
The Treasure, 114–115
The Ugly Duckling, 115
The Village of Round and Square Houses, 116
Caldecott Medal winners
The Biggest Bear, 66
Drummer Hoff, 72–73
The Gardener, 78
The Girl Who Loved Wild Horses, 78
Hey, Al, 81
Joseph Had a Little Overcoat, 85–86

Lon Po Po: A Red-Riding Hood Story from China, 90
Make Way for Ducklings, 90–91
The Man Who Walked Between the Towers, 91
Many Moons, 91–92
My Friend Rabbit, 98–99
Officer Buckle and Gloria, 100
One Fine Day, 101
Owl Moon, 101–102
Ox-Cart Man, 102
Smoky Night, 107
Snowflake Bentley, 107
The Snowy Day, 107–108
So You Want to Be President?, 108
Song and Dance Man, 108
The Three Pigs, 113

J

Jane Addams Children's Book Award winners
Esperanza Rising, 128

N

National Book Award Finalists
The Tiger Rising, 156

National Jewish Book Award winners
The Devil's Arithmetic, 126

NCTE Notable Children's Trade Books
Love, Ruby Lavender, 140

Nene Award winners (Hawaii)
The Best School Year Ever, 122

Nevada Young Reader Award winners
Weird Stories from the Lonesome Café, 116

New York Times Outstanding Books of the Year
The House with a Clock in its Walls, 134

Newbery Honor Books
Annie and the Old One, 63–64
Because of Winn-Dixie, 121
Doctor De Soto, 71–72
Ella Enchanted, 127
The Family Under the Bridge, 129
Hatchet, 133
The Hundred Penny Box, 135
Lily's Crossing, 139–140
On My Honor, 145
My Side of the Mountain, 143
Yolonda's Genius, 161–162

Newbery Medal winners
Across Five Aprils, 119–120
The Courage of Sarah Noble, 70
Ginger Pye, 132
Number the Stars, 144
A Single Shard, 153
Walk Two Moons, 158

W

Willa Cather Award winners
Esperanza Rising, 128